American Kid is a personal story. Told through a child's eyes, it is the 20th century odyssey of an American family returning to their roots in Greece during the Great Depression, before the onset of WWII. Similar to Odysseus, the family faces unexpected challenges including a few corrupt government officials, deprivation, perfidious family members, and finally the ravages of war. Just when the reader thinks the family will be safe, the Nazis invade and the journey becomes more harrowing.

This heroic tale reminds one of the well-known words, "Greeks do not fight like heroes, heroes fight like Greeks!" And in this case, a Greek American family.

~Maria Fotopoulos
Los Angeles-based writer and animal rights activist

Bravo! I loved *American Kid*. The author has captured a vibrant, fascinating portrayal of village life in Greece under Nazi occupation, along with the feelings, painful and pleasant, that innocent civilians endure in wartime. By telling the story through a child's eyes, without the cynicism or jadedness of adulthood, *American Kid's* Johnny brings the reader, scene by scene, into the relevance of historical events. Readers, both young and old who have never been personally involved in war, will find *American Kid* a unique, easily readable, and engaging history of World War II.

~Chris G. Kuchuris, Professor of Social Sciences
College of Southern Nevada

American Kid moved me deeply. It brought back memories of my own childhood growing up in a similarly remote and isolated village in northern Greece during World War II.

In addition to the decimation of Greece's Jews, hundreds of thousands of civilians died, mostly because of starvation. Having a goat and an olive tree made the difference between life and death, and a child's daily question was: "Is today the day we die?" It was an Occupation that influenced and shaped the lives of the Greek people for future generations.

With wonderful ethnographic material about food preparation, festivals, funerals, weddings, and births in a primeval village, Constance M. Constant describes an enduring way of life that persisted despite war and cultural disruptions in rural Greece, not only in the mid-twentieth century but also over many previous centuries and generations. Rich with telling detail, the book brings to life what it is to share fragile survival skills with family, friends, and neighbors.

American Kid is a celebration of the dignity of simple people in the face of unimaginable cruelty.

~Demetrios Liappas, Professor of Greek
Loyola Marymount University

AMERICAN KID

KID

NAZI-OCCUPIED GREECE
THROUGH A CHILD'S EYES

CONSTANCE M. CONSTANT

YEAR
of the
BOOK

Year of the Book
135 Glen Avenue
Glen Rock, Pennsylvania 17327

ISBN 13: 978-1-942430-26-1
ISBN 10: 1-942430-26-4

Library of Congress Control Number: 2015945300

To Bob
   With infinite thanks and all my love

To Nikos, Linda, Athena, Jim, Nick, Amy, Penny, and Harry—
   with endless affection because knowledge encourages more
   thought, better understanding, and deeper love

In honor of Eleni and Nickolas Constant, may their memories be
   eternal

ACKNOWLEDGMENTS

A special *euharisto* to the good people who kept me focused on this project. Each, in his or her special way, helped encourage the completion of my manuscript.

Cleo and George Andrews
Bob Constant
Argerey and James Constant
Linda and Nikos Constant
Father Michael Courey
Aggeliki and Panos Dimaras
Governor Michael Dukakis
Nika Fotion
Maria Fotopoulos
Maita Houpis
Mary Kartos
George Kartsounis

Chris Kuchuris
Demetrios Liappas
Helen Limberopulos
Ilca Moskos
Zora O'Neill
Telly and Collette Sarlas
Christine and Perry Spanos
Demi Stevens
"Surfwriters"
Argie Vassilakis
Stephanie Vlahakis
Carolyn Doyle Winter

And to Zora O'Neill and Carolyn Dolye Winter I bestow a very special *euharisto*. Zora and Carolyn, you are conscientious, thoughtful, patient, and gifted editors. I admire, appreciate, and respect your outstanding abilities with words, your expertise in organizing a story, and the golden suggestions you shared with me that helped enrich this narrative. I am forever grateful. Thank you very much.

MAPS

World War II Greece (not to scale)

"Parnion" Village (not to scale)

"What a strange thing is memory... Memory is history recorded in our brain, memory is a painter, it paints pictures of the past and of the day."

~ Anna Mary Robinson Moses (aka Grandma Moses) 1860-1961

TABLE OF CONTENTS

AUTHOR'S PROLOGUE

"Where have all the young men gone? Gone to soldiers every one. When will they ever learn...? Where have all the soldiers gone? Gone to graveyards, every one. When will they ever learn? When will they ever learn?"

~Pete Seeger and Joe Hickerson

These haunting lyrics, written in 1955 by Seeger and augmented by Hickerson in 1960, address the agony of war—tragically still taking place on our exquisite planet. Clearly, we haven't learned.

The first half of the 20th century was inundated with worldwide disasters. World War I (1914-1918), which technically and more diabolically changed warfare, witnessed uncountable numbers of soldiers disastrously maimed, poisoned with lethal gasses, psychologically wounded, and "gone to graveyards." Between World Wars I and II, Americans and much of the globe's community found themselves financially choking in a 1930s economic Depression. And by mid-1941—a mere nineteen years before "Where Have All the Flowers Gone?" was penned—Adolph Hitler's insatiable greed for power had become temporarily successful; his troops violently occupied most of Europe. Following the December 7, 1941, bombing of Pearl Harbor in Hawaii, the U.S. joined the conflict that became known as "World War II." Until war's end in 1945, soldiers were going to graveyards again—*en masse*—and so were innocent civilians. *American Kid* has its beginnings in Chicago in 1937, during the hardships of the Great Depression.

Problems in the U.S. in 1937

The majority of Americans had been afflicted by economic adversity for eight long years, when in January and February of 1937 the severely flooding Ohio and Mississippi rivers in Ohio, Kentucky, and Illinois left one million more Depression-afflicted Americans homeless. Simultaneously, residents of Oklahoma's panhandle and neighboring areas of Colorado, Kansas, New Mexico, and Texas were enduring the miseries of the brutal Dust Bowl. Vicious winds, carrying devastating black clouds saturated with farm soils, were relentlessly blowing American families, their farms, and their prairie homes out of existence. At the same time, banks had closed across the country, wiping out precious savings accounts; home mortgages were being foreclosed. Businesses continued going bankrupt. Jobs were scarce. U.S. unemployment hit almost 25%. Most Americans were struggling to put food on the table and pay rent or make mortgage payments for the roof over their heads.

World Problems in 1937

In 1935, "average" Americans, bearing the yoke of "hard times," were barely noticing Benito Mussolini's arrogant invasion of Abyssinia (now Ethiopia) in Africa. In 1936, a civil war began in Spain. The Empire of Japan invaded China in 1937; the Japanese military inflicted the worst of atrocities on the innocent civilians of Nanking that year. Hitler and his ally Benito Mussolini, itchy for world domination by means of war, were brandishing their brutal swords in Europe. Yet "Average Joe American," unaware that Buchenwald concentration camp near Weimar, Germany, was already operational in 1937, with more hideous plans in store for its use, saw Europe and Asia as too far away—thousands of miles across our cushioning oceans. Many Americans referred to Hitler's deadly incursions as "Europe's war." One of those Axis-occupied countries was Greece, on the southeastern edge of Europe. *Hellas*, as the Greeks refer to their homeland, is a nation peninsula surrounded by three notably gorgeous and sparkling, sapphire blue seas: the Aegean, the Ionian, and the Mediterranean.

Greece's heroic participation in the Second World War still remains a lesser-known history. The first Allied victory of WWII is credited to Greece's small army and courageous civilians who fought off powerful Italian armed forces in the winter of 1940-41. Italian dictator Mussolini (Hitler's ally in the war) had invaded at the Greek border with Albania in October of 1940. Where it took 43 days for powerful France to fall, it took 219 days for the Greeks to capitulate—from the start of the Italian troubles through to the German invasion. At one point the Greek military, civilians in the reserves, and the Greek women of Epirus in the north were simultaneously fighting off enemy Albanians, Italians, Germans, and Bulgarians: all Axis allies.

This astonishing "David and Goliath" struggle was exalted on the cover of *Life* magazine in 1940 and prompted U.S. President Franklin Roosevelt to remark: "Free people are deeply impressed by the courage and steadfastness of the Greek Nation… which is defending itself so valiantly." But to save Mussolini's face from the shame of being defeated by small, less powerful Greece, Hitler was forced to help his Italian ally by sending German armies over Greece's border with Bulgaria to invade and subdue the feisty Greeks in April of 1941. Some historians suggest that WWII would have suffered a different ending if Greek resistance had not delayed the Nazis in Greece.

The six-week holdup in Hitler's secret plan to invade the Soviet Union was made more complicated for the German army by fearless retaliation from the people of Crete, and by the Greek underground's resistance tactics. Belligerent and intrepid Cretan women and men, in defense of their Greek island, slowed down German troops (Battle of Crete, May 1941). As a result, the Nazis did not arrive in Russia according to Hitler's original schedule. Heavy autumn rains turned the U.S.S.R.'s roads into impassable muddy bogs, and the overwhelming Russian winter of 1941-42 caused worse delay—ultimately disabling Germany's mighty forces. The Germans were eventually defeated.

The people of Greece, scattered in cities, towns, and villages on the northern mainland, southern Peloponnesian peninsula, and throughout the Greek islands of their small, mountainous country, experienced the Italian and German occupations in verifiably different ways: some more brutal than others. Some cities and villages were occupied by Mussolini's armies and saw few German soldiers; in others it was the opposite. Mountain villages drew increased scrutiny from Germans due to the presence of guerrilla fighters hiding further up in the remote crags. Greek villages along the sea suffered different dilemmas. Each war experience was unique.

Most American, WWII-era civilians only observed German soldiers on film while watching black-and-white newsreels in darkened but safe American movie theaters. But John and his family, of *American Kid*, came face to face with them in full, living and dying color: this book relates what happened to an innocent, civilian family when Hitler's armies occupied Europe.

Yet, while *American Kid* focuses on one family, it is also the story of millions of families, regardless of location, trapped in war's violence: past and present. When John of this account writes that it was "the first time in my short life that I asked: 'Are we going to die today?'" he was posing a question no eight-year-old child, regardless of nationality, ethnicity, or religion, should ever have to ask.

For eons, poets, balladeers, artists, and authors of every genre have chronicled human suffering as a result of wars. Yet, tragically, wars are still going on. Is the grasp of power so sweet for the greedy "few" that they cannot be out-swayed by the suffering "many?" With centuries of ethical and moral philosophy, human evolution, advancing civilization, and wide spread education under our belts, why haven't we gained the knowledge, influence, and determination we need to proliferate and maintain peace? Why do children need to wonder if they will be alive at the end of a day? What have we missed that we still need to learn?

JOHN'S PROLOGUE

By the mid-1930s, my father had permanently locked the doors of his formerly successful restaurant, turned the keys and restaurant equipment (Dad had paid for) over to the landlord, and walked away. The financial quagmire of "hard times" had emptied his pockets. Yet, he had resolved to take care of "his own" rather than go on "relief," the public assistance program. Keenly focusing on supporting his family, while only landing "temp" jobs, Dad was distracted and not concentrating on world events. Seeing no improvement in our family economics by 1937, he decided to send Mom and us kids to his Greek homeland for a year. There, we could live off income from a citrus grove he owned in the southern Greek city of Kalamata. At the same time, he chose to stay in the U.S. during our absence to secure permanent employment.

Like the majority of Americans, my father was unaware of the egoistic strategies being hatched by 1930's European and Asian dictators. He, never in a million years, suspected that civilized fellow human beings from northern Europe would viciously invade and occupy his Greek homeland or that there would be a second world war. Dad's naïve plan ultimately and unwittingly plunged my mother, brother, sister, and me into what was to become WWII.

As a result, we didn't learn about World War II on the local newspaper's pages or in library books, like most American civilians were doing in the early 1940s. Instead, we lived it. For us it was daily and genuine. We observed, in-person, how war terrifies, corrupts, kills, and wounds real people. *American Kid* is a war story about real people.

I am now retired and well past seventy, but I clearly remember how, as an American kid, I personally experienced and witnessed the misery Nazi troops wreaked on a particular Greek village during the Second World War. Out of respect for the privacy of the people mentioned in my story, I asked the author to change their names, my own name, and the name of the village where we lived. Because the birthplace of my mother, where I grew up in the middle of WWII, is located in the upper foothills of Laconia's Mt. Parnon, I chose "Parnion" as the pen name for the village of my childhood recollections.

Where my boyhood memory was uncertain about the timeline of certain events, I have taken the liberty of setting them, as closely as possible, to a particular year. One detail of the war clearly remains in my mind: tranquil, "normal" life activities unexpectedly came to an abrupt halt for my mother, my siblings, and me when Axis armies invaded. One day we were free to go about our daily lives, untroubled. The next day we were fleeing Hitler's shiny black boots. As has happened with all conflicts, going back before the sack of Troy—years of indefensible human suffering followed.

"History counts." That is the reason for writing this book, for telling this story. As historians state unequivocally, "History makes sense of the present, as well as the past." I believe that ignorance of what has gone before easily leads to toxic complacency about the future.

Even after seven decades, the atrocities I witnessed as "the American Kid" still stick like superglue to my memories of Kalamata and Parnion. The senior citizen I've become abhors the reality of innocent civilians—and especially children—cringing with fear in the presence of terrorists and daunting, armed soldiers. Over fifty million deaths occurred as a result of the Second World War. Those tragic losses thrust brutal heartache and disastrous grief on millions and millions of families. I personally witnessed some of them. I pray that their survivors eventually found healing and peace.

Heads of state and diplomats of every nation, creed, and color have not yet implemented methods, via smart, cool heads and empathetic, intelligent negotiations, to settle conflicts. And when conflicts arise, governments, militaries, and armament producers get so wrapped up in planning strategies to overcome urgent threats that the tremendous cost to innocent, ordinary civilians is somehow overlooked. Worse yet, innocent victims are insensitively, almost cruelly, labeled "collateral damage." On top of it, wars have become more complicated and vicious with the advances of humankind: perhaps it was better when fists, rather than bullets, flew through the air.

"Peace" remains elusive. "Peace talks" and "sanctions" share a commonality with walking a delicate tight rope spanning two 100-story skyscrapers. The challenge to cross safely is eventually disastrous for the arrogant, bully/show-off. But a skilled, knowledgeable acrobat gets to the other side safely and gracefully.

Humans have worked diligently to minimize the consequences of unavoidable natural disasters like erupting volcanoes, earthquakes, tornadoes, hurricanes, and the rest. War is an *avoidable* disaster, but little has been accomplished toward preventing it. Peace seekers must become more powerful than forces that cause conflict. Ordinary citizens, all over the globe, must demand patience, intelligence—thoughtful give and take negotiations—rather than destructive conflict on our beautiful planet.

1 | CHAOS—APRIL 1941

An hour before, Mother had sternly ushered my two balking, older siblings and me into the middle of the crowd of worshipers, refusing to heed our protests about having to stand for hours in the dimly lit church—we were American kids used to churches with pews. Now, squirming, eight-year-old me, weary of standing on the marble floor, felt sleepy. And while devoted, tradition-bound adults—men standing to the right, women and children to the left—responded to an elderly, bearded priest's melodious chant, I leaned against the sympathetic, arrow-straight torso of my mother and listened. With her arm around my shoulder, I wriggled, shifted from one foot to the other, sleepily eyed rising incense smoke filling the old church's dome, and mindlessly inspected massive chandeliers—not understanding a word.

But in an instant, ear-splitting sirens jolted the adrenaline in all of us. Blaring alarms invaded open church windows from the dusty, outdoor street. Low-pitched and strident rumbling cut off melodic prayers. Chandelier crystals jingled—the roar grew louder.

With alien thunder hanging directly overhead, a horrified man at the back of the church yelled, "Airplanes!" A woman at the front shrieked, "Holy God, save us…" Deafening outdoor explosions shook the old church's thick walls; I felt the rigid floor shudder. "Bombs!" a second male voice screamed. Shrill cries erupted from the stunned crowd. "We're being bombed! Germans are coming to kill us!"

At that moment a huge wooden crucifix, with an icon of crucified Jesus nailed to it, abruptly crashed onto the altar; lit candles fell over. The old priest dashed out of the sanctuary with his colorful vestments flying behind him. I saw him duck head first, under an ornately carved table, which was facing the altar and wide icon screen of time-honored, side-by-side, saints. Yet he never stopped chanting, even as he changed his tone to a desperately loud petition for God's mercy. "*Kyrie eleison. Kyrie eleison. Kyrie eleison...*" he repeated over and over. Anxious voices in the throng joined his prayer—as frantic eyes searched for exit doors.

Outside, zooming airplanes despoiled the clear, blue sky by dropping bombs on the city. Piercing missiles, too close for comfort, were annihilating who-knew-what in the sunny outdoors. Inside, we nervously eyed precariously swinging chandeliers and heard crackling noises in the antique roof. Panicked worshipers screamed nightmarish shrieks, and scattered. Too shocked to cry and so terrified, I put my fingers in my ears to block out booming bombs. But Mother grabbed my hand and pulled me away. "Let's go!" she ordered.

Those first Axis bombs whistled down on the southern Greek city of Kalamata in late April of 1941. Mother, my nine-year-old sister Nikki, fourteen-year-old brother Alex, and I, John, age eight, were attending the ancient Liturgy in that domed Orthodox Church near the port city's harbor. A sunny, peaceful day had spun into hideous trauma. It was the first time in my short life that I asked: "Are we going to die today?"

The only "sure thing" discernable to me in the violence and confusion was my mother's hand. Nikki cried, "Mama! I'm scared!" while religious icons crashed down onto hard marble. Terrorized people pushed toward exits. I held on to the connection with Mom. She and Alex tried to shepherd the four of us toward the front door, but the entrance was already blocked with debris. That holy place was consumed with hellish chaos.

Mother's deep brown eyes grew wider. A fire blazed and spat in front of us, ignited by tens of overturned candles, which had been devoutly lit in the narthex by the morning's faithful.

Mom grabbed Nikki and me with both arms and held us against her tensed body. Skirting flames, dodging fallen wreckage, we fled the church in a super-human dash.

When all four of us escaped, her breath returned. "Where to go? Bombs... Fires... Dome about to plunge ..."

The never-ending siege of anxiety we would endure throughout WWII had begun. Alex, Nikki, and I, running for our lives toward home with Mother, couldn't help glancing back at Kalamata's beautiful, blue harbor. Its now murky waters left us aghast—they were teeming with hundreds of floating, dead fish.

That evening, a half-dozen neighborhood men began excavating a huge trench in the empty field across the way from our second-story apartment; they lined its dirt walls with slabs of rough, oddly shaped pieces of old lumber. Watching from our window, I wondered, "Why are they digging such a huge hole?"

I got my answer the next morning, following the first screeches of blaring sirens. Those same neighbors hastily knocked on our door and directed Mom, Nikki, and me to cross the street. Then we were directed to stuff ourselves into the iffy, makeshift, below-ground, air raid shelter they had constructed the night before. Mom was visibly edgy because Alex, at an early Sea-scouts meeting, was not with us.

The anxiety in my mother's eyes was unmistakable when she stared into the problematic, civilian-built foxhole: it was already filled with neighbors, most crying. Quickly appraising the shelter's obvious vulnerability, Mom took a deep breath, resigned herself to an unknown fate, and carefully helped Nikki and me into it. Then she jumped down, with a neighbor's help, to take her place beside us, murmuring, "Dear God, please help my children live through this catastrophe. Save every one of us from final entombment in this hole."

"Amen!" was the teary response of the gentleman helping her. When the men in-charge positioned long pieces of timber and something resembling used tar-paper over our heads, one woman

3

wryly asked, "Is being buried alive an alternative to being bombed to death?" No one in the terrified assembly replied.

They spread soil over the heavy paper and wood. That's when dirt started sifting down onto our heads and into our mouths, eyes, and noses—collective coughing, sneezing, and complaining followed. After covering the trench, the men squeezed in with us to wait for an all-clear signal.

I remember gagging from the taste of mud in my mouth and the undeniable stink of the suffocating darkness: damp soil and musty mildew mixed with body odors. When whistling bombs pounded, shattered, and shifted the ground around our supposedly protective ditch, gripping fear plunged us into hopelessness: ear-splitting blasts and massive booming scared the hell out of every one of us.

The buried crowd gasped in unison each time shelter walls trembled and dirt crumbled. A panicky male yelled, to no one in particular, "We won't need funerals when this is over. Blown to pieces, we'll already be in our common grave!" One woman fainted. Other women, including Mother, held her up because there was no place to lay the patient down on the ground.

It took a very long time standing and gobs of anguish before a siren's tone signaled safety. When the all-clear finally sounded, the grimy lot of us climbed out of that ghastly black hole. Mom grabbed Nikki and me and we ran—scared, racing to our second-story, rented apartment overlooking the usually peaceful, sapphire Bay of Kalamata.

Deep scars were newly imbedded in the gray stone wall of our apartment building—bomb shrapnel. "Thank God we weren't inside," Mom exhaled, exhausted and distressed, still crossing herself in prayer. "Not that I felt we were safe in that tomb of an air raid shelter either."

Alex finally arrived, following his personal tour of neighborhood damage, and Mother announced, "We're getting out of Kalamata tomorrow. We're going to Parnion. I don't know how long it will take to get there or how long we'll have to stay. But we'll wait in my village until these damned Germans and Italians either get out of Greece—or lose their abominable war. Parnion is so out of the way the Germans won't even want to look for it, children, because nothing happens there. In my grandpa's time, even the Turks couldn't find our Parnion."

But before we could begin our journey the next day, we got word that the German army had already left Athens, where the Greek government had capitulated. Nazis were heading south to Kalamata. The Germans' violent reputation had preceded them: our sources added that the Germans were coming to murder everyone. We had no radio and were not in the habit of getting a daily newspaper. Reports reached us third hand from trustworthy neighbors who told Mother that prior to the expected German arrival, everyone capable of walking was going to evacuate Kalamata. The city's citizens were fleeing to Mt. Taygetos, the giant mountain to the city's northeast.

"That means we can't leave for Parnion now," Mom decided. "What if, on the way, we come across Germans? They'll kill us!" Thinking out loud she continued, "And your father would never know what happened to us. We have to evacuate to Taygetos with the others... we have no other choice. We'll leave immediately... but Alex isn't back yet."

The disturbed tone in her voice was scary. She fought back tears saying, "He went to help the Sea-scouts again this morning. We must wait for Alex." Nikki and I, and possibly our frustrated Mother at that point, were in the dark about my brother's activities with the Sea-scouts. All we knew, so far, was that he had become an accomplished swimmer after joining the group. But Mom's frantic tone in not evacuating, because Alex was not with us, made it evident that all was not going according to her most recent plan.

Yet that was nothing new for our family in recent years. Our parents' plans had gone awry since we had first arrived in Kalamata from the U.S. in 1937. When bombs fell on us in 1941, we were still in Greece and Dad, who had never accompanied us to his homeland, was in faraway America.

5

2 | DAD'S PLAN: UNDERSTANDING IT— BY DIGRESSING AHEAD TO 1946

I got to know my father, to properly recognize this man, when I was a teenager, after we had returned from Greece in 1946, following the end of WWII. Our long-awaited togetherness sessions took place in the evening after Dad's full day of hard work hustling behind the counter and inside the spotless kitchen of his restaurant, the Busy Bee, on Ann Arbor's North Main Street, across from the old county court house. When he arrived home, he would leave his grubby work shoes at the front door, wash up, change into old, but comfy, slippers, and settle into his favorite dark green, easy chair.

Sitting together in the living room of our Ann Arbor, Michigan, house, he shared with Mom, my siblings, and me the events of what happened to him while we had been stuck in occupied Greece. At the same time, we shared our hard-to-believe war experiences with him. Hearing about his life without us, along with stories of his youth, I understood better why he had sent us away before the war. A vital lesson became obvious to me in our personal exchanges: history counts. Yes, even family history.

I found out that Dad's mother had died early in his life, before the turn of the 20th century, leaving him, at thirteen (my age at the time), and his three younger brothers, motherless. The village where he had been born in the prefecture of Arcadia was located in the poorest area of Greece: the middle of *Peloponnesos*. His father remarried; the second wife had five additional children with hard-edged Grandpa. Neither father nor stepmother showed much affection for the four older boys: Andrew, who was to become my father, Demetri, Antoni, and Harry.

"We were poor," Dad said. "We broke our backs farming the little land my own mother's dowry brought into my parents' marriage. But nothing grew well. Arcadian soil had lost nutrients, centuries before. When I was a teenager I left home and went to Athens to get a job."

Dad then filled me in on more family tragedy. His brother Demetri left for America about the same time that Dad went to Athens. Demetri found work at a Carnegie steel plant in Pittsburgh, but tragically died of pneumonia. "We don't even know where my young brother is buried," my father said, on the verge of tears and swallowing a lump in his throat.

Throat cleared, Dad took a deep breath and continued. "In Athens, I got a job in a bakery, shoving unbaked loaves of bread into a scorching oven and pulling them out when they were done. I earned a pittance for spending sixteen hours a day with a hell of an oven. It was like living with the devil... with no hope of seeing paradise. My only salvation was America."

Unlike the grandfather I never knew, Dad was a warm, loving man. Abject poverty worsened by the chronic callousness of a besieged stepmother ultimately drove my twenty-year-old father to leave his homeland in 1906 to immigrate to America. He crossed Europe, sailed the wide Atlantic, and sought out one of the jobs he heard was available to immigrants in the United States.

While most newcomers came through Ellis Island, Dad arrived at the port of Boston and lived in Ipswich for a time; he left Massachusetts when he heard good money was paid to railroad workers in the West. In time, he earned a promotion: section foreman for the Denver and Rio Grande Railroad.

"I finally saved enough to bring my father and my two brothers, Harry and Antoni, to America. I got them jobs on the Denver and Rio Grande because I wanted them to benefit from the good breaks I got in America. But your grandpa and uncles didn't like the Wild West where the railroad traveled through the Rockies of Idaho, Utah, and Colorado. We worked under the clear, blue skies of Pocatello, Grand Junction, Price, and Salt Lake City. And yes, I admit there was too much isolation. But that was the nature of the job. I stuck with it for fifteen years."

Dad's father, hired as a watchman, was assigned to live by himself in a tiny lookout shack to watch for and report landslides, avalanches, rain washouts, and other dangers to the railroad line. But eerie howls of wolves and coyotes terrorized Grandpa during long, lonely nights in his desolate lookout shack. My grandfather and uncles earned more money than they could have earned in the old country, but loathed the West's loneliness and decided to return to Greece.

And when they went back, they took a good portion of my father's money with them to invest in what appeared to be a well thought out, financial opportunity. Dad and his two brothers combined their railroad earnings to purchase, as equal partners, a large citrus grove in the southern city of Kalamata, much further south of their native village in Arcadia.

"I felt good about making a joint investment with my brothers. Together, we could improve our family's economics. Did I want to go back home with them? No, I liked America. But I didn't want to work for the railroad for the rest of my life."

Leaving the railroad job, Dad opened a meat market in Salida, Colorado, but finally moved to Chicago, and opened a grocery store on the West Side. In 1924 he married my mother, Katherine, and finally found the good family life he craved. "The best thing I ever did in my life was to marry your mother. I met her in church... a good sign," Dad said smiling. "I had known her brother John in Salt Lake City. By coincidence, in 1924 both John and I were living in Chicago."

It turned out that John had accompanied his unmarried, younger sister Katherine to America to marry her off. He invited bachelor friend, Andrew, to meet his sister in church one fine Sunday morning. And the rest, as the saying goes, is history. Sadly,

Uncle John got sick and eventually returned to Greece to die. I never met him.

By the mid-1920s, Dad's grocery store was prospering. "I worked hard. Did well. I could support my wife and also help my family in the old country."

Mailing hard-earned cash to his family in Greece was a responsibility Dad carried like a millstone throughout his life. He generously responded to letters requesting money from his younger, adult half-siblings, even though he had never met them; they were born in Greece after 1906, the year he came to the U.S. Dad financed his half-brother Petros's law school education in Athens and shelled out dollars to provide substantial dowries for two half-sisters.

Innate generosity also motivated him to give financial assistance to my mother's family in Chicago when it was needed. This openhandedness prevailed during the 1920s when his business made money. At the same time, Dad felt good about his Kalamata investment with his brothers; it held the promise of pulling his family in Greece out of poverty.

In 1928, when my brother Alex was a baby, Dad sold his successful grocery store, and left the big city's crowded, brick apartment complexes to move to Geneva, Illinois, an attractive, all-American town, located west of Chicago, along the Fox River.

"I had learned how to cook and decided to go into the restaurant business... named my restaurant the Fox River Café," Dad said, "after the beautiful river that flows through Illinois and goes right through Geneva... a few blocks east of my business on State Street... downtown... right next to a movie theater. We had the first neon sign in town! Business was flourishing. And we rented a nice house, too."

Mom, now listening in on our conversation in our Ann Arbor living room, interrupted Dad at his mention of Geneva. She brightened up. "Remember that house, Andrew?" she asked. "It was beautiful—white with a big green lawn. And I had a vegetable garden in the backyard. Illinois's fertile, black soil was perfect for growing everything." Then, smiling less, she added, "But the Depression ruined our perfect American dream."

Dad interjected, "Who expected a Depression in America? No one! My dream had always been to take my family to visit the old country. That damn Depression choked my dream and everybody else's dreams… it infected us like the plague."

Even when economic hardship had crashed down on millions of Americans, Dad tenaciously carried on with business as usual. But soon, vacant restaurant booths and counter stools made him realize that most Geneva residents couldn't afford to be his customers; they couldn't afford anything. Hungry, forlorn Americans waited in long food lines for free, hot soup. Impoverished entrepreneurs hawked fruit for pennies on street corners.

Dad's empty cash register forced him to understand it was no time to be a restaurant owner responsible for monthly rents and purchasing foodstuffs he couldn't sell. His family had grown: he had a wife and three children to support. No longer able to pay the rents, we left our small town utopia and moved back to the big city.

But, arriving in Chicago, Dad discovered "hard times" had caused restaurants all over the city to permanently lock their doors. Each sunrise found him joining the glut of experienced cooks beating Chicago's hard-on-the-feet pavement seeking employment. In the 1930s, Dad said, the going rate for a chef, working 12 to 16 hours a day, was at least three dollars a day.

Now and again, Dad was comforted to take a temporary job as a substitute cook. But most nights he arrived home, dejected and exhausted, having walked the city from sunrise to sunset without a nickel in his pocket because he had not been hired. Yet, as he searched for work in Chicago's jobless market, he dreamed his dream of seeing his homeland again, a wish shared by most Greek male immigrants of his generation, especially during this depressed time in America.

"You know, Johnny, part-time cooks were paid less than three bucks a day," he said. "Our apartment rent was getting harder to pay. I struggled to put together forty dollars to hand over to the landlord for renting the apartment; he got it in small installments. Seeing homeless families living in our neighborhood's Garfield Park shook me up. I wondered if we would end up living in the park. So, I wore out my shoes looking for work.

"I used to tell your mother, over and over again, 'Katherine, I gave a good chunk of my railroad savings to my brothers to invest in Greece. I own productive land in Kalamata. We grow oranges and tangerines that are sold on the market and bring in cash. Why suffer in America when I own land and fruit trees in our *patrida*? Now I kick myself for thinking the way I did back then," Dad admitted.

Mother interrupted, "We couldn't afford to return to Greece and we couldn't afford to live here either. When the Depression hit us," Mom furrowed her brow, "your father talked about returning to the old country. But I told him, 'our children belong to America.' The war taught me many things... the hard way, Andrew," she said as she glared at him. "Opportunities are open to our children here in America that aren't available anywhere else."

Dad walked Chicago's busy streets every day, stopping at each and every restaurant and lunchroom. "There was no work. Even for a substitute. And my feet were killing me. My back and shoulders ached like hell from lugging my kitchen tools around in a damned, heavy suitcase! I was wiped out. I was worried about you—all of you."

"I wonder what our lives would have been like if we had stayed here, Dad?" I piped in.

"Supremely better, Johnny, but I didn't know it at the time. I thought our citrus income would provide a secure home for you and food on the table." Dad's face stiffened with frustration. "I had paid for most of that orchard out of my hard earned savings! I thought that by going back to Greece we could escape the

Depression. I believed it would be good for you kids to meet our families in Greece. To learn our noble language."

"We learned Greek alright, Dad," I interrupted again. "To the point of forgetting English. And now you're paying good money to Mr. Perros to tutor Nikki and me in English."

"But, Johnny, early in 1937, along with my not having a steady job, your mother received a letter from her sister in the village saying your grandmother was about to die. Your mother's pain... pained me."

He leaned forward in his green chair, and looked at us apologetically, "Back in the 1930s, I resolutely saved pennies, nickels, dimes, quarters, half dollars, and occasional dollar bills. When you kids spoke English, instead of Greek at home, I became more determined to spend a year in Greece. As I saw it, we wouldn't be a burden to Mother's side of the family nor to my brothers. We would live on land I owned with my brothers, and enjoy my legal share in the profits from that citrus grove. Your mother would see your grandmother again."

Certainly, my father had never before asked his brothers for his share of the profits—nor had they offered to set aside his share for him. However, he knew that they were kind, generous men, who would be delighted to enjoy the company of their brother and his family. Dad longed to re-unite with his siblings and meet his half-siblings. They were his flesh and blood; in good times, he had helped them as much as possible. My father had no doubt that they felt the same.

By 1937, Dad had convinced Mother of his plan. He had saved just enough money, penny by penny and nickel by nickel, to buy one adult and three children's passages on an ocean liner and European trains, boarded in Paris, that would take my mother, brother, sister, and me to Greece.

It would take years' more work to earn another adult ticket. So Dad decided that he would stay behind in Chicago to work and establish financial stability for our return. "I was relieved. My wife and children would escape Depression poverty! You'd have a secure roof over your heads—in the old country."

As a result, in September of 1937 we prepared to leave for Greece via a great ocean journey. The earth was not considered "small" in 1937. The mindset about getting from one place to another was vastly different for ordinary Americans than what it is today. Geneva, Illinois, seemed so very distant from Chicago, but it was a mere thirty-six miles to the west. The ninety-two mile drive from Chicago to Milwaukee was regarded as an expedition.

Guarded on the east by the vast Atlantic, and on the west by an immense Pacific, most Americans believed that the bottomless and isolating waters of our great oceans insulated our forty-eight United States, keeping the bad guys away.

For most Americans, especially those financially crippled by the Great Depression, the rest of the world was light years away. But while we were living in our American dream house in Geneva, Illinois, in 1933, Adolph Hitler began rearming Germany. For the average American, Germany was impossibly far off—in strange, remote Europe.

When the Empire of Japan invaded China in 1937, as it had viciously enveloped Korea in earlier years, we, in Midwestern America, barely noticed. Americans, like Dad, were concerned with rising homelessness, the expansion of the devastating Dust Bowl, and start of the Social Security Program. As my father readied us for our journey to Greece, nearly as incredible a place for us to go to, in those days, as Japan—or even the moon—he didn't perceive news headlines about Asia, Northern Europe, or Africa as something related to our trip.

Americans had immersed themselves in the romance of Margaret Mitchell's *Gone with the Wind*, and laughed their worries away with the Marx Brothers' *A Day at the Races*—to distract themselves from Depression woes. No one heeded an outraged foreign artist like Picasso and his brutal painting, *Guernica*, a mass of mourning, human forms, ravaged by the fascist disregard for human life.

The 1930s would be described in future history books as the decade of emerging, dangerous dictators. Yet, my father naively understood that China, Germany, Abyssinia, and Spain were unfeasibly distant and unconnected to our family's destination: Kalamata, Greece. And what could possibly go wrong in one year? We were going to be back home before the start of school in September of 1938.

So, in September of 1937, Mom, my brother, sister, and I departed Chicago by train for New York where we boarded Cunard White Star's *R.M.S. Aquitania*, "The World's Wonder Ship." It sailed for Cherbourg, France, at an average speed of 22 1/2 knots. In Cherbourg we transferred onto European trains, which took us from France into Switzerland, Northern Italy, Yugoslavia, and finally to Athens, cradle of Western civilization: land of our great and splendid heritage.

At age four, like I was, kids don't have a concept of time or place; leaving Dad for a whole year made no impression on me. I couldn't fathom 365 days or a journey of thousands of miles. But back home in Chicago, before we left for Greece, I had loved eating oranges.

Mom saved pennies to buy a California navel orange, a Depression luxury, from the Greek fruit peddler who marketed colorful, fresh produce from atop his horse-pulled wagon. The adventure of accompanying Mother downstairs to the alley, behind the apartment house where we lived, and standing next to an immense, real live, brown and white, but smelly horse was exhilarating for four-year-old me. Completing Mom's vegetable selections, the peddler, speaking in Greek and smiling, presented my prize orange to me in a brown paper bag.

Mom held my hand going up the steps to the second floor again, with me gripping the bag. Then she stationed me at our blue and white, porcelain-topped, kitchen table. Perched on one of four, white, wooden chairs, I inhaled a mouth-watering citrus fragrance, as Mom peeled and sliced. Then I blissfully slurped down the luscious, orange sweetness that sloppily dribbled down from my happy mouth and sticky fists—to my little-kid elbows.

So to entice me to leave Dad and Chicago behind with minimal heartbreak in 1937, my parents played a game of distraction with me, promising that a radically thrilling experience awaited me in Kalamata. I was going to a place where I could personally pick and eat luscious oranges from beautiful orange trees, because, they explained, oranges grow on trees. Better yet, we owned an orchard full of orange trees in partnership with the two, wonderful, generous, and loving uncles we were going to meet, once we arrived in our citrus paradise.

It sounded good to me. I bought the deal without a sigh, a whimper, or a second thought.

3 | ARRIVAL: BEGINNING LIFE AWAY FROM THE U.S.—1937

And so, we relinquished my father's scrumptious beef gravy, Glenn Miller's swinging music, banana splits, and thrilling Phantom comic strips for a distant citrus grove with the potential to shelter and feed us. Unknown to us, however, as we left Dad and everything American behind, was that Hitler and Mussolini were revving up their plans to take over Europe.

Yet, demented dictators were not on Mother's mind when she alighted the train with three children in Athens, capital and largest city of her homeland. She was in no rush to get to Kalamata, had no intention of climbing the Acropolis to savor the Parthenon, and never hankered to hang out at fashionable Zonar's, "the" Athenian café. Mom only yearned to see her mother again.

Uncles Tassos, Petros, and Speros, my father's three half-brothers, met us at Athens' railroad station. They comprised the big city-based family of Dad's multiple siblings. Mom's mother, our Grandma, lived in Parnion, a village nestled in the mountains northeast of the city of Sparta, high and deep in the Peloponnesian peninsula, a hundred-plus miles south of Athens. Kalamata lay even further south.

We stayed with my uncles for a few days before departing for Peloponnesos. All three bachelors shared one small, dimly lit apartment that also doubled as a law office for Uncle Petros, the attorney. Good-looking, slim, and fashionable Petros was a 1930s William Powell, without the mustache. The eldest, Tassos, a domineering Churchillian figure, was a high-level bureaucrat employed by the Department of the Greek Army. Uncle Tassos seemed to have the last word on anything that mattered in the family: Petros was his spokesman.

The youngest, newly introduced Uncle Speros was petite, probably shorter than Mom. Sadly, Speros was deaf, but our warmest, friendliest Athenian uncle. His job was being cook and housekeeper for the trio.

Arriving in Athens, officials informed Mother that we needed to retrieve our luggage the next day at the customs office. We had departed Chicago with a bulky trunk, filled with all our belongings. A company called Railway Express made sure it followed us along every segment of our trip. (Lightweight suitcases with wheels hadn't been invented yet.)

On our second day, timid Uncle Speros accompanied us to the customs office to pick up our trunk. The surly customs agent, a short man in a fading navy blue uniform, demanded that Mother unlock the trunk so he could inspect its contents. He reminded me of a Chicago street car conductor having a bad day. She politely obliged; their dialogue continued in Greek. The incident developed into the first conflict Mother encountered in her homeland.

The customs man's icy evaluation: "These are new clothes. You must pay the duty!"

Taken aback by his assessment, Mother was rattled but maintained her innate civility. She looked into his indifferent face and spoke the truth so he could understand why the clothes were, as yet, unworn. "Yes, sir. These clothes are new. You see, sir, we will be in Greece for a year. My children are growing quickly and will need them."

Never glancing at Mother when he spoke, he barked, "Madame, children don't require this many clothes."

"Sir, we will be away from the U.S. for a year. I have three children. One is a girl. The other two, as you can see, are boys. My eldest son is eleven, and the other is four. These three children cannot share clothing. Each has specific needs."

"Madame, children do not need this much clothing. I suspect you brought clothing here—to sell. You need to pay a duty on these items."

Mother, five feet six in her stocking feet, carried herself erectly; she never had to think about sitting or standing up straight. Blessed with a well-proportioned nose, glowing skin, and Mediterranean good looks, she never used cosmetics. Her shiny, dark brown hair was always neatly combed and pulled back into a graceful swirl onto the back of her head. Looking neat, smart, but disbelieving, she listened to the customs officer, then stood up even straighter and directed her intense, dark brown eyes down at the mustached official on the other side of the counter.

"Sir, I have no intention of selling anything. My children need these clothes. I have no money for buying clothes in Greece. I am here to visit my elderly mother and to meet my husband's family. I want my children to be clean and presentable when they call on their relatives."

Bushy black eyebrows shaded the glare in his cold eyes. The pompous and indifferent bureaucrat, acting like the lord of some medieval fiefdom speaking to his stable hands, barked, "Madame, I have no time or interest in continuing this conversation. You either pay the duty or I will confiscate these items. What I do know is that Americans are rich. You'll pay." He announced the amount due. Mother's face lost color.

"This guy doesn't know what he's talking about. He's a little twerp, Mom. The S.O.B. is a nobody!" Alex advised Mom in English. "Let's grab our trunk and get out of here."

Relieved that Alex had only used the acronym for terminology he acquired on Chicago's streets, Mother silenced him. "Quiet," she whispered. "We can't be calling him names. And, we follow rules, Alex. We will not begin our stay in Greece on a bad footing with authorities. These are only threats. He will come to understand that I am speaking to him in earnest."

She addressed the agent again, smiling a little but speaking frankly. "Please understand, sir, that we are not the Rockefellers.

We came to my homeland to be reunited with our beloved families. My husband worked very hard in America to earn money to send us here and to purchase this clothing for our own children to use."

"Madame, don't deceive yourself into thinking that you have fooled me. You Americans are drowning in money." The agent stuck out his chin, produced a disgusting, short clucking sound through his enormous mustache, and in a more intimidating voice insisted on the duty fee.

Mother's smile evaporated; discouraged, she shook her head. Seeing that she was making no attempt to open her purse to take out money, the agent grabbed at sizable layers of clothing and pulled them out of the trunk.

Poor Uncle Speros attempted to speak, but due to his hearing impairment, he pronounced his words oddly. He stepped up, closer to the counter, in an effort to defend Mother but the agent looked down his nose and over his mustache at him. The agent's halting stare silenced Speros and tears came to my uncle's eyes. He shrugged his shoulders, apologetically, and stepped back. "Petros should have come instead."

"If you cannot pay, Madame, the matter is over! I must confiscate these clothes. It is the law." The agent slammed down the lid of the trunk, now half-empty, and affixed his stamp to a handful of forms that he shoved at my mother.

"The dirty bastard is robbing us of our stuff, Mom. He's taking our clothes home for his own kids to wear," Alex protested.

"What's done is done, Alex. I don't intend to accuse him of anything—or call him names either. Let's get out of here." Our raided trunk stayed with us throughout our Greek stay. After Mom's confrontation with the "crook," as we labeled the agent, Alex referred to our trunk as our traveling buddy. So we christened our trunk, "Buddy."

Unlike the friendly, male relatives we left behind in the U.S., my father's half-brothers, Petros and Tassos, were uncles "with attitude," not warm and fuzzy like Speros. Both well-trimmed frames were nattily attired in dark business suits with hair and complexions similar to Dad's: fair and light-skinned. But their conceited personalities vastly differed from my father's naturally smiling, affable behavior. Petros was a lawyer, Tassos a government employee. The village-born boys had developed haughty, cool dispositions.

Both let Mother know that they were "players" in 1930s Athenian society. Even at my young age, I sensed condescension strongly directed at Mother, which I later learned was a throwback to 400 years of the Ottoman Turkish occupation of Greece (in which women were ignorantly looked upon as the inferior gender).

Our visit with them was short. And when we left, we had no way of knowing that we would not return to Athens again for seven-plus years.

***

Also happening—1937:

- ❖ *"Prince Valiant" makes its debut as a comic strip*

- ❖ *Pope Pius XI puts out an encyclical denouncing the Nazis*

- ❖ *Margaret Mitchell wins the Pulitzer Prize for* Gone With the Wind

- ❖ *Coronation of King George the VI of Great Britain*

- ❖ *Golden Gate Bridge is dedicated in San Francisco*

- ❖ *Lincoln Tunnel in NYC first opens to traffic*

4 | TRAVELING TO PARNION:
BY TRAIN, BUS —AND TRUCK

Our journey from Athens to Parnion, Mother's birthplace and home of my grandmother, began with a grueling train ride, heading southwest from Athens. At one spot along the route, Mom suddenly pointed out the train window. "Quick! Look down there, children! That's the *Isthmus of Corinth*." Wide-eyed, we watched as our train precariously navigated a very high railroad bridge to cross a narrow, four-mile long thread of cobalt blue water, located far down below us. The bridge was the only way the train could travel across the dramatic canal that slashed the Greek landscape, separating the northern Greek mainland from Peloponnesos, the peninsula to the south.

The train crawled under a clear sky toward the middle of the mountainous, dry, wheat-colored Peloponnesian peninsula. Nine hours after leaving Athens, we got off at the Tripolis train station where we boarded a horse-pulled buggy that transported us across town to a bus depot. The crowded bus we boarded in Tripolis carried us further south. Leaving Arcadia, it crossed into the prefecture of Laconia, home territory of the ancient Spartans.

Two noisy, white lambs, accompanying a fellow passenger, fascinated me; I had never seen farm animals on Chicago's streetcars. After a few hours of hot, dusty and bumpy riding, with stops to let off other passengers, the bus halted at a narrow road, which formed a T with the main highway, miles north of the modern city of Sparta. The driver announced we had arrived at our stop, a low-slung, one-story, stone building at the side of the road.

21

Gathering us together to get off, Mother spotted a tall man dressed in a long-sleeved, white shirt and dark trousers. He was standing at the side of the road, in front of the stone building. Mom's face lit up when she recognized him. "That's my brother, George."

As soon as the driver released the door, the lanky, handsome, blue-eyed man with graying hair and well-trimmed mustache, leapt toward the stairs. Calling out, "Katherine," he swept Mother off the step and hugged her tightly. After Alex followed Mom off the bus, our smiling uncle quickly turned to swoop Nikki and me down to the ground. He gathered all three of us kids together, warmly embraced us, and put us down to turn and hug my mother again. I was relieved that this uncle was glad to see us.

Descending from the bus, the driver put us in possession of "Buddy," our clumsy trunk, the fifth and most difficult-to-handle member of our traveling party; Buddy had traveled on the roof. Uncle George directed us toward a man waiting behind the wheel of a pick-up truck, parked at roadside. Except for the truck, its driver, and the stone building, nothing and no one else was visible. Trees and greenery indicated we were way out in the country.

"Katherine, children… meet my friend, Sophocles, our fellow villager, who will kindly be driving us to Parnion. And Sophocles, let me introduce you to the American representatives of our family: my sister Katherine, my handsome nephews, Alex and John, and Nikki, my beautiful niece." Following introductions, both men loaded Buddy onto the back of the truck and the four of us miraculously squeezed into the vehicle with Sophocles: Nikki sat on Mother's lap; I sat on Alex's. Making sure no one was hanging out the door, Sophocles asked, "Are we all set?"

"Yes!" Mom answered, "Destination: Parnion!"

Uncle George was ebullient about our arrival and chatted to all of us at once. "Our family is excited and anxiously waiting for you. The women have been happily cooking for days. The only one you'll not see is our sister Joanna who is visiting her son and his family. He works for the government, assigned to far away

Lemnos Island, of all places. I wrote to Joanna to tell her you were coming. She responded that she can't come right now but will return before you go back to America next year. Lemnos is far. Traveling to and from the island is arduous."

Dark haired, mustached, handsome Sophocles, enthusiastically commanding his truck's steering wheel, never took his eyes off the road. Yet, I noticed that he smiled, or wrinkled his brow, or shook his head, displaying an entire rainbow of emotions while listening in on Mom and her brother's exchanges.

"Katherine, I need to warn you," George confided. "Don't be shocked when you see Mother. She is very frail, close to ninety, and definitely showing her years. As you already know, she had been quite ill. Pretend you don't notice her infirmities. Perhaps waiting to see you has kept her alive." Dismayed, Mom's happy face ceased smiling and her eyes filled with tears as she nodded sadly, agreeing to show no alarm.

Riding along a bumpy, dusty, and scarcely one-lane road, enthusiastic Uncle George also directed his remarks toward us children. He explained that Parnion derived its name from Mt. Parnon, their titanic mountain neighbor to the northeast. "It is a very high mountain. But because immense foothills surround Parnon, its peak is not visible from our village." Then he pointed toward the west. "That's the world renowned Mt. Taygetos." We turned our heads and spotted the distant, mountain range; a ring of clouds circled its peak.

"As the second highest mountain in Greece, infamous Taygetos is much higher than Parnon. Ancient Spartans threw the weaklings of their society off the top of beautiful Taygetos! Have you heard those stories in America?"

"Spartans were tough guys," Alex agreed. "Like the 'Outfit,' in Chicago."

"Not quite the same," George responded, smiling and recognizing Alex's analogy to the infamous criminal organization. "But, don't worry, Nikki and John," he teased us. "Our Parnon is a friendly mountain. You are safe on this side of the valley."

Three wide-eyed city kids gazed out truck windows. Sophocles followed a road that plowed through woods interspersed with planted fields. Traveling upward, through the backwoods of rugged country on a road studded with blind curves, we steeply ascended. The dusty topography was strange, like nothing Alex, Nikki, or I had seen before. I eventually came to understand the difference between hills and mountains, but on that first day's journey, the terrain, for a kid from flat-as-a-pancake Chicago, resembled a meeting of the Rockies, the Alps and the Himalayas. "We must be going to the top of the world," I whispered to Alex.

Mom, animated and happy, identified local flora as we rode toward her village. "Look, children. Fig trees...with fruit as sweet as honey!! And the trees with the grayish-green leaves, on the left of the road, are olive trees. They don't grow in Illinois. It's too cold."

I peered out the window, a little puzzled by her enthusiasm. The trees were not as stately as elms and oaks back home in Illinois. In fact, these were short and scrubby.

"George, are there still walnut trees down at the bottom of the ravine? I remember picking walnuts there when I was a girl."

"They haven't moved a centimeter, Katherine. In fact they're waiting for you," George kidded. "You can pick nuts while you're here. It's autumn, walnut season."

But conversation broke off when Sophocles's fast moving truck skidded, almost veering off the road. Tires screeched and dust clouds flew when he pushed the brakes to the floor. We reeled out of our seats, stunned; Alex held me down when I started to fly out of his lap. But strangely, when the truck stopped skidding, Sophocles casually turned off the ignition. Four jolted Americans held their breaths: the road ahead was gridlocked with animals.

"What's that?" Nikki squealed.

Pleased with her reaction, unshaken George explained, "A flock of sheep, Nikki. For thousands of years they and their shepherds have had the exclusive right of way on our roads. They freely meander through these hills and valleys to find grazing lands for food to eat. Take notice, children. We must always stop to pay our respects when we find sheep on the road," he laughed, joshing us again. "Actually, we have to wait. There's no way to go around them.

"Look over there! That's the shepherd, a fellow from Parnion." Then, waving his arm, George called, *"Yia sou, Yianni!"* A gnarled old man wearing a wide-brimmed straw hat and long tunic over his trousers smiled under his prominent white mustache, and waved back at us with a long shepherd's crook.

"What an exquisite sight! I haven't seen a flock of sheep since I left Greece." Our delighted mother was mesmerized by the hundreds of animals occupying the road and actually making docile "baaa baaa" sounds, just like I'd heard in the nursery rhyme. Furry sheep milled about the truck then slowly wandered off to join their pals in the valley on our right. Elegant ribbons of curly, white and beige wool, dotted with occasional black fleeces, gracefully flowed into Laconia's green and straw-colored countryside.

Sophocles explained that the hollow, tinkling sounds, heard through intermittent bleating, came from bells tied around the necks of the flock's leader rams. Stuck in the middle of the narrow road, the six of us watched the ancient scene through modern truck windows. But technology abruptly interrupted pre-historic serenity when our driver revved up the engine again: the shepherd and his barking dog had cleared the flock from the narrow path. Sophocles's truck was the only motor vehicle on the road.

We passed vineyards, and arrived at a simple bridge over a trickling stream. "Water in this river comes from snows melting at the summit of Mt. Parnon," our uncle explained. "It's autumn now, and looks almost dry. But during our winter rainy season these river waters get pretty high." Alex, whose frame of reference was Illinois' mightier Fox and Chicago Rivers, was curious. "Does a river with so little water have a name?"

"Its name is *Oinountas*," Mom answered, "from the ancient Greek word for wine, *oinos*. The river is named for these vineyards. Don't let the trickle of water fool you. When it rains, forceful waters in this river become treacherous."

We passed farmers in their fields; they looked up from their work to smile and wave; we waved back. Closing her eyes and deeply inhaling air breezing through the truck's open windows, Mom was enjoying every inch of the ride to her birthplace. "That's what we call real fresh air, children. Parnion air!" she remarked with pure joy on her face.

Climbing the narrow, curvy road, we spotted a few crudely constructed, stone huts. Nikki asked about them, and Mother explained that the tiny buildings were shelters used by farmers, shepherds, and travelers who journey by foot. "They rest inside during the hottest part of the day, and also during rain or snow storms. Sometimes people sleep overnight in these huts."

"People sleep out here, in the wilds of Peloponnesos?" Alex asked disbelievingly.

He had barely finished asking his critical question when Sophocles pointed up to an outcropping of foliage and structures on the mountain in the distance. "There's our village!"

"I can't believe this," big-city Alex moaned under his breath. "We came half-way around the world to get to the middle of nowhere."

5 | "MIDDLE OF NOWHERE"

Our destination crowned one of Mt. Parnon's steep foothills like a Christmas wreath: the rising bluff, wrapped in an impenetrable collar of deep green, was studded with red-tile and white stucco. More greenery surrounded Parnion than we had seen around any village on our long train ride from Athens or our bus trip from Tripolis.

A clump of trees, on the rock face, allowed the large cross of a Byzantine church to poke higher into the heavens from the crest of a red-tiled dome. Red roofs topped off small grayish stone and white buildings around the distant church.

Mother's voice flooded with emotion. "Children, that is Parnion! That's where I was born and grew up. It's still beautiful and green like I remembered—even in the dry season!" She wiped her eyes with a white handkerchief, and Uncle George warmly reached out with his arm to embrace her. He understood the depths of her feelings better than we did.

But Mother had not forgotten my brother's sarcastic remark. "Parnion is in the middle of nowhere for you, Alex. It's the exact opposite of Chicago. Yet, people have been happy to live in this precious place for hundreds of generations."

Initially we had come upon a distant, full view of Parnion. When the long, tree-lined road we traveled led into a natural left turn, the panorama was gone—and we were inside the village. Individual houses lined the road; high stucco walls fenced off each property. A hundred yards after entering Mom's village, Sophocles pulled to the right side of the road and stopped in front of a walled house.

Mother smiled when she recognized the two-story, white stucco home, topped with a barn-red tile roof. Stone steps climbed up from the street to a matching stucco wall and a plain wooden door. When George helped Mother down from the truck, I was surprised to see her immediately scramble up the stairs. She was no longer a middle-aged wife and mother of three. Instead, she was a young daughter yearning to see her mother.

Our uncle encouraged us to follow her through the door. "Go meet your Aunt Sophia," he advised. "She'll take you upstairs to meet your grandmother."

We trailed Mom into a shady interior courtyard. Glancing up, I spotted casually braided vines, green leaves, and immense grape clusters hanging down from twisted canes, like chandeliers. The emerald arbor's natural air-conditioning brought welcome, cooling comfort: a relief after hours and hours of traveling in Greece's autumn heat. Mom continued hurrying over a cobblestone floor and disappeared into the house through a second door. Squeals of delight, mixed with crying, greeted her. "That's your Aunt Sophia," George reported. We could tell by their murmured cries that my mother's younger sister had already engulfed Mom into a tight, lingering embrace. Then we heard our aunt say, "Mother is waiting for you upstairs by the fireplace."

Aunt Sophia welcomed all three of us with loving hugs and kisses on both cheeks. Shorter and more petite than Mom, her pretty face was surprisingly older-looking because her ruddy complexion was carved with multiple facial wrinkles. Still, Sophia's deep brown eyes were as lovely as Mom's and just as affable. Adoringly examining us, our aunt proclaimed she was proud to be related to three such handsome American children.

When we reached the second floor, Mom was already in the tight, permanent embrace of a tiny, delicate, white-haired, wrinkled woman, who was reclining on a small day bed, close to a stone hearth with blazing fire. Grandmother, dressed entirely in black, whispered words through her tears that I couldn't make out, but Mom understood they expressed the joy of a mother who was finally reunited with her child, after almost two decades. Silently clinging together, Mom and our grandmother managed smiles when they glimpsed the three of us watching them.

Motioning us to come closer, Mother introduced us. "*Mitera*, these are my children. This tall, blond boy, my right-hand man on this journey, is our oldest, Alex. Here is Nikki, your granddaughter who has been so anxious to meet you. She loves to sing and dance, so she will entertain you. And this bashful little guy with dark hair and bright, brown eyes, peeking out from behind Alex, is John." Each of us took a turn to embrace and to be embraced by our frail, smiling, octogenarian *Yiayia* (Grandmother): an ancient woman.

For the first time in my short life, I knew a grandma. When she reached to hug me, I got a closer look at her narrow, creased face, felt the rough skin of her hands, and noticed twisted arthritic fingers. The fragrance I inhaled was eucalyptus, something akin to essence of Vicks VapoRub. Grandma spoke softly and I didn't understand her words; but her eyes were full of tears—and there was love in them. I knew senior citizens in Chicago, but my feeble, wrinkled grandmother was the oldest person I had ever seen.

More relatives than one could remember at a first meeting had arrived to greet us with tears, smiles, embraces, and kisses. Mother's birthplace was full of family who came to be reunited with our mother and meet her children. Fond caresses and friendly pinches to our cheeks from rough, well-worked hands were affectionately extended to our childish faces.

Warm smiles revealed sparkling gold teeth, or gaps where teeth were missing; some grins showed perfect teeth. Male complexions were deeply tanned, leathery, and wrinkled. All the men wore mustaches in a variety of shapes and sizes, some bushier than others. The exteriors of these family members appeared somewhat rougher than relatives we left behind in Chicago, but like their American kin, they were down-to-earth, warm people.

Even as a four year old, I noticed right away that Parnion people dressed differently from Chicagoans. When relatives had visited our apartment in Chicago, men wore suits, white shirts, ties, and fedora hats. Women also wore hats, and carried handbags, as well as gloves. In Parnion, though, there wasn't a necktie or handbag to be found.

Greeting us first was Uncle George's wife, Athanasia, a very slender woman with dark blond hair and blue eyes. Then, Aunt Sophia's husband Vasili, a distinguished gentleman with a Clark Gable mustache, stepped forward to welcome us.

Next came Mom's widowed older sister, Stella. Dressed entirely in black, the scarf around Stella's shoulders distinctly contrasted with her snow-white hair. She cried as she embraced my mother and continued crying when she hugged the three of us. At first, because of her crying and black clothing, I felt she wasn't as friendly as the others; though soon enough, I changed my mind.

We had younger cousins too: Sophia and Vasili's children, Tasia and Kosta. Uncles George and Vasili helped our driver bring Buddy, the trunk, into the house. Sophocles was warmly invited inside to partake of our welcoming feast; it turned out he was the only resident in Parnion who owned a motorized vehicle. After all the hugging and kissing, Grandmother reminded Aunt Sophia, "Bring out the sweets."

"Already done," Sophia answered, as she approached us with a fancy tray holding four tiny dishes. Each dish had a tiny silver spoon set at its side and was topped with a tablespoon of gooey fruit, which looked like small purple cherries. Four glasses of water, on a smaller tray, were offered to us too.

"*Kalos oresate*," the crowd welcomed us, almost in unison. It was the traditional Greek welcome to "sweeten our visit."

"I made these preserves from *vysina* (wild cherries) I picked from our very own trees last July," Sophia proudly announced. I thought she had a wonderfully delicious way of greeting us. After that dusty trip, the cold water was welcome too.

While we enjoyed our sweets, Mom's older sister, Stella, steered her into a conversation that focused on my aunt's late husband. He had immigrated to Chicago, without Stella or their offspring, in the great wave of European immigrants before 1920;

but he had died in Chicago in 1925. My aunt was still wearing black. By the time we arrived in 1937, her children had grown and were living and working in Athens. Stella lived alone in her husband's house in Parnion, further up the road, on the village's major square, near Parnion's main church.

"Do you remember my Manoli, Katherine? Tell me about his life in America."

"Certainly I remember him," Mom said. "He was a very kind man who worked very hard."

"He was in the produce business, was he not?" Stella asked.

"Well, yes. Manoli was a fruit and vegetable peddler," Mom explained. "He owned a horse and wagon and sold produce, house to house, in Chicago neighborhoods. As I said before, he worked hard, long hours, Stella."

"But he died so suddenly." My aunt's tears began rolling down her face, recalling news of her husband's untimely death. "My children and I never saw him again."

"I know. And I know it was unbearable for you." Mom sweetly reached for her sister's hand. "No one knows why he died, Stella. It was probably a heart attack. He had not been sick. One day, he was found, passed away, in his rented room. Please know, Stella, that we buried him with love. All of us in the family attended his funeral."

Just then, a noisy, very large, older man entered the house. Sophia happily announced, "Here's Cousin Nicholas." Mom smiled, probably relieved that the man's presence was about to change the glum topic. The big, boisterous, senior citizen, interrupting the cheerless conversation, enveloped Mother in a huge bear hug. "Welcome back, Katherine," he said warmly, but loudly.

Taking his place on a chair next to Mother, the huge man was introduced to us kids as "Uncle Nicholas" because, by tradition, children were encouraged to refer to their older relatives as "Aunt" and "Uncle." Mom's cousin was an older widower, with no children. His rowdy voice and ruddy face complemented his head of thick, white hair, and prominent, snow-white, bushy mustache. Nicholas was a striking figure—the only person who spoke English to me.

Soon women with steaming platters of food emerged from all the corners of Grandpa's house and we were graciously seated at a long table, covered with a white tablecloth and set with glasses, dishes, and flatware. Grandmother was helped across the room to sit at the head of the table. We ate in the same sparsely furnished room with the fireplace and her daybed. It served as a living room, dining room, and bedroom combination.

Heaps of food: roasted lamb and potatoes deliciously fragrant with lemon and oregano; braised chicken and rice pilaf; tomato and cucumber salad; a rough brown bread we were encouraged to dip into the olive oil dressing; and olives and cheese were set out on the table. A fragrant, clear elixir, produced from the previous year's courtyard grapes, was proudly poured into small, stemless glasses and served to adults. There was cool water for us kids. "Grandpa's grapes make the best wine in the village," one guest remarked to the approving crowd.

Ironically, we traveled thousands of miles to visit our grandmother in the home where Mom and her many siblings were born, yet heard local relatives calling it "Grandpa's house." Grandfather had died twenty years before and Grandma had arrived as his young bride to be the mistress of the house, decades before that. Yet, she got no credit for ownership.

During dinner, adult conversation swirled around me, using thousands of Greek words I had never heard before. But when I looked up at the wall opposite the fireplace, I found a framed picture of someone very recognizable. Smiling down at me, as the only connection to something familiar in that peculiar new world was a photo of my favorite older, Chicago cousin, Mary, in mortarboard and gown. Mother explained, "It's her college graduation picture." The first college graduate of our family—a woman—proudly graced the ancient walls of Grandpa's patriarchal, village home.

The toast to Grandpa's memory brought back warm thoughts of others who could not be present. The first mentioned was John, Grandma's eldest, who had accompanied my mother on her journey to America, but returned to Greece in the mid-1920s and died in the village, still young and unmarried. "*Aionia tou i mnimi*" ("May his memory be eternal") was repeated by our relatives at the mention of his name, and other names too. Grandma's eyes sparkled with tears, especially at the mention of her late son, John. "What's the news about Joanna?" Mother asked, not wanting to see her mother sad.

We learned that Joanna, my mother's widowed older sister, who was visiting her son on Lemnos Island when we arrived, also had a daughter studying music in Athens. Stella explained that Joanna lived on the other side of Parnion when she was at home in the village.

At dinner, I heard more about Nicholas, the uncle who spoke English. He was one of several Parnion-born men I was to meet in the village who had immigrated to Boston and Chicago in the early 1900s. These Greek Americans were financially able to return to their homeland with their hard-earned savings in tact prior to the Depression.

"I remember, Katherine, that before I came back to Parnion from America in 1926, I traveled to Chicago to meet our relatives. You and Andrew gave a dinner for me in your apartment... I think it was on Springfield Avenue. You were newly married. Had no kids yet. And I recall the superb dishes you cooked for all of us.

"My dear cousins, Sophia and Stella, our Katherine is a gracious hostess and an outstanding cook. Katherine, I have never forgotten your kindness and hospitality—and that wonderful meal." Early on, I could tell that even though Nicholas was a huge man, his energetic movements did not make him a fearful presence; his manner of speaking, robust and loud, was quite friendly.

After dinner, while adults continued to reminisce, our cousins Tasia and Kosta invited Alex, Nikki, and me to go outside to play together. My shyness kept me hanging close to my siblings as we played tag with our new cousins. But, to my regret, we encountered some half dozen, scruffy, foot-tall, feathery creatures on the road in front of the house.

I froze when they darted toward me and persistently pecked around my feet. I flinched and whimpered, but the strange birds wouldn't leave me alone, even after I tried what Alex suggested: shooing them away. Nice relatives were one thing; mean birds were another. I didn't like this Parnion place after all.

"Let's go back to Chicago, Alex," I suggested to my brother in English. Naturally, all the kids laughed at me when Alex translated. Seeing my tears, Cousin Tasia felt sorry and walked me back into the house again.

Lowering my head and staring at my feet, I attempted to silently slink back into the house without adult attention, but teary eyes gave me away. Tasia's explanation, "Johnny's afraid of chickens. He wants to go back to Chicago," did not relieve my discomfort. Adult laughter followed—I felt worse.

"Don't you have chickens in America?" Uncle George asked Mom.

"Of course we have chickens, George. But we don't interact with them on our streets. Come here, Johnny. You'll get used to them. They're only chickens."

Mother's words weren't as soothing as she thought they were going to be. Chicago chickens didn't have beady eyes, weird feet, and feathers. Chicago chickens didn't walk all over the city. They quietly stayed on dinner plates—like they were supposed to.

I spent the rest of the time inside the house, in the company of my mother and Cousin Tasia's father, Uncle Vasili—with the movie-star mustache. Even though the others had laughed at my discomfort, Vasili put his arm around my shoulder and winked, as if to say, "You're alright, kid. Just hang in there. Life gets better." As he sat near me, I picked up the scent of wine on my uncle's breath.

Taking his leave in late afternoon, Mom's cousin Nicholas gave me a friendly pinch on the cheek and shook my hand. My little paw had never before been in the grasp of a hand as massive as his. He kindly turned the volume down on his usually loud voice and spoke gently to me.

"Johnny, I found lots of things I thought were strange here when I returned from the States. The good people of Parnion have never lived anywhere else and have no way of knowing how we live in America." Smiling more he added, "Myself, I miss efficient American organization. You probably don't understand that yet."

"Take it from me, John," Nicholas continued. "Parnion is a good place. I wouldn't have come back if it wasn't. Like your mother says, it will take time to get used to the way things are done here. And before you go back home, you'll find things to love in Parnion that we don't have in Boston or Chicago." Vasili and Nicholas made me feel better in my new, very foreign environs.

Evening darkened the unfamiliar surroundings of Grandpa's homestead and I discovered there was no electricity. Small oil lamps were lit inside the house, and I noticed, with dismay, that in dimmer lighting, ominous shadows haunted the home's peculiar niches. So, to keep my mind off scary darkness, I sat with the conversing adults, while cuddling close to my mother. Drowsy from the journey, I followed the sparkle of gold teeth reflecting fireplace flames and flickering oil lamps. With all those relatives buzzing around, I fell asleep in my mother's lap.

Blood-curdling shrieks jarred me at daybreak. The room was full of light and I realized it was morning. Jumping out of the strange bed I found myself in, I ran to what appeared to be a second-story window. Bright-eyed, dark-haired Nikki was already up and looking out of it. We had experienced our first earfuls of crowing roosters.

Gazing out the window, we spotted three women following three live donkeys below us on the narrow road. The animals were screeching even weirder sounds than the roosters had made. Dressed in black from head to toe, only the women's eyes showed between folds of the black scarves wrapped around their necks and heads. Their donkeys were loaded down with densely bundled branches. Parnion was unveiling one peculiar scene after another to us city kids.

Later, we learned village women were extremely careful, outdoors, about exposing their skin to the sizzling sun. No matter how hot the day, they wore long sleeves, long skirts, and scarves around their heads.

Those noisy donkeys in the street, on my first morning in Parnion, persisted at making harsh, scary screams. So, I rushed out of the bedroom to find refuge with my mother. Nikki preceded me into the fireplace room/kitchen where I found Mom, under interrogation. With arms open, grandmother hugged me before I silently slipped into Mother's lap. Nikki made a beeline for *Yiayia*, who smiled, embraced her warmly, and kept Nikki close on the daybed, near the lit fireplace.

The warm reminiscing of the night before—had gone. Now my relatives were speaking about practical things. Grandmother, George, Sophia, and Stella were questioning Mom about life in the United States. "Katherine, we're thrilled you're home again," said Uncle George." Our joy is beyond measure because we missed you so much. But why did you leave America, without your husband, to return here? There you had everything. Here, as you well know, there is very little."

Aunt Stella, mourning the loss of her husband the night before, was matter of fact in the light of morning. "Why didn't Andrew come with you? How will you handle three children and survive without a husband advising and protecting you for an entire year? Why did he allow you to come without him? Katherine, you can't function in Greece without a man's guidance."

Soft, kind Aunt Sophia observed, "Your children are beautiful, may God bless them. But they are Americans. Can they cope with our simple ways? Johnny already appears frightened."

Stella appraised, "You're going to Kalamata. You have never been to Kalamata before. It's not Parnion and it's not Chicago. How will you manage? It's impossible without your husband!"

Mother was getting the third degree. Could she answer all their questions? She, most assuredly, could not. Holding me tight on her lap, Mother gently explained, "I need to follow Andrew's plan. After a few weeks of visiting with you here, my dear loved ones, we will go to Kalamata. I made my promise to Andrew and I keep my promises."

***

While we lived in Kalamata—1940:

❖ *Benito Mussolini drags Italy into the war on Hitler's side*

❖ *"The Grapes of Wrath" with Henry Fonda debuts in American movie theaters*

❖ *Americans laugh as they listen to Fibber McGee and Molly on the radio*

❖ *Frank Sinatra begins his singing career with the Harry James Orchestra*

❖ *F.D.R. wins a third term*

6 | WAR AND OCCUPATION:
KALAMATA, 1938-1941

February 13, 1938

Dear Andrew,

I hope my letter finds you well. We miss you. We are in good health and hope you are too. Loving thanks for the money you sent in your last letter. Every little bit helps. It is paying the rent for the tiny house I rented on Pharon Street, about two blocks from Kalamata's port. The courtyard in back and its little fountain fascinate Nikki and Johnny. The children are adjusting to life in Greece and are enrolled in the city's schools.

At first, local kids made fun of Nikki and John when they heard them speaking "American" to each other. Nikki's reaction was to tell them off. "Too bad you dummies can't speak English like I can because I know two languages and you only know one." But our shy little Johnny was deeply embarrassed. He has avoided the English language ever since. So, whatever challenges we have in adjusting to our surroundings, at least your children are learning Greek as you wanted them to do when we came here.

The neighborhood school wanted to place Alex in a lower grade because he cannot read and write Greek as well as native-born students in his age group. But the first grade teacher, Mrs. Pandora, was very helpful. She feared he would be embarrassed and disillusioned in classes with younger children and suggested placing him at the age-appropriate grade level in a school across town. I am grateful for her efforts. Alex is learning quickly in classes with children his own age. I'm pleased Mrs. Pandora saw his potential. School is working out well for all three. I know this news will please you.

As I mentioned in my previous letters, your brother Antoni continues to claim that I have no rights to the citrus orchard. He says he paid for his half,

Harry paid for his half, and you put no money into the purchase. Without legal paperwork, he is giving me a hard time. Your brother Harry is trying to help me with this problem. We'll see what happens. I'll keep you informed.

I received a letter from my brother George in Parnion telling me my mother's health is worsening. I'll need to return to the village soon. Inconvenient transportation between Kalamata and Parnion makes the trip arduous.

I know that our letters to each other spend weeks in the mail process. News is already old when it arrives. But, as I promised, I'll keep writing. The children join me in sending you our love.

With love,
Katherine

Overwhelming anxieties began haunting Mom immediately upon our arrival in Kalamata when Dad's brother, belligerent Uncle Antoni, announced that Mom had no claim to the land, and ruthlessly accused my mother of trying to steal his land away from him. Mother was shocked and devastated by his bogus assertions that Dad had never contributed money toward purchasing the orchard.

During the eleven months that intervened between the previous surviving letter to Dad and the one to follow it, written in 1939, Mom endured deplorable, mean-spirited behavior aimed at her from Antoni. She felt powerless and overwhelmed, even though Dad's other Kalamata-based brother, Harry, supported Mom's case. Surely, she preferred to leave it all behind and return to the U.S. but there was not enough money to pay for our passages home. With no other choices left to her, Mother stuck it out and went to court, using money Dad sent in his letters to feed and house us.

Meanwhile, in March 1938, a month after Mom wrote the previous letter, Hitler and the German army helped themselves to Austria and annexed it to Germany. Then in late September of 1938, Hitler threatened to take over the Sudetenland, a section of

Czechoslovakia heavily populated with ethnic Germans. Attempting to avert the outbreak of war, France and Great Britain agreed to Germany's takeover. Hitler's world domination had begun, slowly but deliberately, in lands neighboring Germany. Both places seemed so very far away from Kalamata.

January 17, 1939

Dear Andrew,

We have been in Kalamata for over a year and problems with your brother, Antoni, continue to plague us. He does not allow me access to the land you helped pay for. I'm sorry to have to write this to you about your brother but he is a vicious, violent man. He came after me with a garden hoe and threatened to beat me with it. It was not a joke. The children and I are afraid of him. We keep our distance and fear him in the same way we would fear a lurking crocodile— one that's always ready to bite. Your brother Harry, who has been kind and hospitable to us, tells me that Antoni has always been difficult. Didn't you know that, Andrew? Why didn't you share that information with me before I came here? Antoni is a sadistic man. Harry is remorseful for failing to notice your name was not recorded on the original deed to the property. He's sure Antoni purposely omitted it.

Harry has always known of Antoni's treachery. That is why he sold his own share of your joint real estate venture to Antoni and purchased a separate orchard with the money Antoni paid him. Harry and his family live in the home Harry built in his own orchard. He has no business dealings with Antoni whatsoever. Did you know that, Andrew?

I am forced to hire a lawyer and go to court to claim your share of the property. Harry will testify that your money went into buying the land. Petros, your lawyer brother in Athens, refuses to help Harry and me because Petros does not want to get involved in "family squabbles." Your suggestion in your last letter to go to Petros for help is not an option. I remember quite clearly that when we were first married you sent sizable amounts of your hard-earned money to Petros to pay for his law school education. Obviously, not getting involved is Petros's way of showing us his appreciation.

Enclosed you will find a note from Alex asking you to send him an American boy's magazine which he wants to read. And here below is a drawing for you from Johnny. He told me to write you that his teacher's name is Kyra [Mrs.] Pandora and that he's learning how to read. Nikki wants you to know that her teacher's name is Kyra Evangelia. Nikki asked me to tell you that Uncle Antoni was mean to her when she picked up a ripe orange which had fallen to the ground in the orchard. She wants you to write a letter to him to tell him to be nice. You have no idea how malicious a man he is.

I will try to mail this now so that you can get it as soon as possible, which means weeks.

Stay well. We all send you our love.

With love,
Katherine

While Mom struggled to achieve rightful ownership of Dad's portion of the citrus grove in a lawsuit against Antoni, which like most court cases slowly dragged to a final decision, Hitler and Mussolini quickly mobilized their armies to carry out their plans for world domination. The Germans would invade Poland on September 1, 1939. And when Benito Mussolini confidently invaded Greece, without warning, from its northern, Albanian border in October of 1940, we, down in Kalamata, were unexpectedly thrust closer to real-time war.

January 22, 1940

Dear Andrew,

Again, it was good to receive your greatly appreciated letter and the generous amount of money you enclosed. Your stipends keep us going.

The latest news is that we won the case in court. We won because Antoni could not prove to the judge how he was able to accumulate all the money he needed to buy the orchard. As part of the settlement we won the right to own 2 bedrooms of the house on the orchard property where Antoni and his family live. It was decided that we have no rights to the kitchen. We would need to build our own kitchen and bathroom.

Please understand this, Andrew. Living in the same house with Antoni, as the court says I have a right to do, is completely unacceptable. Now that I have won in a court of law, your brother Antoni is more vicious than ever. He is dangerous. I do not plan to put the children, nor myself, in danger by working in the same orange grove alongside him or by living in the same building with him and his hostile family. I decided to lease our portion of the grove to a citrus grower so we can earn some income. So far I have not seen any income from your orchard. Harry will help me find a tenant. Women do not get involved with matters of business here. It is simply not done!

I couldn't return to Parnion again for my mother's forty-day memorial service. My sister Joanna, still with her son in Lemnos, couldn't even attend Mother's funeral. Lemnos is in the northern Aegean. It's very far from Parnion.

The grueling journey I made to visit my mother before she died was so full of detours that I walked much of the way. Mt. Taygetos is located between Kalamata and Sparta. I traveled north on the west side of Taygetos to get to Tripolis, then south again around the east side of the mountain to get to Laconia. Transportation is not easy, like it is in Chicago. I was fearful of something happening to the children. So, I left them behind in Kalamata because I didn't know how long I would be away. I didn't want to take them out of school. Harry and his wife, Maria, looked after them. They were well, thank God.

I realize the Depression has lasted more than ten years in America and that you have not yet secured a permanent job. Yet, one of the things I learned here is that the Depression also hit Europe hard, including Greece, of course. Economic suffering is evident everywhere. I don't feel that winning our case in court was such a great victory for us. Life in Kalamata is not as blissful as you expected it to be. And now this misery is compounded by talk of a looming war. What am I supposed to do? Neither of us has money to buy our return ship passages to the U.S.

Stay well. Know that we miss you. The children and I send you our love.

Your devoted wife,
Katherine

***

November 20, 1940

Dear Andrew,

I hope my letter finds you well. As you must already know, the situation here in Greece has radically changed for the worse.

Mussolini's invasion started a dreadful war. As I write to you, it continues in northern Greece against invading Italy. I belong to a group of women knitting wool socks for our barefoot army. The good news is that Greeks are defeating Mussolini's troops and tanks. The euphoria here over the Greeks' success is overwhelming. The big question is: Are we, down here in the south of Greece, in danger? I don't know, and so far your brother Harry is not able to answer that question for me. The war is hundreds of miles away, at the opposite end of Greece from us here in Kalamata. Hopefully the Greeks will continue winning and the Italians will go away and leave us alone.

We do not have a radio, nor does Harry. He goes to the kafeneion [coffee house] where men gather to hear news on the radio. It is frowned upon for women to enter a kafeneion. I am dependent on Harry for news. He tells me the daily newspaper is tacked on the wall and customers discuss old and recent news from radio and newspapers. The Germans are invading countries in Northern Europe. Austria, Poland, and Finland are very far from Greece. Are we in danger? I remember that during the last war with the Germans, the sea-lanes were open and travelers went back and forth from Europe to America. I am assuming that we could return home to you.

Alex, Nikki, John and I miss you very much and wish we were there with you. The American boy's magazine arrived and Alex is reading it over and over again. I think he has committed it to memory. Alex has joined the Sea-scouts. I'm still trying to figure out if that is good news or bad news. Stay well. We all send you our love.

Your devoted wife,
Katherine

My mother was wrong about being able to travel across the Atlantic as passengers did during the First World War. When WWII started, the Nazis planted explosive mines under the ocean's waters to blow up their enemies' ships. The seas were too dangerous for civilian travel. With no ability to get out of Greece before Mussolini's late 1940 invasion, we were tragically stuck there for the duration. Mom was never able to mail the following two letters. She saved them and delivered them to Dad when we arrived in Ann Arbor in 1946.

April 28, 1941

Dear Andrew,

I hope you are well. The situation here is worse than I ever could have imagined. We never should have come to Greece. We were naïve about your land partnership and about the shaky situation in Europe. People here, including me, are confused and scared to death. There's no respite from this kind of fear.

Today, the Germans and Italians bombed the port of Kalamata while the children and I attended services in a church near the harbor. I thought the deafening blasts were going to kill us. Explosions shook the church's walls. The sounds were unimaginable. Airplanes zoomed outside. Falling bombs shrieked. I thought the old church was falling apart. Thunderous cracking noises from the roof and walls sent us off in panic. People screamed horrendous screams. With icons falling and the crowd pushing in around us, we ran for the door, which was already blocked with debris. The confusion was hellish. Fearing the roof and church dome would descend and crush us to pieces, I grabbed the children, held them close, and we fled, climbing over obstacles of rubble in our rush to get outside. The horrifying noises still echo in my brain. Running toward home, we saw hundreds of bombed, dead fish floating in the harbor. The atrocious sounds and sights will forever be imbedded in our brains. We finally arrived home, in panic and confusion, to find hunks of bomb shrapnel imbedded in our house's outer walls.

The world is coming to an end, Andrew. Where do I turn for safety? How do I save our children from this violence and destruction?

In truth, I can't tell the Germans from the Italians. Both fly in violent, ugly airplanes that make us run for our lives. Now, we run for a homemade bomb shelter our neighbors dug out of the ground when we hear warning sirens. I don't feel safe in the shelter. I don't feel safe outside the shelter. I don't feel safe anywhere. But I am determined to protect our children and keep them from harm. I can control Nikki and Johnny and keep them close to me. But Alex is almost 15. He has joined the Sea-scouts and pays more attention to their rules than to mine. I am sick with worry every minute of the day. Danger is all around us.

Please write. Tell me what you think I should do. It is too late for us to return home now. The tenant citrus grower has not paid rent. Even if it were possible for us to sail to the U.S., I don't have money to buy four steamship tickets. I don't know what to do. I am considering going to Parnion. God help us. We send you our love.

Your devoted wife,
Katherine

***

May 5, 1941

Dear Andrew,

I have a letter in my purse, written to you a week ago. I was advised to not mail it. I am writing this one and will hopefully send both letters to you in a few weeks when all this violence is over. I pray it will be over soon. I need to tell you (and that's why I am writing again) that I definitely plan to take the children to leave Kalamata and escape to Parnion while these horrible events take place around us. From now on, we will live in my village. I think remote Parnion will be safer for us, if we can get there alive.

The German army reached Kalamata last week. Prior to their taking the city, we were warned that they were coming down from the north and killing everyone in their way. Panicked, I grabbed blankets, wrapped up some cheese and a loaf of bread, took our two younger ones by the hand, and followed the hordes of people leaving the city on foot. I searched everywhere but I could not find Alex. So, letting Nikki and John walk toward safety with our neighbors, I decided to turn back to look for Alex. But I couldn't find him! Authorities, herding us out of the city, wouldn't allow me to wait until he showed up. They forced me to return to the escape route. Thank God, I found Nikki and John again. I was sick worrying about Alex. Death is a terrifying shadow that never goes away, much closer to us here than it ever was in the United States.

Escaping and evacuating involved anguish, stress, human misery, and personal prayer on a scale that my words cannot communicate. Luckily, the villages of Lada and Karveli in the mountains above the city offered food and shelter to refugees from Kalamata. The three of us were directed to go to Lada. The people of that little village fed as many people as they could and were helpful to all who were temporarily homeless. Lada's villagers were as compassionate as human beings can possibly be to their fellow human beings. There is no way to adequately thank these good and saintly people.

The children and I lived under a huge tree for several days. Other families were grouped around the tree and all the other trees in Lada. We heard airplanes overhead and were told they were German airplanes, aiming bombs on Kalamata. This is a strange, violent world we find ourselves in. I was paralyzed—sick with fear not knowing of Alex's whereabouts but I knew that I had to keep my wits for the sake of Nikki and John's safety. I am determined, with all the brains and strength that God can give me, to make sure that all three of our children survive this catastrophe and return home to you.

Word finally reached us in Lada that the German army had taken Kalamata. We lived under the sky in Lada until the all-clear siren signaled us to return to the city. We were assured that the Germans are not killing innocent civilians— and that it was safe for us to return. I didn't want to go back to occupied Kalamata. But I needed to find Alex. We were deathly afraid to return. Then again, for the sake of the children's security, I needed to bring them within the walls of our little apartment, again. Thank God, we found Alex hiding in the cellar. We do not know what the Germans will do to us. Andrew, our children have seen things that children should never see. We are all frightened and don't know where to turn. We were shocked to find Kalamata's beautiful beaches—the places where Johnny and Nikki used to play in the sand on happy summer mornings— turned into a cemetery! The beaches are covered with the burial mounds of British soldiers who died during the battle. Kalamata is in shambles. Nothing is the same. We are afraid to breathe, let alone go about our daily routines. People are paralyzed with fear. All the schools have closed.

Andrew, we are packing a few things in the trunk we brought from America and leaving for Parnion tomorrow. I don't know how we will travel there but even if we have to walk every step of the way, we are getting out of here. Kalamata has been bad news for me from the moment I stepped on its soil and met your brother Antoni. Everywhere we turn, we see armed German or Italian soldiers. Your brother Harry tells me that Germans and Italians occupy all of Greece's larger cities. Parnion, a small village in the mountains, must be a safer place to live until this war is over and we can return to America. We hope you are well. The children and I send you our love. I describe all these conditions to you so that you will understand what is going on in case something tragic happens to us. I pray that we will live to see you again.

Your devoted wife,
Katherine

Mom was advised that letters would never reach their intended destinations under Axis occupation; Nazis opened and read outgoing mail, so she never mailed the last two letters to Dad. Communicating with someone in the United States would certainly have brought suspicion and danger to us from the Germans.

My memory easily resurrects a picture of southern Peloponnesos, Kalamata's green valley, and red-roofed Lada clinging to the side of majestic Mt. Taygetos like a precarious rock climber. The village is perched high above the basin's silver-leafed olive groves, fruit orchards, vegetable gardens, and church domes. Actually, two quaint, red-clay crowned villages hang on to the humungous mountain's western side: both Lada and Karveli share giant Mt. Taygetos's stone countenance. A deep chasm separates the hamlets, yet they see each other over the great expanse of a bottomless canyon.

I have never forgotten escaping from Kalamata in a crowd of desperate refugees, primarily women and children; the elderly and infirm who couldn't evacuate stayed put in Kalamata, awaiting an unknown hell. We hiked northeasterly, about twelve miles over difficult terrain; cracks and holes pitted the jagged, rocky ground. We passed a terrified, screaming woman in labor along the evacuation route. A clump of women stopped to shield her and assist with the birth of her baby.

Fleeing real and looming danger was nothing like orderly fire drills I experienced in Ann Arbor's public schools after we returned to the U.S. Refugees do not walk silently, in single file. Terror, confusion, noise, and continuous crying accompanied our quick departure from Kalamata in late April of 1941.

We overheard fellow refugees, walking behind us, suspecting the German army would find and kill us while we were escaping. One woman speculated that Nazis might already be waiting for us in Lada. Mother quietly assured Nikki and me that it was preposterous for Germans to chase and kill powerless women and children. "They have bigger fish to fry," she promised.

We persisted in our escape under the hot sun, for miles: out of breath, scared, thirsty, and on the verge of collapse. But we kept moving. We breathed deep sighs of relief when we finally arrived in Lada; the German army was not there to greet us.

I still remember what we ate in Lada: a stew of celery and pork. As a kid, it was my least favorite food but Mom forced me to eat it. She told me the meal had been deliciously and kindly prepared by heroic, hospitable neighbors, whose kind generosity we ought not rebuff. "Besides," she reminded me, "you might not eat again for weeks."

After living with lots of strangers for several days under a wide plane tree, Lada's authorities gave us rather dubious "you'll be safe in the city" advice. Not knowing what was in store for us, and still surrounded by a stream of anxious refugees, we began the return trek to our apartment overlooking the harbor.

Alarmingly, we came across the frightening specter of wrecked, twisted, and huge, British military transports ditched to the side of the road, and abandoned in ruins, as if they had been discarded tin cans. Colossal, overturned, British supply trucks had been deserted, with contents spilled out on the road.

To our amazement, we found tins of English biscuits scattered on the highway. Hungry, wide-eyed kids darted toward the free bounty of cookies but adults shouted, "Stop! Poison! Bombs!" Mother grabbed my arm with the strength of a wrestler and I staggered back. The tins, we were warned, could be bombs planted there by Germans, and cookies might be filled with killing poisons. Disappointed and frightened, we left the luscious-looking goodies behind. "Times have changed," Mother warned. "Curiosity brings trouble now. Mind your own business and stay out of trouble."

Mussolini had lost esteem and Albanian territory, which he had long before conquered, to the less powerful but victorious Greek army in 1940-41. This defeat prompted his ally Hitler to send in the German army; they invaded from Greece's Nazi influenced, northern neighbor Bulgaria on April 6, 1941. By April 27 the Germans were in Athens and the Greek government capitulated. Greece officially had found itself suppressed, under the heels of Hitler's glossy boots. The battle of Kalamata took place on April 28-29.

Meanwhile, British soldiers, who had previously arrived to assist their Greek allies in the expected Nazi invasion, attempted to escape the country via ports around the coasts of Greece where the Royal Navy could rescue them—ahead of the fast moving Nazis. Rescued British soldiers were then re-positioned at other war-fronts where Great Britain battled the Germans.

Ships in the Gulf of Messenia successfully rescued thirty-two thousand escaping British troops. Ten thousand Brits did not escape. Most of those men were taken by the Germans as prisoners of war and held at Stalag XVII-A in Wolfsburg, Austria, until the end of the war. However, there were hundreds of British soldiers who were neither rescued nor taken prisoner. They found welcome shelter and refuge in clandestine caves and hidden nooks and crannies by Greek villagers who risked their lives to protect them.

As a result of being a loyal Greek Sea-scout, my brother Alex was instilled with ideals of "patriotism and service to country." Those teenagers were so fervently dedicated to the scouts' causes that many parents lost control of the comings and goings of their own children. In peaceful times, before war came to Kalamata, the scouts were taught to swim and dive in the Gulf of Messenia.

But with news of Hitler's advances in Europe, scouts were secretly trained to act as air raid wardens and lookouts for ominous aircraft and parachutists. They were encouraged to have their eyes and ears open to detect out-of-the-ordinary activities that might signal collusion with German or Italian armies, and then to report unusual movements to scout authorities.

When Mother couldn't find Alex the day we escaped Kalamata and walked to Lada, he was on-duty with the scouts. But, Alex was more deeply involved in the war effort than ordinary Sea-scouts. Without Mother's knowledge, Alex, who spoke perfect English and perfect Greek, had become an interpreter for British soldiers hidden in Kalamata and environs. He secretly helped hide, feed, and shelter men of the British army who had not been rescued or taken as prisoners. At the same time, he and his buddies had discovered a stash of guns inadvertently left behind by Allied soldiers who were being rescued by ships in the waters off Kalamata's beaches.

Alex and his fellow teenage friends concealed the weapons, out of German sight, by tying them onto the upper trunks of tall cypress trees; more guns were buried in farmers' fields, olive and citrus groves. Hidden at the start of war, the weapons were a self-defense measure for what might befall the local citizenry as the war heated up.

But as a result of his clandestine activities, Alex was in danger of being arrested and killed by the occupying German army. My brother later surmised that the guns he helped hide were used by the Greek underground resistance movement against Italians and Nazis, long after the four of us left Kalamata for Parnion.

From the time we arrived in Kalamata in late 1937, Alex had spent a great deal of time at Uncle Harry's home, enjoying the company of Harry's children who were fun, affable cousins. All teenagers, Alex and our cousins hung out together at the nearby beach when there was time from schoolwork and chores. On summer evenings, they listened to a sultry, new Greek singer, Sofia Vembo, whose recordings, along with other popular music, were broadcast on the public address system in the city's large public square.

Our cousins knew more about my big brother's activities than Mom did; in time they shared the "hush-hush" information with their father. Before we left Kalamata, Mom finally heard of Alex's covert actions from Uncle Harry.

Alex had visited Harry and his family on the day they returned home from their escape into the countryside following the bombing of Kalamata. During Alex's visit, my uncle responded to a knock on the door and found himself face to face with two German soldiers. My brother, in the next room, merely needed a glimpse of Nazi helmets and uniforms at Harry's door to know why they were there.

So, Alex bolted out the second-story window of Uncle Harry's home, jumping down into the well-irrigated citrus orchard. As Alex landed with a thump and splash between orange trees, three or four German soldiers, blowing whistles and shouting in German, leapt out of a military car the investigating soldiers had parked at the side of the orchard. The Nazis doggedly chased the kid who jumped out the window into the muddy grove.

My brother skillfully darted off through a neighboring cornfield where he buried the pistol he had hidden in his pocket. All the next day he hid in irrigation ditches and olive groves. Fortunately for our entire family, the Germans had more important duties to attend to in occupying Kalamata than hunting down a teenage boy; they appeared to give up the chase.

Nevertheless, if Nazi soldiers had nabbed Alex and discovered the pistol in his pocket while he was in Uncle Harry's home, Harry, his family, and Alex would definitely have been arrested. At the same time, Alex's American mother, sister, and little brother would, no doubt, have been accused of nefarious acts against the German military. That was the reason we found Alex hiding in the cellar, dirty, desperate, and hungry, when we returned from Lada. And that's when Mom made the final decision to return to Parnion.

Civilians in Greece, from Epirus in the north to Crete in the south, were occupied after the German invasion; Mom, Alex, Nikki, and I were trapped in Greece—with no way out. Our economic lifeline to Dad had been cut off and we had no income. In no time at all, others around us realized that loss of life and human rights weren't the only casualties of Nazi occupation.

As soon as the first Nazi soldier stepped over the border from the north in 1941, inflation began choking the worth out of the Greek drachma. The value of Greek currency went into a free fall: the official price of bread soared from 70 drachmas to 2,350 drachmas. One had to stuff a shopping bag with money in order to go out and buy a single newspaper.

War, victims soon learned, is a well-rounded criminal: a ruthless murderer, and a vile, skillful pickpocket. War's foul tentacles clean out its prey's savings: assets, no matter how humble or opulent, are diminished; hard-earned funds evaporate. There's not enough money left to buy bread.

Inflation began devastating the buying power of most Greeks. Exceptions, and there are always exceptions, included the few people who had something to sell, like wheat or olive oil. But those commodities, too, were to soon diminish. Wealthier Greeks in cities and larger towns would sell off their gold and their furniture to buy food. Inflation affected our little family in the general sense, as it affected all Greeks at that time. We had no gold, no bank account, no cash, and only fragile ownership in the Kalamata property that earned no income. Our pockets contained the three "Zs" of negative subsistence: zilch—zip—zero.

***

As noted before, when we were safely back home in 1946's post-war Ann Arbor, Mother, Nikki, and I continued sharing our wartime experiences with Dad when he came home from work. I clearly remember the evening when Mom told my father about our escape to her village after Kalamata was bombed.

"It was dangerous for us to attempt to reach you, Andrew," Mother told Dad. "We no longer received your letters with support money. I had not collected one drachma of profit from the orchard. We were almost penniless when we escaped to my village for safety. You see, there, at least, I had my family. What else could I do? We'd have a roof over our heads and be undisturbed by war. I naïvely underestimated the war, Andrew. I had no idea of the horror in store for us."

Agitated by grief and regret, my father wept. "I am responsible for sending you into that hell!" Listening to our accounts, he angrily hurled names at our occupiers: "Bastards!" "Barbarians!" "Monsters!" "Satans!"

And when Mother described to Dad her dialogue with Alex, regarding my brother's possession of a firearm in Kalamata, I sensed she was still upset over it. It kind of went like this:

"Where in hell did you get the pistol in your pocket, Alex!"

"I found it."

"You found it?? Do you think you are that weird, fantasy character—the Phantom—you read in Chicago's funny papers? Alex, did you consider the safety of your family? You endangered every member of your father's family in Kalamata by having a gun! Where did you get the gun?"

"From a German soldier."

"A German soldier gave you his pistol?"

"He was dead. I took the pistol off the body of a dead soldier."

"*Christos kai Panagia!* (Christ and Virgin Mary!) You approached the body of a dead German? A battalion of Nazis could have accused you of killing him. They would have executed you on the spot. Did you kill anyone with the gun?"

"No. I never tried to shoot it. I just kept it in my pocket for protection."

"Protection? Good thing it didn't go off and kill you."

Mother struggled to keep a firm grip on all of us, especially Alex, repeatedly drilling into all three of us that we were responsible for each other. "I don't want to have to bury any one of you in Greece! You are going back to the *U.S.* and God willing, I'll be with you.

"So, Andrew," Mom said to Dad, "we left Kalamata to get away from the damned war."

***

Inundated with Nazis—Europe in 1940

- ❖ *April 9: Nazis invade Norway and Denmark*

- ❖ *May 10: Nazis invade Luxembourg, Belgium, and the Netherlands*

- ❖ *June 14: Nazis march into Paris*

- ❖ *Roosevelt announces build-up of peacetime army, first peacetime draft*

- ❖ *October: Italians invade Greece under orders from Mussolini*

- ❖ *First victory against Axis: Greek army successfully pushes back Italian army*

❖ *December: In order to help out his ally, Mussolini, Hitler orders "Operation Marita" (German troops to attack Greece from Bulgarian border in 1941)*

7 | PARNION, AGAIN:
LATE SPRING, 1941

We were separated from my brother when we left Kalamata to go to Parnion. Mother agonized over the parting, but Uncle Harry assured her it was the wiser alternative: Alex needed to avoid meeting up with the Axis military. So while Mom, Nikki, and I took train and bus, lugging our ungainly trunk with us to reach Laconia, Alex, alone, hiked mountains and trekked covert back roads on foot.

Up to then, nothing in our Greek stay had gone as Dad and Mom had foreseen. Unexpected shocks had become "business as usual" for us. As we traveled to the prefecture of Laconia, we met other terrified refugees, carrying bundles, baskets, and trunks of their worldly goods to more hopeful locations.

After a long, dusty bus ride we were deposited at the bus stop, north of Sparta, where Uncle George had greeted us on our arrival in 1937. Three-and-a-half years later there was no one to meet us; our relatives in Parnion didn't know we were returning. Communication was complicated. In our haste to leave Kalamata, Mother made no attempt to advise them of our pending arrival.

Mom refused to leave behind our almost-empty trunk, which we had nicknamed "Buddy." "It's the little piece of America that we brought with us," she remarked. I think the trunk was Mother's clumsy security blanket. She said it reminded her of the day she and my father had shopped for it with hard-earned Depression cash on Chicago's Maxwell Street. A mere glance at Buddy metaphysically took her back to Dad, the U.S., and happier times.

Because we couldn't transport our hulking trunk to the village by ourselves, Mother hatched a plan. When we arrived at the familiar bus stop, she led us into the crudely built inn we had first seen in 1937. Nikki and I stood by while she asked the innkeeper if he could hold our trunk at the inn until someone, traveling to Parnion with car or truck, was willing to bring it. The man agreed. Our trunk had an easier journey than we did. We walked; Buddy rode all the way.

We climbed upward and northeasterly, one weary foot in front of the other, into Mt. Parnon's foothills. Two hours later, our energies and breaths expended, we had reached the little bridge over the Oinountas River. Mother, physically and mentally fatigued, kept focused on our Parnion objective. Prodding us uphill and usually out of breath during our laborious march, she continuously whispered, "Each step takes us closer to Grandpa's house and safety."

It was early May and at a certain point Mom hesitated to admire wild, yellow and white narcissus blooming along the roadside. Nikki and I gladly lingered to take in springtime flowers and, more importantly, catch our breaths. Three hours into our trek, we spotted the peaceful, verdant village still hugging the side of Mt. Parnon's foothill. Aunt Sophia couldn't believe her ears when a neighbor, whose house overlooked the green ravine, alerted her that her sister Katherine and two children were walking up the road leading into the village.

Sophia's husband, cordial Uncle Vasili, immediately came over to Grandpa's house to welcome us. Still as sharp looking as ever, he was relieved that we had survived the Battle of Kalamata. "Nikki, you're such a big girl, now. And Johnny, I can't believe you're already eight years old. Where has the time gone?" When he hugged us and admired how much we had grown, I detected the familiar whiff of wine, my uncle's signature fragrance.

When white-haired Aunt Stella, still in black, rushed to Grandpa's house to greet us on the day we arrived, she couldn't resist telling Mom that she, the wiser and older sister, had been right all along about our going to unknown Kalamata. Then Stella remarked, "The children have grown beautifully, my dear little sister, and I notice changes in you too. Do you remember what our parents used to say when they started getting gray?"

"Yes, Stella," and Mom recalled, "'Snow has started falling on the mountains.' I think of it when I glance in a mirror and discover new white streaks. You and I will soon be twins, Stella."

A mere glance at us revealed that we had grappled with problematic challenges since the last time they had seen us. Villagers held us in implausible awe when word eventually spread from one to the other that "The Americans" (meaning us) had walked all the way from the main road.

Mom's older brother George was astonished that we had managed the laborious trek. Mother's tone with him was more sarcastic than jovial. "Did you expect us to fly? Americans have legs to walk too. You know, George, after being scrutinized by Italian and German soldiers all over Peloponnesos, walking fifteen miles to Parnion was the least of our challenges.

"And you'll notice, dear brother, and dear sister Stella," she continued, "that in spite of traveling through enemy-occupied Greece, a 'lowly' woman was completely capable of guiding her young children back to Parnion—without a man to protect and advise her."

We repeated gory details of the bombing and occupation that besieged us in Kalamata. With no radio or newspapers in Parnion, news reports of the Axis occupation and war had been trickling to the village by word of mouth via Sparta. No electricity meant no radio news. When Sophocles drove to Sparta, he brought back what he believed to be accurate world news.

Parnion tongues spread the news in two ways—accurately and inaccurately. Sophocles's latest reports inspired rage and horror: the Nazis had taken down the blue and white striped Greek flag, which flew high above Athens, atop the Acropolis—and replaced it with the abominable red and black Nazi swastika. When Sophocles had shared this detail, Uncle Vasili lamented, "Barbarians have desecrated the holy hill of civilization."

Mother shared with sisters Stella and Sophia, brother George, and brother-in-law Vasili that Alex was traveling to the village on his own, using back roads, so he would not attract Axis attention. Germans and Italians were looking to force young, able-bodied males into their armies. Eventually, Mother told of the obstacles she endured in Kalamata with Dad's brother, Antoni. All of us were seated around the table in Grandpa's living room when Nikki and I heard Mother vow: "I will never step foot in that city again. To hell with fruit orchards, courtrooms, Nazis, and my brother-in-law!"

"Is that the kind of man your husband Andrew is?" older sister Stella suspiciously interrogated. "You know, one brother is usually like the other."

"You're wrong, Stella!" Mother snapped. "My Andrew is a kind and generous man." Then she angrily showed the back of her hand to Stella, palm facing toward Mom, and fingers spread out. "Look at this, Stella. All my fingers belong to the same hand, but each finger is different. It's the same with a family—and the sisters and brothers who belong to that family."

Changing the subject, Uncle Vasili cleared his throat to get the sisters' attention and give Mother an update. "We have news from Joanna," he interjected, interrupting Mom's exhausted glare at her older sister. I had not met Aunt Joanna yet, so she was turning into a sort of mystery woman for me.

"Oh, yes, Katherine," Stella announced. "Joanna is ending her visit with her son and finally returning to Parnion from Lemnos. Joanna's daughter, in Athens, wrote to George that Joanna is planning to spend time with her in Athens before returning here.

"I'm worried about Joanna traveling about, with German and Italian soldiers spread all over our country," Stella continued. "They tell me her son in Lemnos doesn't think she'll encounter problems. But I don't think it's safe. Joanna should not have gone to Lemnos in the first place. I told her to stay put. I told her, 'Let your son come to visit you here in Parnion.'"

"Come on, Stella," Uncle Vasili suggested, "what could occupying armies find suspicious in the movements of an innocent, white haired, elderly widow traveling alone? And remember, she left Parnion several years ago, before the Germans invaded."

"Anything could happen," Stella reiterated. "Katherine already knows that." Yet Aunt Stella could turn from bossy sister to loving friend in a heartbeat. Smiling and looking at Mother, she shared, "Katherine, I'm pleased that you and your children are safely here with us, again. Now that Father's house is unoccupied, it's perfect for you and the children. When do you expect Alex to be with us?"

"Soon, I pray. I can't be at peace until I see him. He departed Kalamata after us."

Since Grandma's death a year before, no one had lived in the house. Six months before, Mom's brother George, its present owner, and his wife Athanasia left the house vacant when they moved to Athanasia's village with their year-old baby boy, Fotis. George was employed by the government as a paralegal and assigned to work in the larger village, closer to Sparta, capital city of Laconia.

In referring to Grandpa's house as a two-story structure, I exclude the partially underground basement where, during my grandparents' lifetime, Grandpa stored barrels filled with the wine he produced from his own grape harvest. I remember seeing his immense but empty barrels in the *ypogion* (basement); during our stay they remained empty and eventually began to fall apart.

Mom told me that when she was a girl, a trap door in the wooden floor made the stairs to the basement accessible. Mother remembered that one of her daily household tasks required her to go down into the basement with pitcher in hand to procure her father's mealtime wine rations. It was a chore, Mom told us, she accomplished as quickly as possible to escape the clammy darkness.

We entered and left the house via the stucco-walled, grapevine-covered courtyard, a few steps up from the street. In Grandma's time, a summer kitchen was located in one of two large ground level rooms off the courtyard. The front one, nearer the street, had been the location for my grandfather's business in the 1920s: the village general store. When our little goat "Bebba" came into our lives, the back room became her living quarters on icy nights; we used the front room to dry out leaves and other silage to feed her.

Springtime blossoms dotted village courtyards when we moved into Mother's unoccupied, ancestral home in May of 1941. Greenery had started replacing flowers on apple, pear, and cherry trees in Grandpa's *perivoli* (garden adjacent to the courtyard). Tiny fruit had already sprouted on the fig tree.

We lived on the upper floor, where the small *saloni*, two bedrooms, tiny space around a balcony, and the house's largest room, with necessary fireplace, were located. Moving into a vacant house, Mom needed to start from scratch—on an absent bankroll; there were no stored provisions like wheat, flour, sugar, honey, rice, or olive oil. We had no flock of chickens in the courtyard or pigs, goats, and sheep to provide us with protein or a basis for barter. We had nothing.

No changes had been made to Grandpa's house since our grandmother's passing. Exterior walls were still whitewashed. Inside, the family collection of religious icons and framed old wedding pictures, along with Cousin Mary's graduation picture, still hung on various greenish-blue walls. The few rugs I remembered from our first trip to the village were gone; now the rough wooden floors were bare and dusty.

Grandma's day bed, several single beds with lumpy mattresses, and a simple but aged wooden table with four unmatched chairs remained. Mom opened an antique trunk she found in the same room as the fireplace and was moved to tears discovering Grandma's own handiwork: embroidered but rough-feeling sheets and pillowcases; loom-woven, thick, wool blankets;

and sweaters: all smelling like mothballs. Walking through the house, Mother opened the lone cupboard and found well-used pots and pans, a few dishes, and beat-up, rusty forks, knives, and spoons.

"Well, children, it all needs a bit of cleaning," she announced. The days that followed found Mother on her hands and knees, scrubbing, washing, and disinfecting the floors, and everything else, with limited cleaning supplies—mere boiling water. Everything in sight underwent her boiling-water scrub and "Mrs. Clean" management, with no vinyl gloves to protect her hands.

While Mom worked hard at cleaning, a few villagers entered the courtyard to welcome us and introduce themselves. Mother suspected they were just plain curious about what was going on in the old house. One was a soft-spoken, friendly old lady, who introduced herself as Maria. She found Mother in the middle of clean-up and sympathized that a house never runs out of chores that need attending. "And you, children," she kindly asked Nikki and me, "how do you like Parnion after living in America and Kalamata?" Of course, Nikki spoke up first, referring to the woman respectfully, as "Aunt," just like Mother had taught us. "Oh, it's much quieter here, Aunt Maria. But I'm happy there are no scary soldiers. And I love the sound of the church bell. It makes a more musical sound than the one we heard in Kalamata."

Huge and noisy Uncle Nicholas with the enormous white mustache also dropped by to welcome us. He was on his way to the *kafeneion* (coffee house), and stopped by to chat. Nicholas, I was to find out, was a regular, late afternoon fixture in the village coffee house.

Entering Grandpa's courtyard, Nicholas shook my hand with his massive paw, commended my sister and me on how handsomely we had grown, and caught up on our survival of Kalamata's bombing. Then, he presented Mother with a sack of lentils: a basic source of protein and a mainstay of the Greek kitchen. "It's a house warming gift," he smiled. Mom would cook many meals for our near penniless family with his vital offering.

And surely, Mother didn't feel comfortable in Parnion until Alex walked into Grandpa's house. He had stayed hidden at Uncle Harry's house in Kalamata and didn't begin his journey to Laconia until after we had left the city. Crossing the mountains on foot, alone, took him four days. All the relatives came to welcome him.

Our Parnion aunts and uncles were not only relatives: they were easily accessible neighbors. Mother's younger sister, Sophia, her husband Vasili, and their two children Tasia and Kosta lived five houses away, closer to tiny St. Nicholas Church; Mom's widowed sister Stella resided alone in her husband's family home further down the road, adjacent to the main square. Uncle Nicholas lived at the edge of town, not far from us; we saw him almost every afternoon when he walked to the *kafeneion*.

From the first day, Nikki and I poked into every nook and cranny of Grandpa's house. Early on, we discovered a small balcony on the upper floor where we could view all of Parnion. We watched village comings and goings from the balcony, over the top of the courtyard grapevines. Springtime greenery was sprouting up all over the village. And when spring rains pounded, we stepped out on the balcony to watch rainwater bounce off red-tile roofs. Nikki and I made the balcony a venue for the games we invented. When the house was thoroughly shining and clean, Mother opened the balcony doors to let in fresh mountain breezes.

A kid's creativity was compelled to work overtime at Grandpa's house; there were no books or toys; there wasn't much of anything. Nikki and I needed to invent childhood amusement in our village world of scarcity. She learned to turn acorns into miniature doll faces. Acorns were free of charge and profusely available under the plethora of Laconia's holm oaks (*pournaria*). Their natural caps outfitted Nikki's nut-brown creations with chic French "berets." I used acorns to play a village version of "jacks;" in a pinch, roundish, gumball-size rocks worked too.

Stella, Sophia, and Mother were afforded an opportunity to renew and strengthen close, sisterly ties, now that we were back in the village. They managed time to visit between the many necessary, heavy-duty chores that village women undertook everyday of their lives, except Sunday. Invariably discussing old times, the three sisters resurrected family events.

One afternoon, after the day's work was done, the three sisters sat sipping tea in the courtyard; Nikki and I were playing jacks with courtyard pebbles. As usual, their conversation turned to family history. That's when Nikki and I learned about Grandpa's motives for Mother's emigration.

"I wonder how life would have been for you, Katherine, if Father had not sent you to America," Stella wondered.

"God only knows, Stella. It's hard for me to imagine any life other than the one I have actually lived," Mother answered. "The Greek dowry system sent thousands of women, like me, to the United States. Most of the Greek women I know, in Chicago, went to America for the same reason I went: their fathers could not afford dowries for them. I think poverty and the dowry came close to emptying Greek villages before 1925."

Well into the 20th century, according to Greek law and "carved-in-stone" tradition, a daughter marrying in Greece received her inheritance in the form of a *prika* (dowry) from her parents at the time of her marriage. A bridegroom with known superior qualities (a good trade, profession, education, wealth, good family background) could demand a higher offering from the bride's father. Prior to the wedding, the agreed-on amount was awarded in cash, property, or flocks of sheep or goats.

My grandfather had provided substantial dowries to Stella, Joanna, Sophia, and his daughter Ellie who married before emigrating from Greece in the company of her husband. But Grandpa was running out of property for his sons John and George to inherit. By sending his daughter Katherine to the U.S., Grandpa saved the money that he would have had to dole out for a fifth dowry. Dispatching single, female offspring to America became a common practice for fathers with many daughters to marry off. Greek immigrant males in the U.S., seeking brides of their own religion and ethnicity, willingly overlooked gaining a dowry. For

Greek parents, it became a bittersweet solution to retaining what little wealth a family owned.

"Our mother cried every day after you and John left," Sophia remembered.

Mom replied, "I cried for days and months too, Sophia. Thank God for our dear sister Ellie in Chicago. I lived with them for four years before I married Andrew. Ellie soothed my loneliness. Her husband and children made me feel like I was a vital member of their family. Dear Ellie was a great comfort."

Sophia kindly saw the other side of the coin. "Surely Ellie appreciated having you with her. Being so far away from Parnion, she enjoyed having her own wonderful sister for company."

Mother explained to her sisters that in spite of the heartache, she was glad she went to America. She married a good, kind, and generous man whose love for her had nothing to do with a dowry's financial gain.

Mom said that by meeting good people outside the Greek community, she enriched her life in a way which was unachievable had she remained in her village. Hearing about my mother's past was fascinating, but I couldn't bear it when the women cried—my cue for checking on village action from the balcony. That's when I ended our game, and left Nikki with the emotional women.

Mother understood, better than her clueless American children could comprehend, that in Parnion, we needed to grow our own food to survive. The garden she planted in the *perivoli* became a vital project that kept Mother super-busy. She also intended to raise a few chickens to help us provide for ourselves. She may have lived in the big city for seventeen years, but Mother never forgot how to live and survive in a primitive village.

She said that she did not intend for us to be a burden to her siblings, yet each of them, realizing our dire financial straits, generously offered her something to start us off: milled wheat, dry beans, onions, a laying hen, and vegetable seeds for starting a garden. Since it was May, there was still a time-window to plant seeds for late summer and autumn harvests. We couldn't live on

Uncle Nicholas's lentils forever, nor hope for other "housewarming gifts."

Mom enlisted my help in clearing away stubborn weeds and persistent rocks in Grandpa's field, on street side, across the main road from his house. With sweat, straining muscles, and blisters, Mother and I painstakingly turned and spaded the soil: my first experience with gardening. Then, we deposited tiny pieces of potatoes in the freshly cultivated field. Mom explained each bit contained a bud (eye) and each eye would produce a potato plant. Through the summer, we watched vigorously developing green leaves give proof that an entire field of healthy potato tubers was thriving below ground.

I was positive we would become the potato kings of Parnion. My mouth watered at the prospect of roasting a portion of our crop with oregano, salt, pepper, lemon, and olive oil to a divine crispness. I planned to devour every luscious morsel. Every time I glanced at the lush garden, various potato dishes I had eaten in my short lifetime mystically raced through my mouth in anticipation: mashed, fried, stewed, baked, and roasted. I eagerly waited for fall harvest.

Adjacent to Grandpa's house, also on street side, was the *litrivio*, an olive pressing business established by my grandfather, decades before. Mom's brother-in-law, our Uncle Vasili, operated the family's *litrivio* for Uncle George, male head of the family who had moved to another village. Olive pressing is a vital industry in a region where olives are grown.

Olive oil has been a basic Greek necessity since ancient times. Since pre-history, cured olives have been a vital part of the Greek diet, even at breakfast. In addition to being a fundamental food source, olive oil was burned in small lamps called *lihnaria* to light homes without electricity, a practice as old as Greece itself. This ancient form of illuminating darkness was the only method at our disposal of bringing light, as meager as it was, into the dim shadows of Grandpa's house.

Payment for pressing a villager's olives into oil was not reimbursed in cash. Instead, Vasili collected a percentage of the oil produced, as payment for the *litrivio* service. We were given some oil and cured olives to inaugurate our household. George assured Mother that she would receive a portion of the oil, collected as payment, when the season ended.

Vasili's olive oil production took place in the small shelter, similar to a family garage, adjacent to Grandpa's house. I would go next door to watch raw, uncured olives being squeezed between two huge stones, which drew out and collected the oil, a fascinating procedure for a kid who had never seen anything like it before. I looked forward to the autumn excitement of olive pressing in November and December, when olives are harvested.

***

What we didn't know until later—1941

- ❖ *May: The Battle of Crete, the Greek island south of Peloponnesos*

- ❖ *Big Band music of Glenn Miller, Harry James and Benny Goodman charms Americans*

- ❖ *Orson Welles' "Citizen Kane" released in U.S. movie theaters*

- ❖ *Tojo becomes Japanese premier*

- ❖ *December: Japanese attack Pearl Harbor, Hawaii*

- ❖ *U.S. declares war on Japan*

- ❖ *Germany and Italy declare war on the U.S.*

8 | FROM THE SECOND-STORY WINDOW

In time, we established our routines and Grandpa's house became our home away from home. Like all kids, no matter the year or season, I had plenty of time to kick around. And in lieu of a yet-to-be invented TV set—I looked out the window for entertainment. I recall curling up in my private window alcove to warm myself in bright sunlight and watch the fascinating "live" show down on the street—unhurried panoramas I had never witnessed in more urban Kalamata or hometown Chicago.

Villagers became the cast of my very own street-play; the vast array of Parnion's animals became supporting players. But, in no time at all, villains wearing tall black boots and swastikas showed up, turning my pretend dramas into real-life tragedies. I was to watch repulsive, authentic, WWII history from the west-facing, second-story window.

Decades before, when our grandparents lived in the house, the sunny, second-story *saloni* with its two windows was a kind of front parlor room for receiving guests. By summer of 1941, gracious entertaining was long gone; yet, the room had inherited a few beat-up ladder-backed, wooden chairs with dusty, woven straw seats, typical of the sort found in rural Greece's coffeehouses and town squares. Fortunately, the almost bare *saloni* still featured two windows with two extraordinary perks: warming sunshine and a view.

Window openings had been provided for in the two-foot thick exterior walls when the residence was constructed in the previous century: six small, framed, rectangular pieces of glass inside a larger rectangular frame were installed as windows with middle openings. Rudimentary shutters constructed of simple, wood slabs covered the inside—there were no curtains. When it was warm enough, Mother opened the shutters, as soon as she got up in the very early morning, to invite light into the dark house. On frigid days she used the shutters as additional insulation to keep the cold out; a dark interior was even darker in cold weather.

The *saloni's* north-facing window restricted looking deeply into Parnion; multiple red-tile village roofs obstructed views of street action—not as much fun for me. The tiny "downtown" section of Parnion, with a major square and church dedicated to St. George, lay northwest of our tiny neighborhood. I couldn't see "downtown" from the *saloni*. Yet, the branches of the neighborhood's old olive tree, between Grandpa's house and nearby St. Nicholas Church, were perfect for monitoring the comings and goings of all kinds of birds. One day I spotted a rare eagle, flying corkscrew turns high above the village, and excitedly ran over to Uncle Vasili's house to share my sighting with him.

Vasili never complained when I popped in to distract him, and I probably did it more often than I should have. He was always approachable. I don't think he realized he had movie star good looks. He was just Vasili being Vasili. I venture to guess he had never even heard of Clark Gable.

When the weather got cooler, I abandoned the balcony, and instead, the wonderfully sun-drenched, window alcove, facing west, became my favorite indoor spot for hanging out. That plain but vital window channeled magnificent light, warmth, and captivating street action into a house where books, knick-knacks, and amenities were absent.

The windowsill I came to know so well was roomy enough to comfortably accommodate the kid—who used to be me—while I viewed life on Parnion's narrow, crude, and only street. It allowed me to monitor plain, domeless, tiny St. Nicholas Church and the little square in front of it that featured the focal point of our neighborhood: a plain, public fountain.

The house's location near the natural, endlessly water-spewing fountain at St. Nicholas Church was a significant asset; village homes lacked indoor plumbing. Water had to be lugged home in heavy containers several times a day. The closer a household was to a water source, the easier. In some cases it was a well, but our water source was St. Nick's fountain: practical, but not particularly picturesque. The fountain was a three-foot high metal cylinder, less than a foot across, with an open spigot at the top.

There was no turn-off valve: day and night water ran into a concrete basin at ground level, then spilled into a dike for downstream irrigation. Villagers obtained water from the spigot, but donkeys, sheep, goats, cats, and dogs lapped water out of the cement basin. The fountain attracted an assortment of animals—and captivating villagers—all within view of my cozy alcove.

I clearly remember two regular characters that visited the fountain; I recall the woman in particular. Her slender face was wrapped inside a fading rose-colored scarf, which covered her head and shoulders. She wore a neatly tucked-in pastel blouse and dark, ankle-length skirt: typical village fashion for a young woman. Yet, it was the animal walking beside her that really caught my eight-year-old eye. Like an obedient dog at its mistress's knee, a gloriously huge, fluffy-white sheep accompanied his willowy shepherdess.

Passing Grandpa's house and then walking under the shade of the village's old olive tree, the tall, pretty woman with the rose-colored scarf took her lone, handsome sheep to drink at St. Nick's fountain each and every day. Remembering a few words of the English I was quickly forgetting, I sang a nursery rhyme I had learned in America, "Mary had a little lamb, its fleece was white as snow..." Then I wondered out loud to Mom, "Does Mary have a whole beautiful flock of sheep just like this one?"

"Her name is Martha, not Mary," Mother advised me when she heard me singing my rhyme by the window. "And Martha is a 'shepherdess' with only one sheep in her flock. Year in, and year out, that beautiful animal keeps Martha and her mother fed and clothed." Mom had learned that Martha was a Parnion spinster who resided with and cared for her invalid, widowed mother. The two women lived alone in their tiny house, downhill from Grandpa's property. Everyone in Parnion was aware that Martha's ewe was a very special animal, with exceptional bloodlines. In a country with tens of millions of sheep, our entire village admired one exquisite ewe.

The ewe was mated yearly and gave birth to two handsome little lambs. Martha sold one lamb for income: the buyer, no doubt, anticipating that his little investment had inherited its mama's special genes. And Martha slaughtered the second to provide meat and meat products for her household. The ewe also supplied milk for drinking, making yogurt, and producing cheese.

Sometime in the spring Martha, with huge scissors in hand, sheared off the animal's heavy fleece. The high-quality wool was spun into yarn for weaving into blankets on their home loom, and for knitting into sweaters and other personal apparel. The two women depended on one beautiful sheep for continued existence: for survival.

Bashful, quiet Martha worked at all household chores, including outdoor work and cultivation of the family vegetable garden, by herself, with possible assistance from her homebound mother in the spinning and knitting department. Single-handed, Martha sheared wool, milked, and then made cheese and yogurt the old-fashioned way—with no conveniences.

Daily, she took her sheep to graze and then always brought her singular animal to drink at St. Nick's fountain. In effect, the ewe provided the women's necessities of life and was their only source for earning an income. For an entire year, they lived frugally on the amount they earned from the sale of a single lamb.

"What would happen Mom, if Martha lost her sheep? Or, if it died? How would she and her mother live, if that happened?" I asked.

Mom looked anxiously at me, "All I know, Johnny, is that nothing is for sure on this earth. We all need to hope for the best.

Let's you and me pray that nothing bad happens to Martha's beautiful sheep, or Martha, or any of us."

From my window, the village looked idyllic, but I knew from the way the adults around me talked that the population of Parnion had its strengths and weaknesses, its vices and passions. Chief among them seemed to be gossip: nearly everyone at the fountain bent their heads together and talked in earnest. Perhaps knowledge gathered at the fountain was as essential as the water. And I know that the fountain wasn't the only place in the village where gossip was traded. I saw the men talking at the *kafeneion* and at the *taverna* when I walked by, after school. And even at church, stories were traded back and forth.

As late as 1941, Parnion's citizens lived and died according to unwritten regulations and volumes of "carved-in-stone" tradition. These tenets and institutions had never been officially declared or recorded on tablets. Yet, they were followed to the letter, "do or die." Social codes were severely strict, and citizens possessed ironclad memories. Recollections of juicy, personal family details spanned generations. A family never lived down its bloopers.

Certainly, respect for elders has always been an integral part of Greek culture, even though as late as 1941 most village elders were illiterate. Compulsory education laws in Greece were not implemented until 1911. Still, like Aunt Stella in our family, Parnion's esteemed senior citizens held a variety of unelected "know-it-all" offices: head philosopher, chief nature specialist, authority on folklore, and revered theologian in the tenets of Greek Orthodox Christianity. Some of Stella's hallowed beliefs were based more on folklore than church dogmas, but because she had heard them from her own elders, she inflexibly believed some incongruous superstitions as having been passed down by Christ, Himself.

All elder citizens were unparalleled tellers of history and unabridged human songbooks. If they had heard a song once or twice, they instantly recalled melody and words. Perhaps their memories were sharp because there was no vast, continuing encyclopedia of information blaring at them from books, classroom, media, or Internet to fill up their brains. Incredibly, they seemed to clearly remember everything they had heard from childhood until old age.

Aunt Stella was regarded as an expert in the art of village food preparation: a chef extraordinaire without benefit of electric or gas kitchen appliances. My aunt had advised Mother that the quality of a homemaker was to be measured by the sheerness of her potato peelings. The thinner the scraps, the more frugal and accomplished the household manager. One day in the courtyard, I overheard Stella criticize Aunt Sophia's potato peelings. "Katherine, our sister is wasteful. The best peelings should be utterly sheer. Sophia's hands are clumsy—she will soon drive Vasili to the poorhouse."

There weren't many places to spend money in Parnion, if one had money to spend. The village had one general store, a *kafeneion* (coffee house), and a *taverna* (primarily serving wine, brandy, and ouzo): a miniscule retail "mall" comprising a primitive 7-Eleven, cheap Starbucks, and "Joe's Bar." Mr. Papadopoulos was the general store's proprietor. Women were not expected to enter the confines of the *kafeneion* or the *taverna*; it just wasn't done. Period. Aunts Stella and Sophia would rather die than rock that tradition.

No one in Parnion owned a car. One citizen, Sophocles, proudly owned a small truck. Calendars and clocks were not necessities for the citizens of Parnion, who as a rule had no appointments to keep. Villagers were skillfully adept at telling the approximate time of day by the position of the sun in the sky, the season of the year, and the shadows that fell on the mountain in the distance, across the deep, green ravine on the west side of the village.

On Sundays we went to church. The Greek Orthodox Church was the living Christian calendar by which villagers kept track of the births of their children: women, most especially, knew ecclesiastical celebrations and saints' days by heart, according to the season. Mom, Stella, and Sophia excelled at remembering feast days.

The clanging of the church bell was radio, newspaper, alarm, and call to prayer for the people of Parnion; they understood its various messages by the nuances of its delightful tone. Villagers did not toil nor did women work at household chores on Sundays or major holidays, except for cooking. Early on, "experts" in culture, folklore, and religion (surely male) must have decided that God approved of and recognized the need for women to cook every single day, Sundays included.

Early one morning, a few days following our arrival in Parnion after the bombing of Kalamata, I heard loud noises on the street and peered out the second-story window to discover a cluster of neighbor women standing in the street below. Animated and agitated, they buzzed to each other while staring into the ravine and pointing up toward the tree-covered mountain in the distance, far across from St. Nicholas Church. They were definitely bowled over about something that was happening. Mother saw them too and decided to go outside to find out what was going on.

Just as curious, Nikki and I followed her onto the street in front of Grandpa's house. Breaking news was traveling from mouth to mouth in the most electric way about—an elopement. Village ladies were attired somewhat differently than the citified women of Kalamata; their full skirts almost reached the ground and every female head was covered from crown to shoulders with a scarf. Their commentary follows:

First villager to my mother: "Kyra (Mrs.) Katherine, before the sun came up this morning, our neighbor, Artemis, eloped with Phillip. See them! They're heading up toward the monastery, across the ravine. Look! They're riding those two mules (pointing) running up the hill in the distance. The frenzied girl is under the devil's spell."

Second villager asking first villager for clarification: "Artemis? Eloping with Phillip? Why? There's no reason for her to run away. That's ridiculous! She's thirty-five years old with no parents to disapprove of a bridegroom. She could marry any man—but until Phillip, no one asked the poor girl!"

First: *"Believe me, this has nothing to do with heaven. It's a sign of the devil's wrath. That movie destroyed her."*

Mother was quickly apprised on Parnion's drama of the month. Artemis, it turned out, was our neighbor who lived four houses away in a typical village house noted for billows of fragrant, red, summertime carnations that drooped over the street from her home's second-floor balcony. A compassionate and responsible woman, Artemis voluntarily adopted her young niece when both her sister and brother-in-law died of tuberculosis.

Aunt and niece lived alone in the house Artemis had inherited from her parents. Having lost both parents and her only sibling, Artemis had been plagued with wretched sorrow for thirty-five years. Describing her as a kind, plump, energetic woman who walked with a limp, a neighbor told Mom that Artemis had unfortunately been "left on the shelf." Someone else in the group explained that Artemis's dowry was not large enough to attract a worthy bridegroom.

Looking at one neighbor woman and then at the others, all sharing the ongoing saga with Mother, I couldn't help but notice the thick scarves around their heads and shoulders: some were black, some yellow. Only eyes, noses, and mouths were visible. By 1941 the customary woman's scarf was probably on its "way out." Yet so traditional a piece of garb in the village, and so vitally used as a sun screen, it took decades of urbanization, following the war, for it to become old-fashioned rather than *de rigueur*. Unlike her sisters, Mom, by virtue of being "American," was liberated; she did not wear a scarf.

One neighbor woman, whose scarf was so tightly wound around her head, chin, and neck that I was surprised she could open her mouth, continued giving Mom the lowdown on the elopement. She carefully confided, with noisy whispers in

Mother's ear, that local bachelors had never been interested in marrying Artemis. (A mere half-dozen villagers overhead the woman's confidential, loudly murmured, hush-hush remarks.)

However, of late, she disclosed, Phillip, a pleasant, hardworking, middle-aged farmer, had shown an interest in the spinster. Phillip had confided that he appreciated Artemis's kindness, her pleasant face, and her renown as a good cook. "But," the woman said, "I never expected an elopement."

First villager (insisting): *"No doubt about it. It's the devil's wrath. The cursed movie twisted the poor girl's brains. It ravaged her soul. Artemis saw it in Sparta last summer. She had never seen a film before but some young relative in Sparta talked her into it. These new fangled devices—movie showing machines—are evils hatched in the devil's workshop. Every time I spoke to Artemis, she talked about that cursed movie. Listen to this... it could only be seen in the dark. How sinister is that? She was obsessed with the unholy thing and said it was American."*

As we all stood there in the street, staring out toward the brush-covered ravine, the crowd turned to gawk suspiciously in our direction: we were Americans.

A look of disbelief flashed across my mother's face. "Trust me. We had nothing to do with it," Mother retorted. "Movies are made in Hollywood, California. We live in Chicago, two thousand miles away from California. My husband is not in the movie business. He's a cook in a restaurant." Seeming to comprehend, the villagers continued their scornful gossip and went back to gazing at the ravine and up toward the monastery.

First villager: *"Artemis took me into her confidence. She yearned for excitement after she viewed the cursed film. She said her life was dull and sad compared to the adventurous woman in the movie who laughed and smiled. This movie woman was*

76

independent and wore a beautiful dress. Imagine. Artemis admired an independent woman who was adventurous. What nonsense! The evil film gave her wicked ideas. She's definitely under the devil's spell."

The story became part of Parnion's unforgotten lore. Artemis had prearranged for a priest to marry her and Phillip in the ancient Byzantine monastery located across the ravine, up on the mountain across from the village. The wedding ceremony followed their electrifying gallop up the mountainside. The following day, bride and groom returned to the village, happily married. Criticism was fierce. Vicious village tongues had condemned Artemis for staging and carrying out her own elopement.

Mother met Artemis the next day, later returning to the house with a different view of the scandal. "It may have been a crazy thing to do, but Artemis embarrassed no one. Phillip is a decent man. I think they are good for each other and make fine parents for her young niece. I wish them a long, healthy, and happy life together. With all that's going on in this world right now, I'm pleased to hear good news."

We eventually learned from Artemis that the sinister but attractive movie heroine who inspired her quest for excitement was Claudette Colbert, and the depraved, handsome hero of the film was Clark Gable. Shown in Sparta's little outdoor theater six years after it premiered in America, the cursed movie, "hatched in the devil's workshop," as well as its stars, won Academy Awards in 1934. Artemis's favorite blockbuster? "It Happened One Night."

9 | THE "AMERICAN KID"

Mom wasted no time putting us in school. Shortly after we arrived in Parnion, she marched Nikki and me up the road, past the *kafeneion* and the *taverna,* through the main square with the lion fountain at St. George's Church, and over to the one-story schoolhouse. Village children, on their way to school that morning, ran around us, tossing curious stares in our direction as they rushed to meet up with old familiar friends. Nikki and I were foreigners to them.

Mother went inside to speak to teachers, leaving us outside: two exotic American newcomers surrounded by a crowd of children who belonged to the village since birth. While we waited to enter after teachers signaled, Nikki joined a group of girls and began conversing. Nikki was good at mingling.

I, apprehensive, silent, and shy, lowered my head when I realized I was being studied by an unofficial committee of village boys, sizing me up and then down with judgmental young eyes that made me edgy. No one smiled or spoke to me, but I heard one kid, perhaps the self-appointed "chairman" of Parnion's "in-crowd," sneeringly refer to me as *"to Americanaki."*

Hearty laughter followed. When their strident chairman callously repeated himself, more laughter assaulted me. Feeling alone and embarrassed, I made it worse: I blushed. "Please God, make me disappear and never set eyes on them again," I wished. But God did not cooperate and I was resigned to my fate, knowing deep in my gut that I had to stick it out.

It was the first time I heard myself called *"to Americanaki"* (the little American *or* the American kid). I realized the nickname noted my nationality, but I also knew my schoolmates had taken the adjective "American" and wedged the Greek diminutive, -aki, on the end. In some cases, -aki was cute, endearing: koritsaki is a cute little girl; arnaki is a cute little lamb. But in my case, they meant it with a negative, mocking note: I was perhaps little, naïve, a tad stupid, even.

Not that I had been given an I.Q. test by my contemporaries that morning and declared "less likely to succeed." But some kids (schools all over the planet are plagued with their like) become menaces—just plain mean—when confronted by someone "different."

I didn't like being laughed at and singled out as the "oddball" by my contemporaries. Certainly, I shared the same humanity as the other kids and even the same Greek roots. Only age four when I left the States, I didn't know and couldn't remember what being American was supposed to feel like. I recalled coming from America, but I didn't feel like a bizarre outsider, no matter what others thought of me. By the time we returned to the village in 1941, I spoke fluent Greek and had mastered the basics of reading and writing in a Kalamata schoolroom. My place of birth was not tattooed on my forehead in red, white and blue, yet the only thing different about me was that I was born in the U.S.

When I bitterly told Mother about my unfortunate nickname, she urged patience in her painfully shy, distressed son, advising, "Swallow it, John. Don't let it bother you. There are worse problems in the world. You're not different. You're a child, just like they are. They'll realize it soon enough—and before you know it you'll all be friends. In fact, be proud that you're American." It was difficult for me to be proud of something that set me apart from my schoolmates. I didn't enjoy standing out.

But Mom was right. Fellow students at P.S. #1 (and only) in Parnion eventually realized I was just another kid, not dense and not different, and I was ultimately included in the fun. Nonetheless, the nickname stuck: I was still "the American kid."

Nikki was not shy and, when annoyed, her confrontational retorts did not allow bullying. She wasn't assigned a negative nickname.

The village school was located beyond the main square, on the other side of the village from Grandpa's house; the one-story building was a two-room operation for grades one through six: one room for girls, the other for boys. Both classrooms were populated with children of various ages and abilities. Students desiring to go to high school (grades seven through twelve) were required to do so in Sparta, the local big city. Alex needed to be enrolled in Sparta's high school, but Mother held off separating him from our family until we were more settled in Parnion.

On frigid mornings, an army of children carrying slates and dry branches arrived at school from every nook and cranny of the village; parents supplied the heating fuel in winter and students took turns at stoking the classroom's wood fire. A map of Greece was a permanent fixture on the wall of the classroom, but I don't know if anyone ever looked at it.

The school was too poor to own a cloth Greek flag, but someone had kindly donated a black and white photo of the patriotic blue and white banner; we had to imagine the blue and white part. There was no Pledge of Allegiance as recited in American elementary schools. Yet, religious training was included in the school day; I learned the Ten Commandments in Parnion's schoolroom.

Incredibly, I don't remember books, paper, or pencils at school. We were expected to learn by rote. Teachers imparted the three "Rs", according to grade level, orally and by writing on a large but worn, fading blackboard. Students sat, two by two, in sturdy seats attached to ancient and marred wooden desks. Using thin pieces of white chalk, each of us recorded lessons and figured out arithmetic problems by writing on an individual, two-sided, hand-held, teacher-issued, black slate, approximately the size of today's iPad.

Busy little chalky fingers wrote quickly on both sides of a worn slate. We were constantly forced to wipe away childish,

Greek scribbles with tiny worn-out rags (brought from home) to clear space for more information. Lack of writing space made it necessary for us to quickly memorize lessons.

Were students' individual differences of learning and comprehension taken into consideration? The answer is: probably not as seriously as that vital aspect of education ought to be considered. My classmates and I were unable to look up anything in textbooks; there weren't any. White chalk dusted our shirtfronts, pants, and extremities, like powdered sugar that showered off *kourambiedes*, the butter cookies I savored on holidays.

The small, stucco building lacked electricity and indoor plumbing. Classroom illumination came through windows in the form of sunlight. It was dark in class on cloudy, rainy days. Young eyes function more efficiently than older ones; it's a good thing our eyes were young. The boys' lavatory was an outside wall on which to urinate. I don't know what facility was available for girls and I'm better off for having forgotten the details.

In spite of the bare bones structure of Parnion's elementary school, the village produced alumni who went on to become teachers, engineers, lawyers, scientists, scholars, clergymen, doctors, mathematicians, university professors, and at least one Greek Supreme Court judge.

For reasons I never understood, teachers (usually single men or women educated at teacher's college) were assigned to classrooms far from their home cities and villages. Parnion's principal/teacher, however, was a married man. He, his wife, and their two children, all from Northern Greece, lived in Parnion during the school year. The second, a single man, was from far away Crete. Teachers rented rooms in village homes or took residence in vacant houses that were empty because occupants had gone to America, or had left to work in Greece's larger cities. The government paid instructors, until Axis armies invaded and the war commenced.

At the beginning of the Axis occupation, our regular teachers returned to their distant hometowns because they were no longer being paid, and local teachers returned from far-off assignments. They would teach classes, without pay, from time to time, even though Parnion's school was not their regular assignment. School attendance was diminished to days when Mom knew the school was open.

Yet, education, for this American kid, extended way beyond classroom walls. There was something new for me to learn at every turn: inside and outside Grandpa's house; from family and other villagers; from the war; from the earth itself; and from animals, namely a wise donkey and a wild goat.

Early one afternoon, a voice in the courtyard shouted, "Hello, Chicagoans! Are you at home? I have a special delivery for you."

Mom and I hurried outside and encountered a familiar, older gentleman, Barba Lambros, under the grape arbor. He had introduced himself to us at church the previous Sunday morning. *Barba*, a form of "uncle," was a title of respect villagers gave the old gentleman, and he seemed to like it. He was one of the male elders who made his miniscule fortune in the restaurant business, in Chicago, prior to returning to Parnion before the Depression.

Barba Lambros was standing in the courtyard with a large, half-filled, cloth sack flung over his shoulder. After warm "hellos" and handshaking were completed, short, muscular, white-haired Lambros easily hoisted the bag off his shoulder and deposited it on the stony courtyard floor. "Open it, *Kyra* Katherine," he directed with a smile on his ruddy face, under his thin, white mustache.

Mother hesitated, but moved toward the sack when he encouraged her a second time. She finally loosened the cord and curiously peered inside. "Wheat??" Mom looked puzzled, but Lambros smiled even more. "Is this... for us?" she asked with hesitation in her voice. "You know, I have nothing to pay you with, *Kyrie* Lambro."

"Did I ask for payment, *Kyra* Katherine?" he asked with the ebullience of St. Nick himself. "This is a belated 'welcome to Parnion' gift," he said in English, "from one Chicagoan to another. I know you'll need bread, long before your wheat seeds grow into grain." He refused money and wouldn't hear of future payment. Lambros wasn't wearing a red suit, or driving a sleigh with reindeer, but the sack he presented us was generously given to us at a very needy time. I have never forgotten his kindness.

Meeting friendly, new people in the village was essential for the shy American kid. One of them, a second cousin, Demetri, became my best friend. He and his family lived beyond St. George's Church, closer to the village school and cemetery. We were approximately the same age and comprised a remarkable pair of buddies, like two side-by-side scoops of ice cream: one chocolate and the other vanilla. I was raven-haired with dark brown eyes; Demetri was blond and blue-eyed, like his father, Paul. His mother, Anastasia, Mom's first cousin, was a willowy, dark haired Mediterranean beauty.

Both of Demetri's parents had been born in Parnion, but Paul had immigrated to Boston when he was a young man. Before the U.S. economy tanked in 1929, he had gathered up his grocery-store-earned savings and returned to Greece to set up a business and find a good wife.

Following his marriage to Anastasia, they moved to Piraeus, Greece's main port city near Athens, where he established a successful building materials company. When the German army invaded in 1941, Nazi military confiscated all of Paul's building materials and made them their own. The couple had no other choice but to take their son Demetri and leave occupied Piraeus to return to what they believed would be the safety of their quiet, remote native village.

Anastasia had received her late father's mill as part of her dowry, so when they came to live in the village, Paul went into the flour milling business a few miles from the center of Parnion, near the Oinountas River. He had learned English in Boston and often tried to carry on a conversation with me. However, by that time, because of my lack of practice, I struggled with my replies—I had forgotten most of the English I knew.

Barba Lambros's gift and Paul's mill came together the day my mother sent me on an essential mission. "Lambros's grain needs to be milled into flour so I can bake bread," Mom explained the day after the older gentleman's visit. "I need you to run an important errand for me, John. But you'll need transportation. So stay put. I'll be right back."

She hastily walked down the road to Aunt Sophia's home, and returned pulling Uncle Vasili's donkey. Hoisting me up to mount the donkey's saddle and then lifting the sack of wheat over the donkey's back, Mother pointed the two of us toward Uncle Paul's water-powered flourmill. My assignment was to have the wheat ground into flour.

Her words reverberated in my brain as the donkey and I set off on our crucial assignment: "Guard this grain carefully. It's more precious than diamonds, Johnny, because I can make bread with it. Hang on to it with all your might."

Most of the year, the Oinountas River contained a trickle of water. The day we returned from Kalamata, we had crossed the little bridge that spans it and the river resembled a bubbling stream, twenty feet wide. But following seasonal rains or heavy rainfalls, the narrow stream swelled and widened to two hundred feet. Unseasonal summer rains had plagued the area a few weeks before I arrived with the donkey, and I was startled to find the usually peaceful stream gushing with white caps. Mother, surely, had no idea of the river's raging condition.

The usual way to go to the mill was to follow the edge of the riverbed. But, I didn't know that when the river was high, there was no "edge of the riverbed." Steep, dangerous embankments at water's edge made navigation difficult. Impenetrable brush was growing out of the dry, rocky terrain on both sides of the stream. As a novice, I didn't know passage through thick brush, even on a donkey, was impossible.

I spotted the bridge. But I knew it was of no help: my route to the mill did not require me to cross the bridge, only to walk along the side of the river. So I naively kicked the animal's flanks to urge him to walk parallel to the torrential current, along what looked to me like the riverbed. But the donkey stubbornly refused. I couldn't let the grain fall into the water, in case the animal moved abruptly. So, to protect the precious wheat, I held on to the animal's reins with one hand and hugged the sack with the other, allowing my feet to kick him. But nothing happened: he wouldn't budge. No matter how I pounded my feet into his flanks and urged him to move, the donkey stayed put. So I dismounted and attempted to pull him along the surging stream. But the animal's feet might as well have been cast in cement. He refused to budge.

"What's the matter with you, stupid ass?" I yelled at him.

Ears pointing up, like two exclamation points, Vasili's donkey silently defied me. I didn't realize it at the time, but his rebellion was communicating a serious message to me in—donkey thought: "Which one of us is the stupid ass, you dumb kid? I don't know about you, but I stay away from danger."

Staring at me, eyes to eyes, he slowly backed away from dangerously gushing waters. Powerless, I didn't know how to make him cooperate. Certainly, I couldn't abandon the borrowed animal. And the sack was too heavy for me to carry to the mill without the risk of dropping it into the water. Lambros's valuable wheat was not to be squandered nor allowed to get wet. Angry and frustrated, tears welled in my eyes. I had no way to make the donkey deliver me to the mill. I was a failure.

All I could do was humbly re-mount the donkey and head home. The animal's stubborn ears still pointed toward the sky, but I was relieved when he fully cooperated with my plan to turn back. With me hanging on for dear life to the heavy sack, we arrived at Grandpa's house. Disappointed and distressed, I presented Mother with un-milled wheat.

"This animal is smarter than the two of us put together," my relieved mother said, after I explained my failed mission. "The donkey's natural instincts saved you from being swept away by the Oinountas. You know, Johnny, for centuries, there was no bridge crossing the river. The reason the bridge is there is that in the past, on a day like today, when the river is full of raging water, many people drowned crossing the Oinountas. In fact, people from Parnion living in the U.S. saw the need for a bridge and sent money to the village to pay for building it."

She explained that in time the powerful current could have dumped me from one gushing stream into another and, eventually, "maybe into the Mediterranean Sea." Uncle Vasili's donkey had saved my life. The following week, Mom heard our neighbor Phillip, Artemis's new husband, was going to the mill; she entrusted him with having our grain milled by Uncle Paul and she finally had ground wheat to bake bread.

I may have failed to get the wheat milled that day, but the project I handled with pride, responsibility, and success was our gorgeous potato field. From that first day of sharing the work with Mom, I fussed over those potato plants. On schedule, I irrigated them by channeling water into the field from the culvert at the side of the road.

Older villagers, passing me on the main road as I weeded and hoed, stopped to commend the American kid on his thriving potatoes—surprised an *"Amerikanaki"* knew anything about growing plants. I smiled shyly and thought to myself that everything I knew I learned from Mom, one of their very own native daughters.

Healthy green leaves sprouted from buds that had appeared lifeless when we had first stuck them in the ground. Mother explained that potatoes were forming under the earth and that we would dig them out for harvesting when they had grown to the size of large tomatoes. She predicted there would be enough potatoes to keep us fed throughout the coming winter; there might even be enough extra potatoes to use as barter for other much needed food supplies.

One afternoon, Mom's brother, Uncle George, made an unexpected visit to us with an even more surprising companion at his side. George entered the courtyard tugging a rope looped around the neck of a little black goat. "Who's your friend?"

Mother teased. My uncle explained that a goat-herder had just leased a piece of Grandpa's land from him, and that the female goat was payment for the lease. "I am giving her to you and the young ones, Katherine. She'll provide milk for the children." Then he turned to me. "John, you can be in charge of her."

Caught unaware, I was elated. Profusely thanking my uncle for giving me my first pet ever, I promised, "I'll take good care of her, Uncle George."

During their visit together, George shared a letter with Mother that he had received from their sister Joanna's daughter in Athens. Conditions were bad in the city, she wrote, but her mother was anxious to leave Lemnos and planned to stop and visit with her daughter in Athens for a few weeks. Joanna would probably be back in Parnion in the next two months. The two siblings shared mutual anxiety concerning their sister's journey during wartime. The planned stop in Athens, a heavily occupied city, worried both Mom and her brother.

"I think it would be wiser for her to stay in Lemnos until this damned war with the Germans is over," George added. "But Joanna has been away so long, she's probably chomping at the bit to get home again. When she makes up her mind about something, Joanna never relents."

While my uncle and mother chatted, my first instinct was to lean down to stroke the little goat's pitch-black mane; its rough, wiry feel surprised me. In time we realized our goat's hair was a reflection of her untamed personality. Nikki and I decided to call her "*Agrimi*" (wild animal), a name suited to her feral disposition.

In the weeks that followed, I unloaded gobs of affection on Agrimi, but whenever her sharp brown eyes spotted me, she'd turn her backside to me, and often used her horns to ram me on my own backside. Not people-friendly and constantly standoffish, she seemed suspicious of my friendly attentions.

One afternoon, I snuck my mother's hairbrush into the courtyard in an attempt to tame the goat's wild black hair. When I applied the brush to her matted coat, she stubbornly pulled away and flashed me a nasty look that said, "Hey, kid, leave me and my hair alone!" I had failed again. On top of it, I got in trouble for almost ruining Mom's perfect American hairbrush.

"Why doesn't she like me?" I kept asking my mother.

"Johnny, there's a difference between wild animals and domesticated animals. It's not that the goat doesn't like you... she's just not used to human attention. Wild goats are not friendly and social like dogs. At least this one is not." I still held the hope that my pet would mellow and become affectionate.

Agrimi and I ventured out on exploratory expeditions together in places where vacant fields yielded goat delicacies: all kinds of wild green delights. She nibbled non-stop, all the way from Grandpa's house, and far out into the countryside, then back home again. Mother worked hard at teaching me how to milk the goat, but most of the time Agrimi scooted away and Mom's strong hands were needed to keep her quiet, until milking was completed. Amused by my attentiveness to the animal, Mom still demanded that I wash my hands after tending to the goat, "And do a good job of it!"

The feral goat was both toy and responsibility for me, until the worst happened. One day, I noticed that Agrimi had begun swelling up, more swollen in the afternoon than she had been that morning. Alarmed and frightened, I found Mother inside the house and begged her to come down into the courtyard to examine the animal. "She's slowly inflating, like a balloon, Mom!!" Mother was puzzled.

"Uncle Vasili will know what to do," I said with hope. Dashing over to Sophia and Vasili's house, I found my uncle sawing wood. My screams startled him. "Please, Uncle," I pleaded, "drop everything and come! My goat is blowing up. She's going to explode!"

Perplexed by my report, Vasili kindly interrupted his carpentry and rushed home with me. After examining Agrimi, he told us that she had probably eaten some poisonous plant in the fields where I took her to graze. Vasili, stroking his thin mustache, advised me in a sympathetic tone, "I'm certain she won't explode. But, Johnny, I'm sorry to tell you—she's not going to live very long." I nursed and tended Agrimi for hours, but she didn't respond. By nightfall, my pet goat died. I was inconsolable.

"What happened?" I cried. "Mama, she was my pal. I was taking good care of her. I didn't know there's poison in the fields." I grieved for my feisty Agrimi even though her naturally wild personality had kept her from becoming cuddly. I cried for days. And as I look back to my childhood, I recognize that losing the wild little goat was my first experience with the heartbreaking permanency of death.

Eventually, village old timers confirmed that poisonous plants had, indeed, contributed to my goat's demise. Experienced goatherds knew where the plants grew, what they looked like, and avoided dangerous pastures with their flocks. But I was a novice goatherd, with more to learn.

It was still summer when my Agrimi died. During that summer of 1941, Nazi occupation had aggravated already appalling conditions in Athens. By late autumn, a fatal famine had commenced in Greece's capital city that severely impacted the rest of the country, including us in Parnion. Conditions were problematical, but they weren't half as bad as the fate still in store for us.

10 | NO NEWS IS—BAD NEWS

We may not have been homeless in Parnion, but we were moneyless and isolated from world news at a time when World War II was about to personally involve us again. A recently arrived woman and her American children, trapped in a remote mountain village *sans* electricity and reliable communication, knew little. Villagers saw us as temporary visitors rather than residents, a standoffish attitude, which kept us out of touch in acquiring dependable news of escalating war. And we couldn't do anything about it.

The little hearsay Mother gleaned was often unreliable. To make matters worse, everyone, except relatives and the few villagers who remembered "the *Amerikanida*" (American woman) prior to her emigration seventeen years before, regarded us as "*xenoi*" (literally, strangers). And strangers in a village were the last to know anything.

Brother-in-law Vasili was Mother's best source for news. He had access to sparse, reliable information, stripped of village gossip and superstition, derived from unknown sources, usually picked up, somehow, in Sparta. One reason Vasili spent time in the town *taverna* was to learn news of the outside world.

When the war escalated, innocent citizens became dreadfully afraid of enemy collaborators who popped up all over the country after the Axis powers took over. In 1943, Nazi-appointed Prime Minister, Ioannis Rallis, organized collaborators into official Security Battalions (*tagmatoasphalites*), which he stationed in various parts of Greece to help the Germans keep tabs on the Greek people. Collaborators carried out immoral deeds to impress

Nazis with their loyalty and friendship. And, acting as overlords of their fellow Greeks, they instilled fear into their countrymen.

By siding with Germans, collaborators counted on being chosen to run the Greek government after an expected (by their side) Allied downfall. In Parnion, and all over Greece, suspicion of strangers and fellow countrymen who might be undercover collaborators instilled the kind of fear that established an atmosphere of silence. "The less said (especially to someone of suspicion), the better." It was a weird version of xenophobia: familiar people were feared because they might be aiding the enemy.

Millions of questions surfaced in ordinary Greeks' minds when Nazi occupation engulfed them. I know that we, in the village, had no answers. War was the dark smog that choked us; fear became the giant ulcer that ate away our spirits. Cut off from reliable news, we didn't know what deplorable hostility would hit us next. At the same time, our ignorance was a tremendous benefit to the Nazis: it successfully aided their vicious "shock and awe" tactics. German violence worsened as we plodded away at surviving under the exquisite sun, the one benefit that Nazis couldn't take away from us. But healing Greek sunshine couldn't lift the contaminating war-fog; it couldn't cure our dread, or keep us safe. Even innocent, arthritic old ladies became targets for power-hungry, collaborator villains with misplaced loyalties.

With scant knowledge of events going on in the rest of Europe, Asia, the U.S., or even the rest of Greece from the start of World War II until the month it finally ended, nearly four years later, we were constantly in the dark about what was happening in the war. Even when we lived in Kalamata, Mother did not know women and children were being evacuated from the city of London on August 31, 1939, the day before Hitler invaded Poland. Mother was unaware that all-night air raids on London (the "Blitz") had begun in August of 1940 as part of Hitler's plan to invade England (which, fortunately, he was never able to achieve).

Village residents, tucked into remote and multiple niches of mountainous Peloponnesos, were not aware of the new 20th century nightmare occurring in Athens. And Athenians were ignorant of village suffering.

Being a kid in wartime, I did not know much of the background for what was going on. I didn't understand the bigger picture until decades later, thanks to historians who had collected, interpreted, and documented stories from all over the country. When I read further into Greece's past, I understood better how WWII had played out the way it did.

By the beginning of the 19th century, world history had witnessed four hundred years of cruel Turkish rule over Greek soil and its inhabitants. That domination carved profound scars on people's souls and blocked Greek advancement in the world. Turkish Ottoman occupation, which began in the 1400s, prevented Greek participation in the European Renaissance; for centuries, it kept Greece out of the technological, social, and cultural progress the rest of Europe enjoyed following the Dark Ages.

The Ottomans had created their own "dark ages" for the Greeks whose ancestors had led the world in advanced thinking— in all disciplines—during the ancient Golden Age. The critical date in modern Greek history was 1821—the year the bloody revolution against the Turks began. Those events took place a mere 120 years before the start of the Second World War.

When the Ottoman Turks were ousted after the 19th century revolutionary war, the European powers imposed a king on the Greek people. Under the Convention of London in 1832, Otto the royal prince of Bavaria, who had no Greek blood in his veins, became King Othon I of Greece. As a result, newly liberated Greek people were still being denied self-determination.

Memories stayed fresh. When Mussolini's Italians invaded Greece on October 28, 1940, grandparents could still relate their own grandparents' grisly tales of Turkish occupation. Being occupied, yet again, by a foreign power brusquely chafed the Hellenic psyche. "Been there, done that!" sighed the intellectuals at the *kafeneion*. Grandmothers asserted "Never again!" while protectively drawing their grandchildren closer. Twentieth-century Greeks took up the torch of independence, demanding "Liberty or death," just as the heroes of the revolution had done to the Turks in 1821.

Greeks were living under the dictatorship of Ioannis Metaxas when the Italian army attacked in 1940. Metaxas had been educated in Germany; he was an admirer of German military organization and a monarchist. In time, he was promoted to General in the Greek army, and when he started his tenure as Greek Prime Minister in 1936, Metaxas began by ruling according to the Greek constitution, which allows multiple political parties to participate in Parliament.

In no time at all, however, Metaxas regarded the law and political opinions of multiple parties as an impediment to his progress. And, a mere four months after the Greek King had appointed him Prime Minister, Metaxas ruthlessly suspended Parliament to remove the multi-factioned political opposition he had faced in the elected body.

Then supported by the Greek King, Metaxas became Greece's dictator. During his tenure he instituted a mandatory national youth organization modeled after Hitler's German counterpart. However, in spite of his admiration for the German military, Metaxas tried to maintain neutrality before the war. By 1939, however, Metaxas understood that an allegiance with Britain would serve Greece better.

When Metaxas was forced to choose sides, he sided with the British. It was not what was expected of him, considering his previous admiration of Germany. And when the Italian minister demanded Greece's surrender to Mussolini's armies in October of 1940, Metaxas flatly refused with a simple but emphatic *"Ohi"* (No!), and ordered the Greek army to repel the Italians at the Albanian border.

Metaxas died in January of 1941, three months before the German invasion and occupation. At the time of his death, the

Greek population was split in its hatred and admiration of him. After his refusal to surrender Greece to Mussolini, many Greeks regarded him a patriot. Yet, he was still reviled by many others because he was a monarchist, because he had suspended democracy in Greece (a concept their ancient forebears had invented) to rule as a dictator, and because he had a history of admiring Hitler.

Some historical evidence indicates that, initially, Hitler had supported Mussolini's attack of Greece, even though he had been surprised by the invasion. By 1940, Greeks and Germans were on opposite sides of the fence regarding the Brits. Hitler was focused on Great Britain as his eventual, most glorious prize for conquest. (Later in the war he would focus on the U.S.S.R.)

However, early in the decade, he had decided that instead of initiating a German land invasion of England, he would begin his conquest by assaulting and taking peripheral parts of the British realm, starting with Egypt and Gibraltar in the Mediterranean.

As well, Hitler had decided that he was going to allow Mussolini's Italian armies to concentrate on conquering those British lands in the Mediterranean. But since Greece and Great Britain were allies, it was vital to Hitler's plan to keep the British Navy out of Greece's seaports.

After the Italians invaded Greece, Hitler advised Mussolini to capture and dominate the entire Greek peninsula and its southern Mediterranean island of Crete. Once Greece was captured by his Italian ally's forces, the country would be theirs for establishing Axis air and naval bases in the Mediterranean: Greece would become Hitler and Mussolini's passageway for getting their armies and war equipment to North Africa.

However, Mussolini's 1940 plan to take Greece was poorly conceived—a genuine shock and disappointment to Hitler. Early on, the Italians were in trouble. The winter of 1940-1941 found the Italian military suffering great losses at the hands of the defending Greek army, which blustering Mussolini dismissed as "ragtag." That's when Hitler, angered by his ally Mussolini's lack of appropriate planning, decided to send in Nazi troops to assist the Italian army.

Twenty-one days after their initial incursion from Bulgaria in the north, German forces had reached Athens, and the Greek government capitulated. Nazi soldiers installed the red-and-black swastika flag on the Parthenon: modern Greeks continued to be deprived of self-determination. It is easy to understand that Greek hate and hostility toward the occupying German army instantly blossomed following the Nazi takeover.

After the German invasion of Athens, several trucks full of captured British POWs on their way to German prison camps were spotted on the city's streets. Local Athenian residents brashly applauded and cheered the prisoners as heroes—in open defiance of their German military occupiers.

Therefore, to discourage approval of the well-received British, Nazis quickly put out a decree that "contact with soldiers or civilian POWs under the guard of the German army" was a punishable offense. Another decree prohibited listening to foreign radio broadcasts (like the BBC or Voice of America); eventually the Germans confiscated all of the country's radios.

The Third Reich also punished, by death, any assault or sabotage on the German army. Nazis were plainly gearing up their decrees to discourage a Greek homeland resistance movement. Greeks may have been horrified by the appalling invasion, but they were not discouraged by Nazi diktats.

The city's streets filled with Athenians boldly demonstrating against the German occupation. Marchers also condemned Greek government officials who had capitulated to the Nazi regime and condemned, at the same time, the catastrophic downturn in the economy resulting from the Nazi invasion.

Less than a month after the Germans took over, two heroic Greek teenagers snuck up Acropolis hill during the night, and tore down the hated Nazi flag from the Parthenon. By dawn's early light, the glorious blue and white Greek standard was seen flying over Greece's sacred monument, until the Germans ripped it down, replacing it, of course, with another reviled swastika flag.

By June, two months following the German takeover, the formidable, clandestine Greek resistance movement had begun in urban areas and in the provinces. Known as *antartes* (guerrilla fighters), they eventually hid out in the mountains outside Greek cities and villages. Their intent was to sabotage and deter the Italian and German armies from accomplishing their ominous goals, an offense the invaders punished with death.

I was nine years old and unaware that several men and even two women from Parnion left the village to join the resistance. Moreover, families of known resistance-fighters were at risk of being harassed or punished by Nazis. So, as meager protection, guerrillas usually fought far from their native villages.

Then, again, in Parnion, information about the resistance movement was not shared with children because kids have a tendency to inadvertently spill the beans. It would have been exceedingly dangerous for our village neighbors and for kids themselves to have these "beans" revealed. The obligation to intentionally keep children out of an extremely perilous loop was understood by all adults. For the safety and security of an entire village, kids were to be kept in the dark; it was unwritten law in Parnion. Period.

As a kid, I asked questions, but I didn't get answers. Mom told me to keep my mouth shut about everything I knew, but I really didn't understand why—because I didn't know anything. It was clear that German soldiers were the plague I was to fear and stay away from. By the time I was a year or two older, I picked up on obvious village clues regarding collaborators who worked to instill deadly Nazism and I became aware of *antartes* who were fighting to wipe out the Nazi plague.

Shortly after we arrived in Parnion, while Nikki and I, soundly in the dark about resistance details, bumbled around getting acquainted with our new surroundings, our very own mother was drawn into a very dangerous loop. After we came from Kalamata, gossip channels instantly lit up. The *xenoi* (outsiders) included my fifteen-year-old brother Alex, who spoke Greek very well, considering he was from Chicago.

Late one night, Uncle George and Uncle Vasili made a visit to our house. They explained to my mother that British soldiers, who had not escaped from Greece following the Axis takeover, were hidden in the recesses of Mt. Parnon's foothills. The soldiers were concealed, fed, and protected in outlying mountain caves by several patriotic citizens of Parnion who spoke no English whatsoever.

Obviously, we had arrived in the nick of time. My brother Alex's bilingual abilities were vitally needed. At the urging of our uncles, Mother allowed Alex to assist the British. As a result of her heart-wrenching decision, dismal fear constantly overwhelmed my mother. At the same time, she could share her dread with no one. I learned of her situation only after we had returned safely to Ann Arbor.

11 | "LAST SUPPER" IN PARNION

Dark-haired, handsome Uncle Vasili was Parnion's skilled carpenter who also took the role of chanter for St. George's Church on the village's main square. Vasili could chant, from memory, both Liturgies composed by our venerated church fathers, saints Basil the Great and John Chrysostom, along with hymns which accompanied holy days, baptisms, weddings, funerals, etc. Vasili, who had been blessed with a naturally clear, tenor voice, was a pleasure to listen to during the almost three-hour service celebrated on Sundays and holy days. Even in wartime, church traditions carried on. My uncle, a good friend of Parnion's only priest Father Haralambos, was very involved in church affairs.

By tradition, Orthodox Christian priests in Greece wear long black robes all day, every day, and never cut their hair or shave off their beards. Haralambos gathered his long, snow-white hair into a simple coil and secured it at the back of his head under the traditional, tall black priest's hat, known as the *kalymmafhi*.

He was an amiable and devout man, with few wrinkles and a ruddiness that lit up his face like a Byzantine Santa Claus. A married priest, he and his upbeat, white haired *Presvytera*, as villagers addressed the priest's wife, had long before raised their family and were grandparents. She was a cheerful woman, even though she was stooped with age, bent at a ninety-degree angle over her cane.

Parnion's villagers recognized Haralambos as a sincere, good man of the cloth. I often spotted Father sitting on the bench outside St. Nick's Church warming himself in the sun, devoutly concentrating on his constant companion, a well-worn, black

98

prayer book. Most days, he shared passages from his holy book with Panagiota, a mentally handicapped middle-aged woman, who made it a habit to warm herself on the bench too.

When he read to her, Panagiota either stared blankly at the priest or, avoiding his glance, stared down at her feet. Panagiota may not have grasped all the nuances of Father's spiritual message, but he provided her with a few moments of well-needed, heart to heart, human-to-human contact. Assured Father wouldn't notice her when he meditated or dozed off with eyes closed, bashful Panagiota craned her neck to stare at and examine the priest's stately *kalymmafhi*.

Once, when a bunch of boys and I played tag outside St. George's church, and happened to continue our chase in the narthex, I saw Father on his knees, head bent to the floor in front of the altar, so lost in communication with his God that he was completely oblivious to the gaggle of noisy boys. Local old ladies, appalled by our sinful behavior, frowned and acidly scolded us. Haralambos smiled when one of the crones tattled, but he never reprimanded. "I'm pleased they are comfortable enough with our church to play in here," he countered to the shocked busybody. Perhaps being a husband, good family man, and grandfather was the basis for Father's compassionate understanding of human foibles and the occasional but aggressive game of tag.

Unlike many other priests whose liturgical chant I have strained to understand, I recall Father Haralambos' style: he enunciated every word, spoke or chanted prayers with passion, as if it was the first time he was invoking them. He never rushed through petitions even though as an older priest, he had uttered them a million times before.

Uncle Vasili regularly assisted Haralambos as a kind of "gofer" during sacraments, liturgies, and countless church rites. I had watched my uncle light candles, sweep the church, ignite incense in the silvery censer, fill the simple baptismal font with water, even reprimand unruly altar boys. Vasili enjoyed working at church as much as he liked working with wood.

One morning, Vasili and his wife, Mom's younger sister Sophia, walked to our house loaded down with the makings of a very fine supper. Since our pantry was almost empty, I judged that we were happily going to feast royally that night. "What's going on, Uncle Vasili? What's the holiday?" I asked, eagerly expecting to fill my stomach with the meat and potatoes that I was helping them unpack.

"Johnny, we're going to have a very special visitor tonight. The Bishop of Sparta is coming to interview me. He wants to see if I'm a good enough candidate for the priesthood. But we can't be feeding lowly bean soup to someone as prestigious as the Bishop," my uncle said. "So we're cooking a special meal."

I knew Uncle Vasili was active at church, but his desire to become a clergyman took me by surprise. Noting my stunned expression, Vasili attempted to elicit a reaction. "He wants to make me a priest. Isn't that exciting, John?"

I asked, "Do you want to be a priest, Uncle Vasili? You're a terrific carpenter. I love the stuff you make out of wood."

"Certainly I'd like to be a priest," he answered. "It would be an honor to serve God in such a special way. Don't you think so?"

"The Sunday Liturgy is okay, Uncle Vasili. But could you stand going to all those funerals? Weddings and baptisms are fine—but burying dead guys is creepy."

Patting my shoulder, and winking at Aunt Sophia, Vasili smiled at my reaction. "I guess it's something I'll have to get used to, Johnny."

"How come Aunt Sophia came here to cook for the Bishop? Are we going to eat with him here at Grandpa's house?"

Vasili replied, "Your mother and aunt are both extraordinary cooks, so they are collaborating on this extra special feast. But, you and Nikki won't be able to stay to meet the Bishop tonight. Before dinner, you'll go over to our house and spend the evening with your cousins."

"We don't get to eat roast lamb and potatoes? None of us kids? Why? That's not fair." I objected. "Why can't all of us eat together with the Bishop?"

"The Bishop will be having a very serious talk with me here tonight," my uncle answered. "And he said he doesn't want any distractions. He asked that our meeting only include him, your aunt because she would be the *presvytera*, and me. But the Bishop said it's okay for your mother to be part of the group too, because she's the lady of your grandpa's house now."

Making one more plea for sharing roasted lamb and potatoes, I said, "You know, Uncle Vasili, I remember something I heard in church a few Sundays ago. Didn't Father Haralambos read something to us about Jesus liking children? His apostles were going to shoo some children away while Jesus was talking and Jesus said, 'It's okay for the little kids to come over to me—I like kids.' Doesn't the Bishop know that part of the Bible? I think Jesus would want us kids to eat here at Grandpa's house with the Bishop tonight."

Laughing, my uncle commended me on my knowledge of the Gospels and told me he would remind the Bishop of that particular verse during his interview. Still, I was completely let down knowing I wouldn't be able to partake in the final results of culinary activities surrounding me.

I hadn't smelled my mother's savory roasting meat, steeped in its bouquet of garlic, oregano, and lemon, since we left Kalamata. Even as I argued with my uncle, the cooking had begun. Now these luscious aromas—a desirable fragrance that Coco Chanel could never match—began to envelope me, and I wouldn't even be allowed to taste.

"Children, before you leave for Aunt Sophia's house, I want you to wash your hands at the *niftera*," Mom directed. As I washed my hands with cold water, I thought of her common response to my complaints about washing my hands so often, "At least water is plentiful in Parnion, children," she would always reply.

Our mother had learned more complete hygiene habits in the U.S. than were practiced in the village at that time. Since there was no running water in Parnion homes, the *niftera*, a water receptacle resembling a small cylindrical tank with built-in, off-on spigot, was a permanent fixture in village courtyards.

Water, procured daily from the nearby fountain, was poured into the *niftera* to keep it full and ready for washing hands and faces. Ours must have set a record for most used *niftera* in the prefecture of Laconia. Mother had me fill that thing multiple times a day with water I had to lug home from St. Nick's.

Nikki and I presented our dripping hands for inspection, and Mother saw the famished look on our faces. She disappeared into the kitchen and returned with a succulent, gourmet potato slice for each of us. "The Bishop won't miss them," she said with a wry smile, as she shooed us down to Sophia's house.

As far as Nikki and I were concerned, that was the end of the story. We went to sleep that night filled with envy for the Bishop. In the months to come, I often thought back on that night as my last supper, even though I barely partook of it. Those were the last aromas of a complete, cooked meal I ever inhaled in Parnion. And although I didn't know it at the time, our family's unexpected odyssey was about to connect us to greater danger and further nauseating hunger.

***

Years later, when we were safely in Ann Arbor with Dad, I overheard Mother relating episodes from our war experiences that had occurred in the years we were parted from him. Curious, I listened. Her story regarding that special meal in Parnion was slightly different from the one I recalled. Mom described the familiar scene of Vasili arriving at Grandpa's with bundles of meat and a sack of potatoes, Then she went on to tell him about cooking the big meal, alongside her sister Sophia, in the crude kitchen facilities at Grandpa's house.

But Mother's story took a different turn when she explained what happened after sundown, in the hours when Nikki and I were at Sophia's house playing with our cousins. Mom reported to Dad that when it was completely dark, her dinner guests arrived—five bearded British soldiers dressed in black clothes.

Mom's account stunned me and I listened, intently. She continued telling my father that her first sight of the men had frightened her because they had blackened their faces with burnt cork to camouflage themselves in the dark of night. But then Mom went on to say that she finally relaxed after the men introduced themselves to her; the Brits had good manners, pleasant personalities, and were more than grateful to be invited visitors in her home. I was even more astounded when she explained to Dad that Alex had smuggled the soldiers into the village and into our house from the cave where they had been hiding.

Mother shared with Dad that she had been very anxious about the scrumptious aromas of roasting lamb deliciously drifting from the kitchen—afraid that villagers would notice the mouth-watering cooking fragrance coming from Grandpa's house, possibly making some of them wary of what was going on inside. Cooking a huge meal with roasted meat when it was not a holiday—during the beginning of occupation when food was getting scarce—could easily bring suspicion. We could never be sure if villagers we didn't know well were siding with Nazi collaborators.

Mother also explained to Dad that, for security reasons, the younger children had to be kept completely unaware of the clandestine dinner. Word of the big meal and special dinner guests could not be revealed via innocent childhood chatter. Any hint of the "American woman" feeding foreign soldiers, with the help of Sophia and Vasili, would have endangered our entire family. "So Vasili took care of that detail by making up a story for the children," Mom told Dad. "He told them the Bishop was coming over to discuss making him a priest."

I couldn't believe what I was hearing. I had always wondered why Vasili never became a priest. It had bothered me that the Bishop didn't think my uncle was good enough because I believed that Vasili was one of the best men in the village.

Knowing too well and—first hand—about our frightful wartime circumstances, I teased my mother, feigning annoyance that it was all a lie. "Mom, you are tighter lipped than the Secret Service. Why didn't you save a few scraps of food for your own children? What happened to the leftovers?"

"Leftovers? After feeding five ravenous soldiers?" Mother tossed an incredulous stare in my direction. "There weren't any!"

***

1942: Bing was ..."dreaming of a White Christmas..." We had
nightmares about Nazi soldiers:

- ❖ *U.S. gas rationing goes into effect, allowing 3 gallons per week*

- ❖ *Count Basie records "One O'clock Jump"*

- ❖ *Bing Crosby first records Irving Berlin's "White Christmas"*

- ❖ *Walt Disney's Bambi" released in American movie theaters*

- ❖ *"Archie" comic book debuts*

- ❖ *Anne Frank and her family move into their Amsterdam hiding place*

- ❖ *First European bombing-run undertaken by U.S. forces*

- ❖ *Japanese invade Burma*

- ❖ *Japanese troops land on Bali*

12 | EXODUS—1942

Mother relished the company of her sisters, relatives, and neighbors in Parnion, along with the roof over our heads: her sole benefit in returning to the village. In the early 1920s, when she had first arrived in the U.S. lacking English skills, Mom had found it difficult to make friends with neighbor women who spoke no Greek. That hurdle, compounded by missing her family in Greece, brought her loneliness until she married my father.

Then, having suffered stressful, antagonist relations with Dad's brother Antoni in Kalamata, when we first arrived from the U.S., the warm ties Mother rekindled in Parnion made wartime woes more bearable.

One of Mother's most encouraging friends was skinny and energetic *Kyra* Margarita. Black garments of widowhood framed her ancient and wrinkled face but never dimmed her cheery smile. Old in years, our dear neighbor was a dynamo: sharp-witted and forever in motion. Nephews, who lived in the village, regularly came to check on their elderly aunt's wellbeing. But as Mom observed, Margarita was probably in better shape than those young men. Our plucky neighbor took pride in having survived eighty-eight years with every one of her own teeth, almost a miracle in a place without dentists, toothbrushes, or Pepsodent.

Kyra Margarita felt a connection, and took a liking to us because she had two nieces who, twenty years before, had emigrated from Greece and were living in Chicago. Margarita was disappointed when Mother reported we didn't know her relatives. "Chicago is an immense city of over two million people. *Kyra* Margarita, thousands of Greeks live in Chicago. I would have remembered meeting your nieces from Parnion. When we return, I will make it my business to meet them."

"Katherine, how many people live in Parnion?"

"I've heard over a thousand," Mother replied.

"That means Chicago… " and the old woman paused to calculate in her head, without using paper and pencil or ever having attended a day of school in her life. "Let's see, one… single American city… is like… a combination of… two thousand villages with populations like Parnion's. No wonder you haven't met my nieces. How about my nephew Christos who lives in Kansas City? Have you run into him?"

Mother smiled. "No. I've never been to Kansas City. It's probably five hundred miles away from Chicago."

Margarita was fascinated by the vast expanse of the U.S., and flabbergasted by the sizes of huge American cities with great populations. "My dear Katherine, I wish my father had sent me there when I was a girl."

I also recall our good neighbors Artemis and Phillip, who lived four houses away from us. They were the couple whose elopement had taught me the power of gossipy tongues when we first arrived in Parnion. They lived happily, lovingly parented her orphaned niece Maria, and worked alongside each other in their fields.

"*Kyra* Katherine, God brought you into my life," Artemis told Mother one day in our courtyard. "You know, I'm the laughing stock of Parnion. I could kick myself over whatever it was that got into my head. You know, my parents and sister died while I was still a young woman, leaving me alone, except for my niece Maria. I needed change.

"I needed happiness and excitement," Artemis continued. "Everything in my life was black. Black dresses, black scarves, black stockings—black was choking the life out of me. Villagers didn't understand how I was feeling. And their condemnation will outlive me. I'm a joke to everyone, except you, *Kyra* Katherine. You actually like me. And so does old Margarita."

"Of course we like you," Mother hastened to say. "You're not a joke. I plainly detect that villagers are only secure in sticking to unbroken traditions. Parnion's people believe the 'Parnion way' is the only way. Artemis, you did no wrong. You harmed no one. And, you are blessed because you have a happy marriage."

Mom explained, "I have lived in America for seventeen years. I've learned there's more than one way of doing something, and no sin in acting differently, if it doesn't bring harm to others. Most of our Chicago neighbors were Irish, Italian, and Polish, all Roman Catholics—not Orthodox like us. The kind Swedish lady, next door, is a Protestant. They are good, caring people. Artemis, I learned that even if their ways are not my ways, their ways are good too." In response to Mother's American pluck, Artemis shook her head with regret, "That attitude would never translate well here, *Kyra* Katherine."

"Most people here look at my children and me as outsiders," Mom continued. "I was born here and I still feel connected to this place. My father was one of the village's leading citizens when he was alive. Yet, those who don't remember me say I'm a *xeni*. But I don't feel like a stranger. I know people think what they want to think, dear Artemis, and I can't change them. Just remember, you did no wrong."

Artemis shook her head again, "*Kyra* Katherine, I didn't come here today to talk about my problems. I, actually, came today to warn you... about someone. God may not have blessed me with beauty but He blessed me with good hearing. I know what's being said about everyone in this village—some true, but some dirty lies."

Then Artemis lowered her voice. "The champion of cruel gossip is *Papadopoulina*. Mrs. Papadopoulos often has a group of women gathered around her. They share the latest news, whether or not it's true, and they pass the latest judgments. Be careful of her. Be nice—but cautious.

"Her exaggerations and spiteful words have tragically wrecked fine reputations. I should know. Villagers realize she has an evil tongue, but too many of our neighbors hear and believe the garbage she tells. From my own experience I know she spreads hateful lies. And what makes her dangerous is—she believes her own lies. Avoid her, *Kyra* Katherine."

Mom nodded. "My sisters warned me, Artemis. I'm to be pleasant but to stay away because Papadopoulina retaliates maliciously when she thinks someone is snubbing her. Her husband owns the store on the square. I don't shop. I have no reason to run into her.

"I appreciate your concern, Artemis," and Mother smiled. "I'm blessed to have my sisters and good friends, like you, who care about my safety and the welfare of my children here, in my own village."

Our neighborhood was populated with a cast of unforgettable and loveable characters. Along with *Kyra* Margarita, Artemis, and Martha who walked her fluffy, white ewe past Grandpa's house every day, there was Panagiota, who was always fascinated by Father Haralambos's tall black hat.

About fifty years old, docile Panagiota lived alone in a somewhat rickety cottage, five or six houses from Grandpa's house. In good weather it was her habit to walk to St. Nick's and sit on the bench near the fountain to warm herself in the sun. The heart-wrenching image that remains in my memories is of this harmless, mentally handicapped woman sitting, huddled on the simple, wooden bench in front of the church, often talking to herself.

She wore the same threadbare, dark blue sweater drawn around her shoulders every day and an old, brown wool scarf typically slipped off her matted, graying hair to reveal her head— sadly hung down, almost to her lap. Because her shoulders were slumped over, Pangiota's blank but pleasant face was rarely visible. Yet, when she looked up, I noticed she avoided eye contact and rarely smiled. Poor, shy Panagiota was such a pathetic figure that even village bullies didn't bother her.

The fame she unknowingly enjoyed among fellow villagers was that she was related to some very rich people, while having no means of support herself. Panagiota was cousin to a famous family of Greek ship owners. Born in Parnion, as were her deceased parents and wealthy relatives, she had no siblings. Her millionaire relatives made money in shipping, via a fleet of immense cargo ships that sailed the earth's oceans, years before Aristotle Onassis amassed his fortune.

Some in Parnion referred to the woman as *"Panagiota ton Ephopliston"* (Panagiota of the Shipping Magnates), sadly making it into a cruel joke about the unfortunate woman. The glitzy branch of Panagiota's family tree enjoyed the luxuries of high society and life in London, headquarters of their commercial enterprises. Panagiota subsisted on the compassion and handouts of village neighbors.

I recall a warm, sunny day at the end of our first summer in Parnion, when I was still getting to know the village and its characters. Mom and Aunt Sophia were busy kneading dough for making a large batch of *trahana*. The village staple, eaten in winter, consists of cracked wheat cooked with milk. The two women were working on a table they had set up in the courtyard, under the spreading grapevines, when Panagiota silently wandered in to watch.

She stood there, observing them form crumbles of dough by hand, then spreading the tiny pieces on a clean white bed sheet, to leave them to air-dry. As they worked, Mom and my aunt attempted to explain the steps of the process to Panagiota in simple terms, like they were speaking to a small child. She watched, asked no questions, but when their backs were turned, Panagiota grabbed handfuls of raw dough and stuffed them into her mouth.

Sophia spotted her and compassionately warned, "Panagiota, please don't eat un-cooked dough. Eating raw *trahana* will give you a bad stomachache. Come back after it has dried and we'll share some with you. And we'll give you enough to eat all winter long, but only after you boil it." Panagiota returned the following week and took them up on their offer. Recalling the activities of that first summer in the village for us, I remember, most sadly, that the German occupation ended the summertime tradition of making *trahana*. In fact, for residents of Parnion, like us, German occupation would come close to finishing off the fine old, revered practice of—eating.

When the Nazi military machine took over Greece, they did not transport food from Germany or German army cooks to prepare communal meals for their forces. In contrast, American soldiers in WWII were relatively self-sufficient. They carried K rations as a daily, portable source of nutrition. I don't know if the Germans who came to Greece had anything equivalent to K rations.

There were no German mess halls, nor did they transport tents to provide sleeping facilities for the thousands of invading Nazi soldiers. With no chow, office space, or sleeping accommodations, they solved their shortages by simply taking over Greek real estate and Greek food supplies, at will, to house and feed their armies and run their war.

As far as I know, the Italian military did not have a major presence in Parnion. I have been told that small groups of Italian soldiers had come to Parnion, but they were not deemed as brutal as the Germans whose atrocities became harsher with time. Eventually, Nazis replaced the Italian army in Peloponnesos. Due to the Nazis' ruthless reputation, German entry into a Greek community stirred more fear than the appearance of Italian soldiers, who as a rule were usually more laid-back in military demeanor. I never saw Italian soldiers in Parnion.

***

Parnion's green ravine, the village's western border, was not visible from Grandpa's house; nor could we see from our windows the bend in the road leading into town. However, the main artery into Parnion, where the road bends, was visible at a distance from St. Nicholas Church and houses overlooking the ravine.

Curious residents peering out over the verdant canyon easily observed travelers approaching Parnion. Shepherds, goatherds and their sprawling flocks, even lone trekkers were plainly noticeable against the mountainous panorama on the tree-lined entrance to town. With the exception of Sophocles and his truck, few motor vehicles came to the village. Motor sounds were quite uncommon.

I don't recall the month or exact year—late 1941, or maybe 1942—when that all ended; we had no calendar on the wall to make note of events. But I do remember the haunting morning when clamorous engine sounds emerged from the distance, like alien thunder. The frightening noise surged at us from beyond the bend in the road. Mom, my siblings and I were inside the house when we perceived motor vehicles approaching. Heavy cars were maneuvering Mt. Parnon's curves: screeching brakes shrieked in high-pitched cacophony.

Hushed, we held our breaths hearing the booming "vroom-vroom-vroom" of engines coming closer. Hearts dropped witnessing the ominous parade that churned road dust and spewed stinking exhaust. Black and shiny foreign vehicles appeared and momentarily disappeared behind the trees lining the road into town. Startled eyes understood the sinister procession of long black cars and military trucks was arriving to deliver... terror. The startling invasion of little Parnion was beginning.

But fast-thinking village brains, always super-alert to looming peril, collectively abandoned momentary paralysis. Alex ran to look out the *saloni*'s window; I jumped to my feet and pulled on my shoes. Together with Mom and Nikki we darted out to the courtyard, then stopped to listen and clearly make sense of the jumble of shouts coming from beyond the *perivoli*. Oral cautions were erupting over courtyard walls from house to house, neighbor to neighbor. The four of us breathlessly stared at each other. My pulse stopped when Mr. Kostas, two courtyards away, screamed a dreaded warning into the air. His terrifying words flew over Grandpa's outdoor walls. They exploded in my ears:

"Erhontai oi Germanoi. Erhontai oi Germanoi!'
("The Germans are coming. The Germans are coming!")

Mother's face went blank. A second later, she was planning our next move.

"Let's go!" she shouted. "Follow me to the *mantri!*" I knew what she meant. Once, I had taken Agrimi to graze near the walled corral for goats. The sturdy, stone *mantri* seemed as good a hiding place as any.

"Stick together—Run!" she commanded with the confidence of a general. In no time at all we fled Grandpa's courtyard. Mom was shepherding us through tall grasses, scratchy holm oaks, and thorny shrubs. Frantic, we were dashing toward village outskirts.

No mass village departure strategies had been pre-arranged. But, like Mother, villagers instantly herded loved ones together to evacuate homes and fields—to run. They scattered away from the village into caves, remote churches, and fields of tall-grown wheat. Many fled into nearby woods, remote niches in the ravine, and hidden recesses along the Oinountas River. To a five-mile radius, isolated nooks and crannies, which village natives knew from childhood, became silent hiding places when the unexpected German army emerged from hell for the first time. The exodus was hushed and immediate; only the very elderly and infirm stayed put.

Herded together, we pulled each other along, running for our lives over rocky fields. My skin caught on painful, prickly undergrowth. After thirty breathless minutes, we arrived at the *mantri*, along with other terrified, fleeing villagers. Artemis accompanied feisty Margarita, while Phillip and their niece rushed a confused Panagiota to the goat corral.

Petrified with fear, we spent the day dreading the possibility of being discovered by approaching soldiers. Thirsty, hungry, and dirty, we huddled down in stinking, decaying goat dung, keeping as still and silent as possible. Small children were gently muzzled and shushed: a mere sneeze or cough could fatally reveal our hiding place. *Kyra* Margarita had taken charge of Panagiota. With her arm around the frightened woman she compassionately played a silencing game with her to keep Panagiota from uttering her usual moans.

A horrified, collective gasp evaporated from the corral when shattering bullet volleys exploded from the direction of the village. Distant sharp blasts of penetrating gunfire terrorized the lot of us; each and every refugee made the sign of the cross, over and over again. I heard Artemis whisper, *"Panagia, philaxai"* (Holy Mother, protect us) and Phillip plead, "Dear God, save us."

Startled and petrified, I silently wondered, "Are our neighbors being slaughtered? Will we ever return home safely? Will we die today?" There were no answers. Without blankets or coats, we spent the night in the corral, wide-eyed, shivering with fear and bone-penetrating cold.

In the morning, the air was cold and utterly silent. Alex volunteered to sneak back to the village and assess the situation. Ninety minutes later, he returned with news. The German troops had vanished. Old Mr. Apostolis, unable to flee, had been terrorized at the doorway of his courtyard, and was now resting in bed. Old Georgenna reported that her pantry was empty and her sheep had been stolen. Still, it appeared safe to return.

Each time we heard Germans nearing the village, we ran scared, then returned home when the coast appeared to be clear. No one had been gunned down, yet. Heartless Germans shot off their guns to frighten the elderly and infirm who were unable to flee the village. However, along with our neighbors we discovered that, in our absence, soldiers plundered our vacant houses of food and personal property.

Soon we learned that our cold overnights in the dung of the *mantri* had been, more or less, unnecessary. "We can't be running every time Germans come," Mom uttered with disgust. "If they kill us—they kill us," but then added, *"Panagia, philaxai."* Her beseeching, prayerful words were ingrained, as automatic as applying the brake pedal in times of life-threatening danger. Other villagers certainly murmured similar imprecations, "*Thee mou, sosai mas*" (My God, save us) was a common one. And some simply crossed themselves, a wordless prayer letting God know that they knew He was there for them.

Germans usually, but not always, left Parnion and other mountain hamlets before nightfall because they knew they were at risk of being trapped in darkened villages, vulnerable to guerrilla violence. *Antartes* (guerrillas) emerged from mountain hideouts after dark.

At the start of the war, when the Greek government capitulated to the Germans, the government-sanctioned Greek army was officially disbanded because the politicians had agreed that there would be no fight against the occupying Axis military.

In no time at all, however, resentment and resistance to dastardly occupation took root in the souls of Greek citizens, and unofficial, underground guerrilla bands of fighters were secretly forming throughout the mountainous country. *Antartes* became the only forces fighting against Nazi brutality. In Parnion, guerrilla "freedom fighters" also helped the hidden British soldiers. As the only combatants observably helping the Allies and—fighting back—they were considered "good guys."

Mother and Aunt Sophia never made another batch of *trahana* together. When *trahana*-making season came around the following year, cupboards and larders were bare; Nazis had helped themselves to the ingredients needed for making the traditional winter staple.

Eventually we experienced terror-filled nights when Nazi soldiers, taking up residence in village homes, stayed in Parnion overnight. In fact, there was even an unbearable two-week Nazi layover. To deter *antartes'* attacks on the Nazis when they were present in the dead of night, the German military brought in a greater force of motored vehicles, soldiers, and weapons.

Mother had moved us to Parnion to get away from Nazis in Kalamata, not realizing that the guerillas' resistance movement was underway in the mountains surrounding her village. Nor did she know that the Third Reich had issued edicts for retaliation to discourage rebellious Greeks in Parnion and beyond. We learned the hard way—Mom's village was no safe haven. After our fourth escape to the *mantri* when Germans, again, had invaded the village, Mom decided that we would stay put if the Germans screeched down the road again.

13 | CARS, TRUCKS, AND MOTORCYCLES

Alien thunder and smelly fumes assaulted our pristine air, yet again, one morning when out-of-the-ordinary tremors shook the village and shattered our peaceful Parnion sunrise—an earthquake would have been preferable. Reverberating vehicles were approaching Parnion from the main road. It was probably the fifth German "visit." The dreadful clatter assaulted us from a distance, far beyond the thick walls of Grandpa's house. I halted morning chores and held my breath to concentrate on the sounds.

Rather than fleeing to the *mantri*, we stayed put. Mother nervously demanded that Nikki and I stay close to her in the *saloni*; Alex was not home, but Mom didn't seem overly concerned about his absence. Adrenaline pumping, the three of us huddled together to observe the bizarre, real-life drama which was about to play in the street outside my special window.

Safety was uppermost in Mother's mind; she held us back from the window, closer to the opposite wall, by pinning Nikki and me back with her arm. But when the alien racket reached its peak outside Grandpa's house, we dredged up the nerve to peek out—and my heart plunged to my knees. A fleet of highly polished, loud, vexing trucks, black cars, and shiny motorcycles was slowly, but triumphantly, rolling into Parnion. It was my first glimpse of the enemy.

Shivering with dread, I managed to remain upright as we eye-witnessed a bona fide invasion of Nazi soldiers, mere yards away from our window. Three serious looking canines with pointy teeth (surely German Shepherds) rode alongside well-armed soldiers in

116

the open-cars and trucks passing below us. Roaring lions on the loose could not have terrorized us more.

I felt the tension gripping Mother as she squeezed my hand and reached out to draw Nikki even closer. A dozen or more hard-faced German soldiers garbed in dark grayish-bluish uniforms had breached the sanctity of my mother's beloved village. Silvery buttons, elaborate military insignias, shiny black helmets, and villainous guns glistened in the Greek sunlight. Then I felt the release of Mom's hand on mine and I glanced up. *"Thee mou, sosai mas"* (My God, save us) she murmured as she crossed herself. Mother's cheeks were wet with tears.

Precariously staring down onto the street again, my eyes zeroed in on highly polished, panther-black boots rising up to every soldier's knees. Some Nazis wore helmets; others sported military caps with fancy crests and emblems. My heart pounded hardest when my eyes focused on their steely firearms. Glaring, hostile soldiers were aiming machine guns toward the left and right of the slowly moving motorcade.

One stone-faced, helmeted Nazi set his sights on Grandpa's second-floor window, aiming right at us. Nikki pulled away and ran to hide under the bed. I stayed glued to Mother's side until the caravan moved out of sight. Trembling, Mom whispered, "They're heading for the main square. And we'll stay inside the house until they leave the village."

Mother locked all the doors. We barricaded ourselves inside the second-story *saloni* all day and never dared to drift away. The outer walls of Grandpa's house had been constructed of solid stone, two feet thick. So the interior, like all village houses in those days, was relatively cool, but dark. Fortunately on that day we enjoyed illumination in our prison fortress because my mother had opened the shutters when she got up in the morning, and didn't dare shut them for fear of attracting attention.

On a normal day, we would have been outside playing, going to school or doing chores, and taking the magnificent Greek sunlight for granted. Being cooped up all day in dim, interior surroundings made me notice how important windows were to a house, no matter how small. With armed Nazis in town, Mother kept me from curling up inside my comfy window nook. Nothing was comfy that day. Unbearable fear held us its hostages.

Nikki remained under the bed, sobbing her little heart out. For hours and hours we agonized, waiting to hear the sound of vehicles leaving the village; it didn't happen. Strange daylight silence at our end of town, both comforting and terrifying, was interrupted by the bray of a donkey, dogs barking, a rooster's screech, and cackling chickens. Those poor creatures didn't know the Germans had invaded our village. Yet birds were silent. When the birds saw Germans coming, they must have bolted into the blueness and flown out of town. But we were stuck there. I wished we could fly away like the birds.

With no way of knowing what was going on at the other end of Parnion, we waited, immobile and quiet for hours and hours. Restlessness assaulted our frightened bodies, so we rotated positions from sitting on the *saloni*'s stiff chairs to resting on the bare wooden floor, with our backs leaning against the hard wall.

Only Nikki's occasional sobs and inquiries of, "Are they coming to our house?" interrupted our gloomy silence. Mother would always reassure her, "No, Nikki, they aren't. Why don't you come out from under the bed and sit with us?" Finally, an hour before nightfall, trucks, motorcycles, cars, dogs, and soldiers still wielding machine guns, passed our house again on their way out of Parnion. Nikki was finally coaxed from under the bed; Mother shut the heavy shutters and lit the oil lamp. The day felt like an eternity.

"They're gone," Mother said, as we followed her and the oil lamp to the fireplace room. "They've seen how beautiful our Parnion is and they keep coming back, children. But by now they've had enough of climbing that difficult road, and we'll probably never see them again." More disheartened than we were, Mother attempted to alleviate our fears with comforting words she, herself, knew were lies.

While we had stayed put in dreaded fear with the first sounds of military vehicles heading toward Parnion, every physically able man and male teenager had fled into the mountains. Our men knew that one of the Nazis' aims was to force healthy, strong males into the German army or into the infamous Greek Security Battalions. Those were Greeks who collaborated with Nazis and were responsible for spying on civilians. Resistance to Nazi conscription of any sort resulted in arrest, imprisonment, forced shipment to work camps in Germany, or the possibility of being shot on the spot.

Parnion's men had participated in the war against Mussolini's forces in Epirus during the winter of 1940 and spring of 1941. When Germans invaded their country, and the government in Athens capitulated, Greek men scattered along with the rest of the Greek army. Veteran soldiers returned home, barefoot and disheartened, refusing to be available to occupying Nazis. Throughout Greece, whenever Nazis entered a town they usually found only women, young children, the handicapped, and elderly.

The Germans were successfully establishing a precedent of fear and intimidation. We quickly understood that Nazi soldiers could do anything they desired and—we would stay in line. We were afraid of everything having to do with them: from their boots to their dogs to their guns. Hitler's men knew we feared them.

The morning following the Germans' fifth visit to our village, the one we had spent in our *saloni*, Aunt Stella came to visit us. Her anxiety was obvious as she pushed open the heavy door of Grandpa's house and stood in the threshold. Dressed in her widow's black dress, covered by a clean but faded black apron, my aunt took pride in being neat; her pure white hair was always pulled back and carefully tied in a compact bun at the back of her head.

In her haste to see us, the black scarf she wore outdoors had slipped and was loosely gathered around her neck. We welcomed her inside and proceeded to the room with the fireplace to visit. I pulled up one of the ladder backed chairs and she seemed grateful to sit in it. My aunt was agitated, out of breath, and full of information; the Germans had concentrated their visit at her end of town. The Church of St. George and Stella's house were located on Parnion's main square.

Knowledge of the village's goings-on was Stella's passion. She knew who went to church on Sunday, whose kids played in the fountain on the square, which men hung out at the *kafeneion*, and who shopped at Papadopoulos's general store. Without ever having entered its confines, Stella could recite by name and age the local *taverna*'s steadiest patrons, regularly reporting to Aunt Sophia the number of times per week she spotted Uncle Vasili there.

I noticed that Sophia never asked for or cared to hear Stella's tattletale statistics. Once, I was startled to overhear gentle Sophia raise her voice in anger to explain to her older sister that in so very many years of marriage she had never once experienced a drunken husband. Vasili's enjoyment of the fruit of the vine in its barrel-aged, liquid form was a touchy subject between the two women.

That morning Stella did not touch on any of her usual conversation. She had fearfully spent the previous day peeking out through open shutters, while camouflaged behind the starched lace curtains she displayed with pride. I ingested every detail as she provided Mother with her eyewitness account of Nazi activities.

"When the Germans halted their monstrous vehicles at the square, they encountered old Barba Lambros waiting for them by the lion fountain." My aunt was breathless. "I still can't believe what I saw from my window! Lambros manfully and daringly strode out—right in front of the first moving motorcycle in the German procession. And, *Sosai mas, Thee mou,* Lambros held up his hand to stop them. I was positive they would run him over."

Mother's eyes widened, "He what?"

Mesmerized, I gasped hearing my aunt describe Lambros's heroic confrontation—with armed Nazi soldiers. I liked Barba Lambros. The wheat he gave us provided our family with bread at a very needy time. And he cheerfully greeted me as his "fellow Chicagoan" whenever he saw me. "Then what did he do?" I asked.

"Lambros said something to the Germans," my aunt said, shaking. "One soldier seemed to understand him. They exchanged a few words."

"Does Barba Lambros speak German? What did he tell them?" I blurted.

"Don't interrupt, Johnny. Take a deep breath, Stella. Relax your shoulders." Trying to comfort her sister, Mother focused her "keep quiet" look on me.

"Coming over here this morning, Katherine, I passed Lambros on the street and asked him." Still panting, Stella continued. "He told me that he asked them, in English, if he could help them with directions because... they seemed to have lost their way."

Mother couldn't believe her ears. "*Thee mou*! Barba Lambros had the nerve to suggest the Germans were lost?"

"Yes! The old man has guts galore," my aunt answered. "But they arrogantly ignored him. They brought out maps as huge as bed sheets and unfolded them on the front of one of their big German cars. Then, they bent over their maps and concentrated on the maps for a long time.

"Then Lambros, again, asked if he could help them," Stella continued. "The Germans didn't give him an answer—or even a glance in his direction. Lambros told me he knew that they knew exactly where they were. He wanted to start a dialogue."

"They chatted with him?" Mom asked, pulling up another chair to sit face to face with her sister. "I have to sit now too, Stella. I'm overwhelmed."

"No. They completely ignored the old man. When they took their maps into Papadopoulos's store, Lambros took a seat on the bench in the square and kept his eyes on them for the entire day," my aunt reported. "Three or four soldiers remained inside the store for more than an hour. Papadopoulos came out with them and he, personally, took the Germans to most of the houses in my neighborhood."

"Did they come to yours, too, Aunt Stella?" I asked, looking into her eyes and holding my breath.

"No! They skipped my house, Johnny," she answered. "I was praying that they wouldn't come to my door and God answered my prayer. Papadopoulos accompanied them to every house they visited. He doesn't speak German or English, and I don't think they speak Greek. So why was Papadopoulos with them?" Black scarf still resting on her shoulders, Aunt Stella raised her eyebrows. "I don't know but—I am suspicious.

"They knocked on my neighbor Stamata's door," Stella reported, "and the Greek interpreter—the Germans brought one with them—asked about her husband and sons. She told them that her husband had left to work in Sparta, several months before, and he had not yet returned to the village. When they asked about her sons, she told them they had gone to Scala to work in the citrus groves and have not come back either."

"But I have seen her sons, Aunt Stella," I interrupted. "Why did she tell them that?"

Losing patience with me, my mother raised her voice and looked at me sternly. "Because it's none of the Nazis' business. They have no business knowing anything about anyone in Parnion, Johnny. We don't share anything with German soldiers. Remember that!"

Stella looked me straight in the eyes too. "Your Mama is right, Johnny. We say," and she emphasized the words, *"nothing* to Germans. We keep far away from those soldiers. Far away!"

Mother continued, "What else, Stella?"

"The Germans went up and down the main road and along all the intersecting village paths but couldn't travel any further than the cemetery. The path beyond the graveyard, as you know, is too narrow... only wide enough for a donkey to get through.

"And with pistols drawn, they searched all the animal stalls and chicken coops at our end of the village. From my window I watched Papadopoulos fetch good Father Haralambos. The Germans, together with our priest—and Parnion's own filthy German collaborator"—as Papadopoulos had become in my aunt's eyes—"went into St. George's. They spent an hour or so in church.

I'm sure they weren't praying." And here Stella paused dramatically, letting us imagine what atrocities they were committing in that sacred place. "After that, the Germans entered and searched unoccupied houses. They inspected the empty school, inside and out, and went into the church, again. They examined every centimeter of my neighborhood, except for a few houses, including mine."

"What are they looking for, Stella?" Mom asked fearfully.

"I don't know. Nobody knows. Except, perhaps—Papadopoulos knows. One of my neighbors told me she went into his store this morning to ask about the soldiers. But Papadopoulos cut her off, saying that he doesn't know anything because he doesn't speak German. Let me tell you, he was pretty chummy with those Nazis. I'm positive Papadopoulos is a dirty collaborator. Katherine, I don't trust him."

"They found most of us at home yesterday," Mom said. "Their goal was to scare us. The way they rode into town, aiming guns at our houses. It was their way of saying, 'When we speak, you do as you are told. We are your masters! And don't forget it.' When will it end, Stella?"

"I never thought I would see the day when armed soldiers would arrive to threaten us in our quiet little Parnion. What happened after dark, Stella? We heard them leave town before twilight, but I was afraid to go outside in case any of them stayed behind. I kept the children inside, too."

Like the good reporter she was, my aunt knew the end of the story. "Our village men came back when the coast was clear. My neighbor assured me that no Nazis remained in town after dark."

It seemed Stella had brought us up to date on village news. But she had one more tidbit to relate. My aunt leaned forward and touched my mother's arm. In a low voice she confided, "Katherine, my neighbor's husband told me that they are looking for hidden English soldiers... for *antartes*... for able bodied men and... older boys. That's why I rushed here this morning. I'm advising you. I'm warning you.

"Be mindful of your children, my dear sister—especially Alex. Katherine, make sure the Nazis don't know about Alex. Make sure they can't find him."

14 | MY VILLAGE—1942

I don't remember the exact month when enemy soldiers first showed up to terrorize us. The women of a family insightfully kept track of months, days of the week (especially Sundays), church holidays, and fasting days without tacking a piece of paper with intersecting lines on the wall to announce year, month, and day. The clanging church bell reminded them instead.

My young memories of the U.S. were already blurring as circumstances beyond our control forced us to remain in Parnion. While typical village life was new to me, German incursions were new to every one of us.

We left Chicago when my family was living sparsely to survive the Depression, so I didn't miss or even remember the few conveniences we left behind. I was either eight or nine years old when we fled to Parnion, a suitable age to adjust to rural life. The almost primeval village grew to feel "normal." Mom kept reminding us kids to be grateful we were still alive because death and destruction were enveloping many around us. She promised that the frills of good living would come later, when we returned to America.

With no alternatives, I was forced to learn to enjoy the true down-to-earth delights of nature, as only a boy can know them, when there are no books or electricity-dependent devices to keep him indoors. Even though I had lived in the second largest U.S. city, I was young enough for village life to feel usual and acceptable.

Initially, I had been fearful of live chickens, men with weathered complexions and bushy mustaches, so scratchy and rough compared with the clean-shaven men I'd known in America. I had also been afraid of village women who were dressed, head to toe, in black. Live, roaming, domestic animals and malicious, biting roosters unnerved me.

I was even frightened by the daily sight of poor Panagiota sitting woefully on the bench, near St. Nicholas Church, a stone's throw away from Grandpa's house. I'd uncomfortably approach the harmless woman with my head down, looking away when I passed her on my way to the fountain. Peaceful Panagiota scared me. Mother finally enlightened her timid son.

"Try smiling at Panagiota, Johnny," Mom advised. "She's not scary. The unfortunate woman is harmless. Do you like being ignored? How would you like it if every time people passed you, they'd automatically turn their heads? Panagiota needs to feel you like her. It will be good for both of you." Next time I came within sight of Panagiota lingering on the bench, I straightened up and flashed her a big smile. And I was stunned, but pleased, when she lifted her head, looked me in the eyes, and smiled back. We even came to waving at each other.

Even with German soldiers arriving, unannounced, in our village, Mother still gave me freedom to explore the countryside. The experience afforded me a matchless opportunity that I never would have had as a kid growing up in Chicago.

Instead of shopping at a grocery store, like the one my Dad had owned, I learned most villagers grew their own food; that donkeys and mules needed to be fed and watered to provide transport; that un-milled wheat grain had to be ground to produce flour for bread. And, flour, in turn, needed to be mixed with other vital ingredients; kneaded; raised twice; and baked—otherwise, we didn't eat bread. I came to appreciate that the soil we walked on produced food for humans, and provided grazing lands to nourish animals. I made the connection between human survival, animals, trees, grains, fruits, and vegetables, all nourished by generous earth, in a way I would not have realized in the big city.

The 1940s had been a time when "No Trespassing" signs were unknown on open lands surrounding Parnion. Villagers were free to roam those open lands to collect branches for cooking fires and home heating; to help themselves to ripe fruit and nuts from wild trees that subsisted in the countryside; and to graze their animals.

When war and food shortages minimized our food supply, my mother walked to communal lands she had visited as a girl to pick walnuts for our sustenance. Walnuts helped us survive. Seventy years ago, I gathered walnuts from trees growing in Parnion's "boonies" that 21st century nutritionists tell us are vital for human health.

As a kid, I made fascinating discoveries about birds in the sky and insects and rocks on *terra firma*. Swallows constructed their mud nests under the eaves of St. George's Church and partridges ran down the village's main road—especially when I chased them. Honing my ability to identify birds by their songs and appearance, I remember the chubby, brownish-gray *tsihla* (thrush) whose beautiful song could be heard after the rain. Thrushes preferred to hang out in Parnion's nearby woods. But in winter, when they sought additional food, they spent more time pecking about in dormant, frosty fields closer to town.

On forays into the hills, I looked forward to spotting the occasional eagle circling high above, giant wings spread into the heavens and sharp eyes searching ravine and mountains for prey. Most assuredly Mother had issued strict orders for me. "Johnny, be alert. Your ears must act like twenty-four ears. Run home immediately if you hear trucks, cars, and motorcycles. You know that means the Germans are on their way."

Besides Nazi invaders, there were natural hazards in rural life. Prickly *pournaria* (shrubby holm oaks) verdantly cover valleys and hillsides of rocky Peloponnesos. Their tender, bright-green leaves are gourmet munchies for goats in spring. But when *pournaria* leaves and branches dry and toughen in summer's heat, they become like brutally sharp stilettos. Animals instinctively stay away from *pournaria*. I painfully recall countless times when my sleeves, pants, and skin caught on their razor-sharp protrusions.

Night and pure darkness blotted out village shadows. Superior nights brought us moonlight. With no electricity, we went to bed an hour or so after dark. Villagers were cautious of wasting olive oil in dim lamps to illuminate rooms where reading couldn't be comfortable. Reading—when one had something to read—was left for daylight hours. Roosters were our natural, very independent, alarm clocks; they introduced us to welcome, morning luminosity. Those cranky birds crowed at the first hint of glowing sunlight, although sometimes they goofed up and we'd hear crowing at midnight. Curses erupted when welcome sleep was interrupted, but no one argued with roosters.

Parnion's early mornings were extraordinary because we had no electricity to brighten the darkness. After hours and hours of murky night, sunrise created a peaceful and gorgeous "special effect" which finally brought us illumination. Waking when it was still dark, I watched dawn slowly begin spreading blessed sunlight on surrounding hills, red-tile roofs, and the village's dark green, holm-oak-studded ravine. We continue to live on beautiful Earth because this marvelous event still happens, each and every day.

Greek light has always been a marvel. Surely, nature's light is a special blessing to all the earth's peoples, but most especially to those who live without electricity. The ancient Greeks believed that each day, beginning at sunrise, Helios, their sun god, slowly drove his chariot carrying the sun across the sky to light the earth. As far as I know, there was no god of electricity, even though the word is derived from the ancient Greek: *elektron*. Since the beginning, earth's sun has most definitely been the "star" of Greek existence.

At the end of the day, when the golden sun sank into the ravine, twilight pulled nature's unseen curtain aside to open the heavens and I experienced a free, natural, light show that took my breath away. Nightfall brought us the effervescent sky. Brilliant, white light emanated from zillions of glittering stars and glowing planets. Archaic, deprived Parnion became exquisitely illuminated with fiery diamonds.

The wide path of stars, known since ancient times as the "Milky Way," gloriously cut its swath above me as I took in the elegant universe while lying on my back in the *perivoli* (Mom preferred I stay close to home after dark). Villagers referred to the phenomenon as "The Jordan River," replacing pagan mythology with a Biblical reference. Yet, I understand their analogy: staring up from my spot on the hard ground during a luminous Parnion night, I marveled at the concentrated Mississippi of sparkling stars gloriously tattooed across the sky's black "river bed."

I have never forgotten the diamond-like brilliance of a crystal-clear village night and have never experienced the dazzling phenomenon anywhere else. And the best part was that I could watch for free, nearly every night. Only clouds canceled the stupendous light show.

Distinctions between Chicago living and life in Parnion were obvious to me at the start, when I was four. Live chickens didn't stroll Chicago's streets. Big city homes enjoyed indoor running water and inside bathrooms with very useful fixtures called "toilets;" villages were burdened with rudimentary outhouses. Fast-moving, gasoline-powered vehicles filled Chicago's wide boulevards. Parnion had donkeys, mules, sheep, goats—and a zillion brilliant stars.

In the early 1960s, when I was on leave during my stint as an officer in the U.S. Army's Signal Corps, I returned to Greece for the first time after WWII. During my visit, Uncle George's wife, Aunt Athanasia, reminded me of an incident she remembered from our 1937 arrival in Parnion.

She said the first time I was served fish, prepared Greek style—whole from head to tail—I sat and stared at it for a while because it was not typical of American fish *filet* dinners that I had known. After four-year-old me studied the fried sea creature, with its one steely eye staring up at me, I announced, "I don't eat faces."

That kid didn't know, yet, that nothing is wasted in a Greek village.

Centuries before the word "ecology" (a Greek word) became commonplace in the U.S., Greek villages were living ecologically balanced existences with no plastic bags or garbage cans, and few paper bags or boxes. When a box came into one's possession, it was carefully saved to store something truly precious. In Parnion, potato peelings, discarded cabbage leaves, apple cores, and the rest of kitchen refuse, when available, were fed to the live chickens one was required to own so that a household could be provided with eggs, or to the pigs a wealthier villager might be privileged to acquire. Discarded eggshells were recycled into the soil.

With no refrigeration, fats were rendered down to preserve sausages and spiced meats. Mother used discarded fat to make soap for personal and household cleaning. After a lamb, goat, or pig was slaughtered, recipes were followed to cook all parts of the animal's anatomy, including innards, brains, and heads. Leather was produced from an animal's skin. Annually, the hair of sheep and goats was shorn, spun into yarn by hand, and woven into fabric for clothing and blankets on home looms. The act of "wasting" directly affected survival. The 21st century notion of "green" and "recycling" came naturally.

Self-sufficiency held fast in the early part of the war, when Parnion felt no immediate wartime effects. But this complex system broke down when the Nazis confiscated village farm animals for their consumption. Soldiers deprived us of food, and of all other products that animals yield: a deficit that dispossessed all Greek people.

Fruits and vegetables are incredibly versatile and Greeks use them creatively in their cooking. Zucchini was one of many vegetables grown in the village that produces a variety of dishes, prepared at various stages of its maturation. Greek recipes utilize tender zucchini leaves; bright yellow zucchini blossoms which are stuffed with savory morsels of rice; and the part of the zucchini with which we are most familiar: the gourd. Tender young grape leaves were gathered in spring for making *dolmades*: stuffed grape leaves. Grapevines not only produced grapes for fruit and making wine, but also for *mousto,* a thick syrup, somewhat like molasses, used to sweeten foods instead of expensive sugar.

Survival aimed at unifying with nature, not fighting it. Agrarian village life blended with the four seasons. Feeding and caring for the family donkey, chickens, and probably a few goats or sheep was a year-round responsibility, but some vital activities were cyclical.

Spring was the season for preparing the fields, planting crops, and—gloriously celebrating Easter, the Greeks' supreme holiday. Summer demanded the backbreaking labor of cultivating crops planted in spring and savoring luscious cherries, peaches, pears, and figs, cut fresh from trees, a luxury not available in winter. Autumn was the time to harvest, gather fodder to feed animals in the coming winter, and relish freshly gathered walnuts, washed down with multiple clusters of sweet, succulent grapes. Lastly, winter was for recuperating—roasting chestnuts, Christmas, New Year's, and looking forward to the return of spring.

Unlike many Greek villages, the one resource Parnion had in abundance was water. Mt. Parnon's melting snows fed the artesian well located at the town's higher regions. Good old gravity caused it to flow downhill in the direction of its fortunate citizens' homes. Legend has it that Parnion was founded in its niche on the mountain because of its plentiful water.

Elders explained that, centuries before, a goat herder had noticed his lead goat returned to the flock with wet whiskers. When the curious goatherd retraced the goat's steps, he discovered a running spring—and the village was ultimately established at that place. Because the male goat had discovered the area, one could say that an old goat was Parnion's founding father.

Residents eventually built a reservoir to save the spring's vital resources. When waters were abundant, the icy overflow ran down trenches that villagers had dug along the sides of Parnion's street and narrower byways. Farmers were allowed to divert plentiful water from troughs along the road to irrigate their fields. We regularly watered our flourishing potato plants by diverting water from the nearby trench.

Most opportune for residents of our little neighborhood was the fountain at the entrance to tiny St. Nicholas Church. Every day, we filled our buckets at St. Nick's fountain and lugged them home; the chore occurred multiple times a day in my mother's household because she was "Mrs. Clean."

Word of plentiful water in Parnion must have spread afar through centuries of the village's existence. High animal traffic was a common sight. Trekking sheep, goats, horses, mules, donkeys, stray dogs, and cats stopped by to lap up fresh water running in open trenches. Visitors and strangers traveling through the village made a beeline for the public fountain in front of St. Nick's Church to quench thirsts.

In summer's heat, they poured cool water over their heads and bodies. Shepherds, shepherdesses, and goatherds from out-of-town purposely drove flocks through our village so their animals could drink Parnion's ample waters. Nikki and I enjoyed spying on them through the second-story window. But local and visiting flocks, along with the folks who brought them, disappeared after Nazi soldiers arrived.

Sometimes I walked over to the other side of town, to the main square in front of St. George's Church, to admire Parnion's prominent fountain, far grander than the one I looked at from my window. The lion fountain was Parnion's distinguished piece of long-standing public art. Four, eight-foot, gray marble, rectangular columns support a small, gray marble roof embellished on its four sides with classic pediments: an early 20th century rendering of a mini-temple reflecting Greece's Golden Age. The elegant cover protects a short chunky obelisk where four delicately carved lions' heads dispense fresh water from open jaws, 24/7.

Even now in the 21st century, as citizens of Parnion enjoy indoor plumbing, electricity, television, computers, mobile phones, paved roads, and other conveniences of comfortable living, the lion fountain in the main square continues to provide cool, refreshing water, day and night. But when I lived there, abundant water was our only convenience.

Still, the natural world of the village was less than perfect. Nature can smell revoltingly bad. The only way I armored myself against bad odors was to stop breathing and pinch my nostrils for as long as possible. Taking the next breath was a real bummer. I've already mentioned the stinking *mantri*, the goat corral we used as a sanctuary when the Nazis first came to town. Outhouses, pigpens, rotting plants, and dead animals were a few of the uncountable bad smells that brought on instant nausea.

Body odor was a major culprit. Villagers appeared neat and presentable. But the "Downy" freshness of Parnion's hardworking people was compromised as they toiled directly with the earth (without benefit of farm machinery) all day, under the searing sun. Soiled clothes were worn over and over again, without laundering in-between, because laundering was so incredibly labor intensive. And, so was bathing.

Parnion may have had oodles of water flowing from its natural spring, but its lack of running water inside a home's courtyard (forget about inside the house) and the inconvenience of gathering, heating, and holding adequate amounts of water for laundry loads made the chore of washing clothes primitive, problematic, and grossly exhausting for the homemaker.

Mother forced us to bathe regularly, even though facilities were pre-historic and uncomfortable, especially in cold weather. To begin, a bather needed to transport adequate amounts of water from a source, like St. Nick's fountain or a well, to his house.

For us, the second step required lugging water up stairs with minimum spillage. Water was warmed to a comfortable temperature in huge pots positioned in the family's living room fireplace on the upper floor. Dry twigs and branches, personally gathered in the woods by the bather or other family members, provided fuel for the fire. (There was no Home Depot in town selling ready-to-ignite fireplace logs.)

When the water was warm enough, family members were chased out of the room, for privacy. Stripping off clothes was the worst part in the cold, damp house. One shivered as one bathed, standing ankle-deep in water, inside a shallow wooden tub called a *skafidi*—it doubled as the laundry tub on washdays. Using a pitcher, one poured clean, warm water over oneself while attempting to coax lather out of a brownish bar of harsh, homemade soap: the same soap was used as shampoo. No matter how tightly I shut my eyes while shampooing my hair with that smelly soap, the stinging solution seeped underneath my sealed eyelids and burned my eyes.

Mother encouraged soaping and rinsing hair three times, which meant my eyes stung, not once per stand-up bath, but three times. At the same time she reminded us of a village superstition: "Shampooing three times ensures a happy marriage." After all this, I now understand why many of my Parnion neighbors tended to avoid the bathing process as much as possible.

The relieving natural fragrances of sweet basil, carnations, roses, oregano, mint, rosemary, honeysuckle, and sage were grown and savored by villagers: they offset wicked odors. Instead of discarding leaking olive oil tins, they were re-cycled as rectangular flowerpots with drainage to accommodate billowing plant growth on almost every Parnion balcony.

Growing flowers and herbs with pleasant fragrances encouraged public pride. Villagers, by habit, would snip a single leaf from an aromatic herb, rub it between fingers, inhale the enjoyable fragrance, and deposit the spent leaf in an apron or shirt pocket so its delicate scent could be enjoyed again.

Another drawback of Parnion's wild, isolated life was that medical help was hard to come by. When the German army overtook the country, most of us stayed put in the village for four years. During the war, there was no possibility of consulting with a dentist or ophthalmologist in Sparta, the closest big city, even though teeth and eyes change and deteriorate in wartime, perhaps more than they do in peacetime. No "911" existed to dial in case of emergency; there was no phone to dial for any reason. We didn't go to Sparta to watch films in the outdoor movie theater or to shop, even if we could have afforded a shopping trip or going to the movies.

I was a mere kid, yet I realized that life was tough for the hardworking villagers. Living in Parnion was especially tough for my mother. She did all the sun-up-to-sundown work, with the added stress of having no income and no husband at the head of our household. She tended chickens, hauled water, preserved food, and collected wood for our fireplace, which doubled as our kitchen.

Mom cooked our daily meals, such as they were, during the war, in the living room fireplace using branches and twigs we had gathered as fuel. I didn't realize how out-of-date our village cooking methods were until we repatriated ourselves and lived in Ann Arbor. My junior high U.S. history textbook showed pioneer American women of the 1700s replicating 20th century Parnion food preparation. Even as a nine year old, I understood my mother, alone, could not bear the sole burden for our destitute village household. I needed to be more helpful.

Nikki was already helping by cooking, cleaning, and learning to sew. With no clothing or fabric stores in the village and absolutely no opportunity or money to go shopping, mending was vital. Ready-made clothing was not commonly sold, even in big cities. Village girls were expected to be adept with needle and thread, so Mother began teaching Nikki how to mend, embroider, crochet, and sew. I don't remember if there was a tailor or seamstress in Parnion; our little family had no money to hire one. Repairing and mending clothing was the only way we could stay covered.

Alex, on the other hand, was not often seen helping around the house; watching potatoes grow was not his style. Six and a half years older than me, my brother was a city boy, and he specialized in collecting information. He picked up war news from men at the coffeehouse and read newspapers on those rare occasions when papers trickled into the village. Alex delighted in risk and danger for excitement. He read every book he could get his hands on and enjoyed discussing politics with our uncles. Nikki and I were in the dark as to why he was away from home so often and having to meet with men in the village.

When Nikki complained that Alex should be participating in tasks around the house, Mother replied, "He needs to study so that he can enter high school when the schools open again. And Alex is doing important work that you and Johnny are too young to do." Essentially, Alex had never been my playmate when I was a kid. He always had more important things to do. Then of course there were those unknown (to Nikki and me) activities that took him away from home.

The church bell could be heard over all of Parnion: it was the village's major means of mass communication. Hanging from a sturdy tree branch in the main square, near St. George's, it summoned people to worship, announced death, and alerted danger. The bell tolled quickly and continuously to announce good news, like a wedding. Two slow gloomy clangs announced the passing of a fellow villager. On Saturday night, the *kambana* (bell) reminded villagers to attend evening vespers. During Sunday and Holy Day services, one clang announced the start of the preliminary Orthros, two advised the beginning of the Liturgy itself, and three rings proclaimed that Consecration was taking place. Along with Parnion's fountains, the church bell remained undisrupted by war.

Even though I lived in Parnion for almost four years without once exiting its environs, most villagers considered me an outsider. But my soul knew better. From ages eight to twelve, the village where my mother had been born was my hometown; I remembered no other. I was not a *xenos*. Parnion was *my* village. The shame was that I had to live through a war to know it so well.

***

In the thick of World War II—1942

- ❖ *The Japanese occupy Manila in the Philippines*

- ❖ *President Roosevelt asks baseball commissioner to continue baseball during the war*

- ❖ *German and Italian armies occupy Benghazi, Libya*

- ❖ *American auto factories switch from commercial to war-related manufacturing: car and truck production stops for the war effort*

- ❖ *700 Polish Jews sent to Belzec concentration camp*

- ❖ *Food rationing begins in the U.S.*

- ❖ *"Casablanca" starring Ingrid Bergman and Humphrey Bogart debuts in U.S.*

15 | INVADERS

Nikki screamed, "Trucks! I hear trucks, Mama! It's the Germans!"

Right away, we gathered to stand guard in the *saloni*. Holding our breaths, we watched Nazi vehicles enter the village—again. With Mom's arms around both of us, we gawked at approaching armed soldiers.

She gripped my shoulder even tighter when the last truck stopped below our window. The Nazi contingent had halted, smack dab in front of Grandpa's house. Nikki ran from the window and slid herself into Buddy, our trunk, stowed against the *saloni* wall. I froze in place.

"Please, dear God. Not here!" Mom whispered.

The caravan had stopped and, worse yet, a gang of soldiers shoved off the back of the shiny, black, military truck—like ferocious jackals hunting their prey. My sorry eyes followed their advance, directly into our field, across the road from Grandpa's house. The Nazis were landing—on our potatoes. Mom and I cringed when tall, menacing, black boots began stomping over our carefully tended, green plants.

"Hey!" I objected, as soldiers hoisted heavy shovels. "They're wrecking our field."

"Shhh!" Mother scolded. "They must be searching for something."

"What?" I asked.

"I don't know," she said, in her "keep-quiet-I'm-trying-to-find-out" style.

Murmuring sobs came from the trunk. "What are you doing in there, Nikki?" Mom asked.

"Praying," my sister said. "Please, God, make them go away. Don't let the bad men come to our house."

Staring down on feral soldiers from inside the window, I still had enough nerve to protest. "They're ruining our plants, Mom... after all our hard work!"

"Quiet!" Mother's annoyance broke through her fear. "This is not good. They must suspect something—something that will get us into trouble. Five soldiers wielding five shovels—digging from one corner of our field to the other. This looks bad for us."

Invisible Nikki called out, "Please God, keep them far away."

"We didn't find anything in the ground when we planted, Mama. What's in there now?" I asked.

"It might be... they think guerrillas have buried guns or ammunition in our field. Dear God, I pray it doesn't cast suspicion on us."

"Too bad Barba Lambros isn't here. He'd tell them to get out." I whispered. My thoughts naturally went to our village hero, the one who had confronted the Nazis in our main square.

"I'm afraid that someday they will shoot that feisty old man, Johnny. He has to be more careful when...." Then Mother let out a gasp. "Wait! They found something. Look!"

The true mission of the German expedition became evident when laughing, evil clowns in Nazi uniforms triumphantly showed each other their treasures: tangles of vines and dangling roots. Nazi fingers joyfully pulled small clumps of garden dirt away from trailing tendrils. Greedy fists voraciously and victoriously held up their treasured booty.

"Our potatoes!" Mother declared under her breath, far more agitated than fearful. "Tiny potatoes, not even close to harvesting. Look! They've wreaked wholesale destruction on our garden... and haven't got enough potatoes to—fill one Nazi belly."

Like a delinquent gang robbing a candy store, soldiers stomped all over our well-kept field, laughing, shouting to each other in German, and recklessly tearing green plants apart to grab at tubers that were no bigger than thumbnails.

"Daddy had told me," Mom grumbled, "Germans love potatoes. He knew from working in the restaurant. Nazi locusts found their delicacy in our little field. But if those stupid soldiers knew better, they would have waited and robbed us when our beautiful potatoes were grown to full size. That crop was going to keep us alive for six months!"

My dreams of eating savory, crispy potatoes, roasted in olive oil, and flavored with lemon and oregano, quickly evaporated. "Mama, our potatoes weren't meant for filthy Nazis. We did all the work and the bad guys eat all our potatoes? It's unfair."

"This is what war is all about, Johnny," Mom replied. "Unfairness! Nothing will be right until these Germans lose. And, if God forbid, they win, we will be their slaves and fairness will be gone forever. Innocent people need to be free again. We need to go back home to America!"

Nazi soldiers had arrogantly ruined our potato field, and by early 1942, the German army was standing most arrogantly on top of the world. They had taken Europe, and to make matters worse, the Japanese had joined the Germans in their ambitious quest to conquer the earth; Pearl Harbor was attacked in December of 1941.

It was 1942 before we found out the United States had joined the fighting. We were, literally, in the middle of it all, and did not know what was going on. The only fact we knew for sure was that Nazis were continuing their daytime visits to Parnion. At the same time, an insidious famine was slowly infecting the country. Those lamented potatoes would have helped.

German occupation started in April of 1941. Two months later, a notably scorching and arid summer season hit Greece and precipitated a food crisis of biblical proportions. The true tragedy of the Greek famine, which eventually resulted in tens of thousands of people in Athens and throughout the country dropping dead of starvation and malnutrition, began during that unusually hot and dry summer—while our spuds were still thriving.

The abnormal heat was not as intense in mountainous Parnion as it had been in the agricultural Greek valleys and plains where wheat and other produce were grown for the market. At that time, Greek agriculture consisted mainly of small farms throughout the country.

There were no organized trucking conglomerates hired to deliver produce to the marketplace. Farmers themselves transported their goods to sell in local markets. That year, when crops withered, a shortage of foodstuffs ensued; the harvest in 1941 was 30% lower than it had been the year before. But then the winter of 1941 brought frigid temperatures, quite uncommon in a country with a Mediterranean climate. Destructive military occupation made conditions worse.

When the Italian army had invaded in 1940 and the German army overtook the country in 1941, immediately before the sizzling summer, Greece filled up with Axis soldiers. The small country was bursting with combatants who needed sustenance to keep their military machine going. As a result, they seized food, at will, to fill their stomachs.

They also confiscated horses, mules, donkeys, and the few motorized vehicles available in Greece at that time from small farmers; Axis armies needed them to run military operations. Without transportation, it was impossible for farmers to take to market the meager foodstuffs that had survived the extremely low harvest.

By October of 1941, the situation worsened. Field Marshal Göering decided Belgium, Holland, and Norway, all German-occupied countries, had priority—over Greece—for food supplies doled out by the Third Reich. To add insult to grave injury, while Nazis plundered the Greek food supply, they laid the responsibility on their ally, Italy, to supply Greece with food. As conquerors, the Nazis felt free to take anything they desired out of the country without putting anything back. Mussolini grumbled, "The Germans have taken from the Greeks even their shoelaces."

Certainly there were healthy stockpiles of wheat in the western world, which could have saved the Greeks from starvation made worse by vicious Nazi occupation. British and American citizens finally learned of the devastating famine thanks in part to a Greek-American lobby in the U.S. known as the "Greek War Relief Association." The people of the U.S. and Britain were outraged to learn that valiant Greeks, their now occupied allies who had successfully fought off Mussolini in 1940, were starving and literally dropping dead of hunger.

Outrage increased when it became known that the British government had set up an embargo to keep wheat supplies out of German hands in Greece. The British embargo was tragically denying bread to the desperately suffering Greek people. Even the Vatican had tried to intercede in September of 1941 to convince Britain to lift the blockade.

The Brits finally agreed to end the embargo. However, the process from beginning to end took an interminable amount of time, and in the interim Greeks were dying of starvation. In February of 1942, the British allowed the shipment of wheat to travel and enter Greece under neutral supervision.

However, it took *seven* additional months for the first shipment of wheat destined for Greece to leave Canada. During this everlasting course of action, starving people, especially in cities, died of hunger, famine-related diseases, and vitamin deficiencies. Distribution of grain was conclusively realized in Athens, but long after tens of thousands of Greeks had died. The Red Cross calculated that a quarter of a million Greek deaths between 1941 and 1943 were directly related to the famine.

Was this wheat ever distributed to relieve hunger in Parnion? Never. I first read about the distribution in a book, sixty years after I returned to the United States.

Another detail, which directly affected our welfare but that we didn't know about while we were trapped in Parnion, was a pronouncement that Field Marshall Hermann Göering sent to his

Nazi commissioners and military commanders in German-occupied territories on August 6, 1942:

> "In all the occupied territories I see the people living there stuffed full of food, while our own people are going hungry. For God's sake, you haven't been sent there to work for the well-being of the peoples entrusted to you, but to get hold of as much as you can so that the German people can live. I expect you to devote your energies to that. This continual concern for the aliens must come to an end once and for all... I could care less when you say that people under your administration are dying of hunger. Let them perish so long as no German starves."

I personally know that we were not "stuffed full of food."

16 | GETTING WORSE

We had left the U.S. to escape the Great Depression in 1937, and began living in Greece on less than a shoestring budget. The lawsuit Mother tolerated over ownership of the Kalamata orchard cost her both money and tears. Bombing and invasion turned us into penniless, frightened refugees. By the time we arrived in Parnion in 1941, the war had severed all our communication with Dad who had sent money to us in his letters.

When Agrimi, the wild goat, died, our source of milk dried up. Nazis seized our potato crop. Our egg supply was short-lived when Germans plowed through the village and stole all the live poultry. By then I had outgrown my fear of chickens, but the Germans left the ornery rooster behind; he was too vicious for them to snatch comfortably. Nazis confiscated Sophocles' truck, Parnion's only motor vehicle; Phillip and Artemis lost their donkey to them; and Uncle Vasili's donkey, the one that saved my life at the river, was gone, too.

Not everyone in the village was a farmer. Uncle Vasili was a carpenter, Uncle George was a government legal aid. The priest didn't farm, nor did the teacher, the *taverna* owner, or doctor. I also recall that Parnion had a blacksmith, a barber, and a shoe repairman. These village citizens depended on making money via their businesses, trades, or professions to buy food.

When no money came in, and on top of it no grain was available, there was no bread. We were in the same boat, except— even worse off—because we owned no property and possessed no hidden larders of grains, olive oil, dry beans, or other goods saved for emergencies as some villagers did.

Parnion is not one of those Greek "basking in year-round, warm Mediterranean climate" villages that beguile tourists from travel posters, even though as the crow flies, it is relatively near the Mediterranean Sea. Located in the upper reaches of Mt. Parnon, the village is perhaps not as drastically icy as Chicago in winter, but not warm enough to grow foodstuffs.

Village winters are very cold, especially without shoes, heavy coats, scarves, and wool pants with thick pockets to keep hands warm. We had no gloves, and Nikki and I had already outgrown and worn out the shoes we brought to Greece from America. Thank God, Mom had remembered to enclose in Buddy, our faithful U.S. trunk, wool blankets she had purchased in Kalamata.

The winter of 1941-1942 for us was the season of scrounging for food. Martha, the tall, willowy spinster with the elegant, robust ewe was still in possession of her beautiful animal; we heard she hid it inside a little nook of her house when Germans came to town. Villagers desperately held onto as much food that still remained in their households, hiding whatever they could from German soldiers.

Aunt Joanna had not arrived; Mom, Stella, and Sophia were beyond anxious, continuously sending messages to their brother, George, in the neighboring village, to ask if he knew whether or not Joanna was in Athens with her daughter. It was impossible to know if messages or messengers ever reached their destinations; the Germans interfered with mail and other means of communication. The ladies nervously waited to hear news of Joanna's whereabouts. At the same time, Nazi harassment worsened, and what we had painfully dreaded happened.

One day in late 1942, after multiple Nazi raids on our village, a well-decorated German officer knocked on our very own door, accompanied by a Greek collaborator. When we spotted them on the road in front of the house, Nikki and I rushed to the little balcony to silently observe the Nazi and his civilian henchman, a short, balding man with sparse blond hair who hurried along, following the officer's sober footsteps. My sister and I cautiously peered down on the crown of the officer's flashy, military cap as they approached; a shiny visor shielded his face from us.

"I could land a great big wad of spit on top of that fancy Nazi hat," I bragged to Nikki in a whisper. "I've got just the right amount of spit in my mouth."

"They'll kill us!" Nikki lashed back in a murmur.

But she quieted down, realizing I never intended to follow through on my bogus threat. We raced downstairs in time to see Mother, with eyes closed, bracing her shoulders—steeling herself to answer dreaded knocking. Seeing us, Mom ordered me, in a barely audible command, to take my sister and hide in back of the house. "Silence! I don't want them to see or hear you."

She forced her shoulders down, closed her eyes, and with unwilling resignation, slowly pulled open Grandpa's heavy door. She told us later that her mouth dried with anxiety when she gazed up at the tall, rigid-faced German on the other side of the threshold; the polished visor of his cap shaded a clean-shaven, handsome, but chilling, expressionless face. Cap and face alone were enough to make her heart fall to her toes. Mom said the officer's manner was so stiff and his suit fit him so well that he resembled a Chicago department store mannequin.

The smaller, blond man spoke first, in Greek. Mother understood he was a collaborator, acting as interpreter. She did not recognize him and was positive he was not from Parnion.

"This officer of the Third Reich has a few questions he wants you to answer," he barked.

Mother remained silent. The collaborator translated the Nazi officer's clipped and strange-sounding German words into a startling and belligerent first question: "Where is your husband? I want to speak to your husband."

Stunned, Mom weakly answered, "He is not here. He is in America."

"You are lying," the Nazi officer menacingly announced through the short, blond Greek.

Intimidated by his response, Mother earnestly replied, "No, I am not lying, sir. My husband is in America."

The icy Nazi insisted, "Yes, you are lying. Your husband is an American agent in Greece. He is hiding in the local mountains."

Shaken but provoked by his far-fetched remarks, Mother steeled herself and spoke out more firmly. "He is not. I have already told you. My husband is in America."

Coldly eyeing her, the rigid Nazi officer persisted, "You lie again. Perhaps he is an American agent—in Athens!"

The officer's last statement totally annoyed Mother, she told us later, because it was so preposterous. In seconds, she boldly gathered up enough pluck to present some facts to him in the form of questions.

"Do you think that if my husband was an American agent in Greece he would abandon his family to starve and suffer in this poor village?

"Would my husband want his children running around threadbare, barefoot, and hungry—like waifs? Does that make sense to you? Sir, I tell the truth. My husband is in America!"

The officer paused, turned his gaze away from Mother's face and concentrated his cold stare, beyond her, into the house; cold, blue eyes scrutinized our bare surroundings. The meager, miserable state of our living conditions must have convinced him of the logic and truth in her explanation. The interrogation continued, on a different subject.

"Do you know Elpida Katinas?" the translator asked.

"This is a small village," Mother replied. "I recognize the name, but I don't know her, personally."

An intimidating stare demanded, "Where is she?"

Mother replied in her no-nonsense manner. "How should I know where she is? I don't personally know the woman."

A final frosty question followed. "What does she do?"

Mother showed even more irritation. Perplexed, she responded, "I don't know! I don't know her and I don't know what she does."

The German coldly gazed into my mother's determined eyes and said no more. With a startling click of his heels, he abruptly turned around, and marched off with the collaborator, who was struggling to keep up with the German's quick steps. Mom numbly watched them exit the courtyard. When Nikki and I heard the outer gate shut, we cautiously left our hiding place. Seeing us, she sighed deeply and embraced us.

Mother had heard about Elpida Katinas from Vasili and Sophia. Elpida's family lived near Grandpa's house. Mom could not deny having heard of the woman because that kind of response would have sounded suspicious; further dangerous Nazi probing more than likely would have followed.

My aunt and uncle had told Mother that, of late, Elpida had joined the resistance and was fighting with guerrillas in some other part of Greece. Mom instinctively knew the less she said about Elpida, the better. The Germans obviously had information about her, and Mother feared Elpida's family was in danger of Nazi reprisals.

After our neighborhood was clear of soldiers that afternoon, soft and kind Aunt Sophia came to see us. She had learned from our mutual neighbor, Artemis, that a German officer visited Grandpa's house. Poor Sophia, unnerved by the report, needed to sit down after Mother described her bold and straightforward answers to the officer's questions. Nikki and I listened in on their conversation as they visited in the *saloni*.

"Katherine, you are a brave woman. Far more daring than I gave you credit for. I would have fainted from fear," Sophia confided when she started breathing again.

"I was petrified and I'm still petrified," Mom said. "Call me stupid, but please don't think of me as being brave. My blood boiled when he accused me of lying. And before he left, that Nazi stared long and hard at me. Will he come back? What will happen to my children if the Germans arrest me, Sophia?"

Mom continued, "I'm positive the German and his dirty collaborator came to our door because someone in this village suspects me of 'something.' Some villagers are suspicious because we came from America. They call me '*the Amerikanida.*' Can't these people get it through their thick heads that I was born in this house?"

Mother nervously paced around the *saloni.* "Something else bothers me, Sophia. Stupid people in Parnion, whoever they are, must stop referring to us as 'rich.' We 'rich Americans' who came to Parnion were never rich. We're in danger of arrest and worse yet—of losing our lives because ignorant people put out malicious, false rumors.

"Dear sister, they don't know the miserable circumstances that brought me back here. All I want is for my children to get out of this alive."

Fear and sickening frustration had overpowered Mother's stoicism. She started sobbing, while Aunt Sophia sweetly embraced her and held her tight for a long time.

"Dear Sophia, I'm trying to be strong. I don't want to see harm come to anyone, especially to those I know and love. This damn war has come to our village and we are stuck here. I can't do anything about it. But, by God, my children must survive."

Appreciating Sophia's compassion, Mother returned her younger sister's hug, held on to her for a few moments but finally straightened up and pulled her sagging emotions together. Gazing directly into my aunt's eyes, Mom probed, "Dear Sophia, do you ever question what kind of naïve, misguided mental state I must have been in when I left America to come back to this God forsaken country?

"I do. Every day! I ask myself, 'How could you have been so brainless, Katherine?'"

***

"As Time Goes By," 1942:

- ❖ *First self-sustaining nuclear chain reaction accomplished at University of Chicago*

- ❖ *U.S. Presidential order relocates West Coast Japanese-Americans*

- ❖ *Service stars decorate windows of millions of U.S. homes, one star for each of eight million men and women involved in the armed forces' work effort, most fighting abroad*

- ❖ *Japanese suffer first losses of the war in the Battle of the Coral Sea*

- ❖ *Popular U.S. songs: "Praise the Lord and Pass the Ammunition" and "As Time Goes By" from the movie, "Casablanca"*

17 | CELEBRATION
(EVEN IN WARTIME)

When Greek hearts flutter in anticipation of a celebration, Greek party planners implement (no matter how humble) the centerpiece of Greek events: food. Music and décor follow, usually in that order. This "set in granite" practice holds for baptisms, engagements, weddings, and "nameday" festivities. *Joie de vivre,* or *"kefi,"* as Greeks call it, is imbedded in Greek DNA.

Even funerals and memorial services, which recoil from happiness, music, and sweets, more often than not include food and wine. At a "memory meal" following the funeral service, family and friends eat together (fish, by tradition), mourning their loss and commemorating in subdued celebration their loved one's earthly existence and entry into heavenly life with God.

In the midst of war's fear and misery, residents of Parnion insisted that when it came to the church of St. George, Nazi occupation would not interrupt centuries of tradition. St. George's Day had been commemorated in Parnion for generations, as long as a church dedicated to the good saint had existed in the village.

Tradition is integral to a civilization like Greece, which has existed, uninterrupted, since pre-history. Therefore, it was decided that on the saint's special day, in April 1942, Father Haralambos would celebrate the Liturgy in the morning as he always had, and a bash would begin when services ended. The faithful of Parnion planned to celebrate the virtuous saint's feast day with music and dancing: dancing being as integral to a Greek celebration as vodka is to a Russian one. Nikki was thrilled.

Much as we dreamed about eating meat again (one tiny morsel would suffice to satisfy vacant stomachs), we knew succulent lambs were not going to turn on spits over hot sizzling coals in the main square, as they had in peacetime celebrations. Contrary to Greek tradition, there would be no food at this Greek party. In spite of this stark reality, Nikki and I became excited with the wisp of a wild rumor that sweet goodies might possibly be proffered at the event.

Parnion's people loved St. George. They spoke of the highly esteemed Christian martyr as if they knew him personally, like he was a favorite uncle or likeable next-door neighbor. A religious icon depicting the good man on horseback, aiming a spear into the heart of the metaphorical dragon he battled, held a place of honor in the icon corners of village homes. Many of Parnion's men, including my mother's gregarious brother who now lived in a near-by village, were christened with the name "George." St. George's Day was celebrated like a Greek wedding—combined with a Fourth of July picnic.

"We can't celebrate with soldiers aiming machine guns at us," Barba Lambros warned. "What if a German motorcade appears that morning?" Plan "A" assigned villagers to watch out for our regular Nazi intruders on the morning of the planned gala. If a convoy were to appear, "Plan B" would postpone the festival to a day when Nazis were absent.

Our cousin Tasia, Sophia and Vasili's daughter, was a bubbly teenager who, like Nikki, loved to dance. But the war had subdued Nikki's bubbly personality. Mom told me that even when my sister was a carefree toddler back in Chicago, she loved to listen to music and move to it in rhythm. Mother hoped that the fear affecting Nikki's *kefi* would ease up with Tasia teaching us old songs and traditional dances. Mom counted on the distraction to cheer us up.

Tasia had learned Greek dances in school and was a willing teacher for her little cousins. She was assigned to instruct us in the fine points of Greek circle dancing. Nikki, who looked forward to showing her dance "moves" on St. George's Day, was our cousin's most motivated student.

But Tasia needed more students to round out the dance line. So she enlisted her brother Kosta, our cousin Demetri, and me. I preferred playing tag or kicking around an old sock stuffed with rags, but Tasia chided me, "Two dancers don't make a circle, Johnny."

Poised Tasia took the lead, showing us, step by step, how to move to the music while she sang. With no electricity to turn on radio music or play a phonograph, we learned the words and melodies of the songs we danced to from Tasia, and we sang together to provide our musical accompaniment. As a good dancing teacher should, Tasia worked at showing us how to lead the line as well as how to follow in step and rhythm.

"Show good posture! Hold your head up!" she instructed us as we stumbled around Grandpa's fireplace room. "Move the semi-circle of followers around gracefully when you lead. Hold your right arm up above shoulder level. Then forge ahead and snap your fingers to the beat. Show your enjoyment! Smile!" Here in the middle of the war, with no food and no music, our Tasia was actually having a good time, perhaps because she was essentially so pleasant and warm-hearted.

Tasia's lovely brown eyes sparkled, as, chin up and smiling, she demonstrated the acme of grace and elegance in dancing. Her lithe body moved us around the circle with the assurance of Pavlova in Swan Lake. She also filled us in on all the rules of Greek dancing. Experienced dancers were to lead, and they held a white handkerchief in the left hand, to connect to the next person in line.

The hankie provided the leader freedom of movement to perform fancy steps and leaps. A gentleman held a handkerchief to dance next to a woman so he didn't actually touch her hand—considered the polite way to dance next to a lady, Tasia said. The unwritten rule of Greek dancing was to take turns at leading. "Let someone else have a chance. Only show-offs hog the front of the line," Tasia concluded her lecture. "So, don't be a dance hog."

By our third meeting at Grandpa's house, most of us could remember the words to sing, and we weren't tripping over our own feet quite so much. We even remembered to stand up straight. Our cousin delighted in our progress. "You make Terpsichore proud." Tasia's mention of the ancient muse of dance made us, even those of us who had preferred kicking around a rag-filled sock to dancing, swell with pride. We were counting down the days to the festival.

I wasn't yet old enough to appreciate the significance of the dancing, but Tasia was; it may have explained why she was so excited about it. The annual church celebration offered the unique and rarest of opportunities for single young women and young men of a certain age to be observed at their best, especially when dancing. At that time, parents still arranged marriages by determining the value of a girl's dowry. Dating was forbidden in villages like Parnion. Teenage girls were not even supposed to speak to teenage boys who were not related to them.

The festival was the perfect occasion for parents to show off a daughter as beautiful and graceful, yet modest—and a prospective good wife, without the girl personally mingling or even speaking with eligible young men. Wearing that one special dress saved for Sundays, a single young woman could demurely show off her best traits, even if a girl's unfortunate wartime "diet" made her dress hang a little too loosely.

An eligible maiden might possibly attract the observing eye of a handsome young man by modestly showing female grace, spirit, and beauty, while dancing the nimble *syrto* to the tune of *"Samiotissa."* At the same time, an eligible bachelor could show his fondness for fun and tradition when, with virile leaps and sure-footed masculinity, he led the ancient, slow-moving *tsamiko.*

On a bright spring day, April 23, 1942, to be exact, Father Haralambos celebrated the Liturgy while a team of five villagers stood guard on the road, ears pricked for the sound of Nazi engines. Shortly before noon, after services concluded, they conferred with the priest and Barba Lambros. The road was silent—the festival could begin. The civic-minded owners of the *taverna* and the *kafeneion* quickly set up their ladder-backed, wooden chairs, facing St. George's Church—across the square from Papadopoulos's store, the *kafeneion*, and modest, white, stucco houses lining the ravine.

As part of the preparations, Barba Lambros had invited a trio of musicians from a neighboring village to come and play. The men settled on three of the small woven-seat chairs, under the shade of a plane tree, in front of St. George's Church and began playing spirited folk music on bouzouki, clarinet, and mandolin.

The very first strains of melody lifted village spirits. This was my first experience hearing live music, and it gave me a newfound energy. My happy heart inspired my feet to tap to the rhythms. In no time, we kids joined the dancing circle, and moved to the live music, better than we had to our childish singing.

I was disappointed, but not surprised, to learn that the rumor about sweets being proffered on the big day was hollow and false. In addition to missing the usual roasts and sweets, the festival was also missing a significant number of villagers who were mourning the loss of loved ones. But despite all this, those who attended gladly united with fellow villagers to celebrate the goodness of St. George, the exemplary Christian martyr, who allegorically had "slain the evil dragon" of bygone times.

Even Mother, who said her heart was not joyous enough for dancing, joined the circle when Vasili and Sophia, ignoring her reluctance, pulled her out of her chair and onto the dance area— still wearing her big black "Chicago coat" to ward off cool April breezes.

After a few trips around the circle with Sophia and Vasili on either side of her, Mom gracefully dropped out and returned to sit with Aunt Stella who was wrapped in her usual heavy, black shawl. The two sat facing the church, under the thick branches of newly budding plane trees and they conversed with other women, while admiring dancers and enjoying music.

As my cousins and I danced, Mother chatted with women she had known since her youth. I was relieved that the dreaded Papadopoulina, wife of the suspected German collaborator, was busy tending the counter of her husband's general store, so my mother would not have to bear that woman's suspicious glares. Mother smiled when she spotted Tasia, Nikki, Kosta, Demetri, and me dancing at the tail end of a wide circle of dancers.

Parnion's senior residents including Kyra Margarita, the white-haired woman we called Aunt Maria, and Uncle Nicholas, sat on the sidelines: men sat with men; women sat with other women. Older folks chatted quietly, but I noticed them tapping their toes to the beat. The one older man who did dance was the unstoppable Barba Lambros.

He led his specialty, the *tsamiko*, to the music of *"Enas Aetos"* ("An Eagle"). Lambros, our own white-haired village eagle, slowly leaped and twisted backward and forward in rhythmic motion, while hanging on to the white handkerchief in the strong grip of the muscular man on his left. My village hero soared, moving perfectly in step and cadence to the treasured music. Demetri, Kosta, and I joined Uncles Vasili and Nicholas, and the rest of the crowd shouting, *"Yia sou, Barba"* (good health to you, uncle), and we burst into enthusiastic applause when his dance ended.

A few hours into festivities, when the musicians took a break, I spotted Nikki energetically approaching the mandolin player. I was thoroughly bowled over when I heard her ask, "May I please borrow your mandolin to play two songs that I know?"

My sister Nikki's bubbly personality may have been subdued by the presence of Nazi soldiers, but while we had lived in Kalamata, before the war started, Nikki demonstrated an inherent musical gift. My sister's interest in music had inspired Mother to pay for a few mandolin lessons in Kalamata.

Nikki had not touched a mandolin since we had evacuated to Parnion, and unlike me, my older sister was not shy. When the mandolin player saw Nikki oozing with confidence and enthusiasm, he graciously lent her his mandolin, and even sat down to watch her short but confident concert. I ran over to my mother and Aunt Stella to announce, "Look at what Nikki is doing!"

I held my breath as my sister commenced her performance by selecting "*Ta Kimata tou Dounavi*" for her curious listeners. To the audience's surprise, the little American girl could play, and her rendition of "Waves of the Danube" was pitch-perfect.

Delighted with herself, Nikki strummed away, and with the confidence of Judy Garland, she pleasantly belted out her second number, "*San Pas Stin Kalamata*." Perhaps this was why I still remember the lyrics: "*San pas stin Kalamata kai ertheis me kalo, mantili na mou fereis na valo sto laimo*... (When you go to Kalamata, and safely return, bring me a scarf to wear around my neck...) Kalamata was renowned for its silk industry, which produced lovely scarves. The image of the town in the song was very different from my own memory of it after fleeing the German bombardment.

Finishing her segment of the day's entertainment, my beaming sister bowed graciously and returned the instrument to her colleague, the mandolin player, who encouraged the audience to give her a round of applause. Mother smiled for a second time—and I resumed breathing.

I couldn't fathom how my sister had the bravado to volunteer to perform in front of an audience. Nikki smiled more than I had seen for months, looked confidently at the crowd, and bowed three times. A few weeks before, she had been whimpering inside our family trunk, but now she was strutting around the town square, smiling graciously at every compliment, as though the Nazis had never set foot in our village.

By late afternoon, the older men had gathered around a large, rectangular *taverna* table at one end of the square, near the lion fountain. By evening, the spirit had moved them and they began singing "*Kleftika*," hundred-year-old songs about the struggle and revolution that had finally set the Greeks free from atrocious, Ottoman Turk domination.

Impromptu solos by raspy, leathery-skinned, mustached, and snowy-haired old lions, like Mr. Apostolis, Barba Lambros, and Uncle Nicholas, brought tears to elders in the crowd. Father Haralambos joined the nostalgic singing session with his clear baritone. Out of respect for the man, his vocation, and his beautiful voice, the older gentlemen encouraged a solo. When the priest finished, one old woman was moved to yell out, "We're in the same stew, yet again, Father Haralambos! We are enduring barbarians who starve us and dominate our land. When will our beloved *patrida* ever be free?"

***

Despite the war, 1942 brought another occasion to celebrate. On December 6, the feast of St. Nicholas, Father Haralambos recited the Liturgy at tiny St. Nick's, near our house. Men named Nicholas made merry by attending services in the morning and later, at home, hosting guests who stopped by with good wishes, by serving them five-star, homemade wine. Ordinarily, the lady of the house would have made traditional name day goodies for her Nicholas, but this year, she lacked the necessary ingredients. The festive tone carried on throughout the month in anticipation of Christmas.

Christmas Day, an extra special feast is traditionally accompanied with delicious sweets. Mom ached because there was no flour to bake traditional *melomacarona*, the delicate, cinnamon- and clove-spiced Greek Christmas cookie. "I miss the perfume of baking *melomacarona*... the fragrance of Christmas. Even during the Depression in Chicago, I made *melomacarona*."

Caroling was one holiday tradition that was retained unspoiled during the Nazi occupation. The holiday custom was for children to go door-to-door singing carols, known as *calanda*. Heavy, war-battered souls lightened when children's voices intoned the story of Christ's birth. Singing continued on New Year's Day, which was also the feast of St. Basil the Great. In better times, gifts would have been exchanged on this feast day, but on that first day of 1943, we stuck to singing carols about generous St. Basil.

Mother suggested it would be a good idea for Demetri, Nikki, and me to go caroling. She regarded it a good exercise for her shy son and extroverted daughter, deciding it was the perfect opportunity for Nikki to perform and for me to interact with others. I was hesitant about singing in public even though I knew the words of the carol and was comforted that my sister and cousin Demetri would be my partners.

I kept my apprehension under wraps but, at the same time, felt an iota of wartime joy because rare, pleasant excitement was entering our lives. Nikki insisted that the three of us rehearse the ancient carol together. We would be the smash hit of the village.

We were energized at the prospect of traveling through our winter-cold mountain village and going door-to-door to sing our little hearts out, while wishing happiness to fellow villagers at a special time of year. Mother informed us that, by tradition, households in mourning were to be skipped, editorializing, "It's too bad. Those are the people who need the most cheering up. But Greek traditions are Parnion laws." The stipulation greatly lessened the number of families we could visit.

So Nikki, bubbling with gusto, led our joyful but sallow-faced, skinny, and tattered trio down the street. Shivering in icy mountain air, we approached the first house and knocked. Our neighbors, Artemis and Phillip, opened their door, smiling, our cue in centuries-old Greek caroling tradition to ask, "*Na ta poume?*"

Their cheerful response: "Certainly you can sing to us! We've been waiting for you. Come in out of the cold."

We filed into their small, warm living room and began: "*Kalin imera archontes ke an einai orismos sas Christou tou Thea Yennisis na po to archontiko sas....* ("Good day, masters of the house, if it is your wish I'll tell of Christ's Holy Birth...")

But only a duo sang. Nikki was so into her performance element, she was oblivious to the fact that only she and Demetri were vocalizing. Demetri gave me a nudge and a quizzical glance. And I tried, but the old carol refused to come out of my throat. I was, mysteriously, soundless.

Meanwhile, Nikki continued, *"Christos yennate simera en Veethleem ti poli..."* (Christ is born today in the city of Bethlehem...). By now, Demetri had stopped singing to stare at me, and Nikki finally realized she was singing a solo. She flashed a disapproving look at her two bashful companions. Demetri pointed toward me and whispered, as if it needed to be said, "He's not singing."

At that, Nikki directed a sharp shove to my ribs. "Sing, for God's sake," she ordered, in the pause between verses.

Artemis and Phillip were trying not to laugh, but not doing very well. To help me out, they mouthed the familiar words and nodded encouragingly. Burning red with embarrassment, I, again, opened my mouth. I hadn't forgotten the lyrics—I just couldn't sing.

That didn't stop Nikki. She hooked her arm around Demetri's, as if to say, "Forget him!" and they crooned the last verse together. While taking her applause and "Bravos," Nikki dragged our cousin down, into a deep bow, like they were the leading soprano and tenor on N.Y. Metropolitan's stage.

Demetri, standing again, looked over at me in sympathy. But Nikki, after receiving her ovation and reward goodies, grabbed him by the arm and directed Demetri to the next house—leaving me in the dust. My cohorts continued their door-to-door concert tour of Parnion, singing duets.

Artemis and Phillip kindly treated us to the traditional reward: nuts and dried figs, their own homegrown produce, which had been stashed away from Nazi food raids. Clutching a walnut and dried fig in my hand, I ran home, red with humiliation, certain that "the American kid" would never, again, be able to emerge into our village neighborhood without inspiring whispers, finger-pointing, and scornful gales of laughter. In my shyness and anxiety, I had lost my voice.

***

More war news of which we were unaware—1942:

- ❖ *Japanese launch new offensive in China*

- ❖ *Germans enter Stalingrad*

- ❖ *Feb. 16: Britain finally lifts sanctions against food being allowed into Greece and agrees to permit shipments of wheat to Greece under neutral supervision to help stem famine and starvation of Greek civilians*

- ❖ *Aug.1: Wheat destined for Greece to relieve "Greek famine" leaves Canada*

- ❖ *Axis armies retreat from El Alamein, Egypt: first major Allied victory of war*

18 | MORE GLOOM

Filing out of church one Sunday morning, Mother heard someone calling her name. Mom, Nikki, and I turned around to see none other than the tall, robust form of Mrs. Papadopoulos, wife of the general store owner, striving to attract my mother's attention. Mrs. P.'s blondish hair stood out in the crowd because, like Mom, she did not wear the traditional scarf around her head and neck.

Mother pretended not to see the hard-faced woman's hand motioning for her to pause. Intentionally ignoring "Papadopoulina's" persistently cold stare, Mom was not surprised when the determined woman elbowed herself through the crowd and "accidentally" bumped into her.

"*Kyra* Katherine, we don't see much of you." Mother, who had never spoken with the woman before, later surmised Papadopoulina lived on a diet of tart lemons, reporting, "Acid dripped from her mouth when she spoke."

Managing a brief smile in self-defense and attempting to move on, Mother realized she was trapped by her innate politeness. "We live at the other end of the village, *Kyra* Papadopoulou. I don't get down here much, except to attend church."

"*Kyra* Katherine, did I hear your husband lives in Athens?" Stunned with the question, Mom could only stare at the woman. Mrs. P. may have considered it an original question, but Mother had heard it before—from the Nazi officer.

"If you heard that, *Kyra* Papadopoulou, you heard *mis*information. My husband is in America. He hasn't been to Greece since he left his village for America in 1906."

"Oh, has it been that long?" the woman questioned sourly, suspicion accenting her starchy tone.

"He has never returned," Mom answered firmly, trying to move on.

"And how about your oldest son? His name is Alex, isn't it? Does he live in Parnion? We don't see much of him."

Mother stopped breathing. The woman's menacing attitude, accompanied by her inappropriate line of questioning—exceeded "just plain nosy." But Mom pulled off her reply rather smoothly. "Yes, of course he lives here. Alex spends a good deal of time in the house studying to enter high school. My son is a very serious student and he wants to be well-prepared when the high school in Sparta opens again."

Mother had contained her anger, but I could see that mention of my brother's name clenched her jaw. It was clear to Mother that she was speaking to a woman whose husband had the questionable reputation of being a "friend" of Nazis.

Papadopoulina's interrogation abruptly ended when our neighbor Margarita, black scarf properly in place, popped out of the crowd to fling her arm around my mother's shoulder. The elderly woman smiled kindly at the cross-examiner and apologized. "Excuse me for taking my neighbor away so abruptly, *Kyra* Papadopoulou. For the past two days I have forgotten to tell her something very important.

"I'm just an old lady and forget so easily. I must tell her right now before it flies out of my brain again. I know you'll understand. Do have a good Sunday." Margarita slipped her arm through Mother's and walked her hastily toward home.

"You needed to be rescued, dear Katherine," Margarita said as we trotted back across town. "I hope I came in time. I know my reason didn't make sense, but time was of the essence. I couldn't think of anything else to say."

"I'm grateful, *Kyra* Margarita," Mother said, half-smiling. "If that nosy woman's questions were only a matter of gossip, I wouldn't care—even though what she wanted to know was none of her damn business." Mother's face stiffened again. "Sinister motives hide behind her questions. Did she think I was too stupid to notice? What a horrible person!"

Mom recalled the officer who had paid us a visit. "Now, I know why that German came to interrogate me about my husband. I'm scared to death the Nazis will come back to take Alex." Reaching Margarita's house, Mother dropped her voice even lower, "Now I'm positive Papadopoulos is a collaborator. He puts his wife up to gathering information for him to turn over to the Germans."

"Neither is to be trusted, Katherine," Margarita agreed. "I've known that for years. Even before the war."

As I learned later, my brother was still secretly translating for British soldiers who were trapped and hiding in the caves of Mt. Parnon. After Mother's questioning by the German officer, she heard from Vasili that Nazis were becoming more vigilant of the comings and goings of villagers. The Nazis knew there were British soldiers in the area, and wanted to arrest them, as well as destroy Greek guerrilla fighters who were hiding out in the mountains. I knew none of this at the time, so I was puzzled to see Mom so anxious after her encounter with Mrs. Papadopoulos.

***

Years later in Ann Arbor, Mother filled out this story for Dad and me. She explained that Uncle Vasili had rushed over one morning to bring her news about three teenage Parnion boys who had been apprehended, trucked to Sparta, and jailed by the Germans—accused of covert activities with the concealed British. Mom said she went to bed with a pounding, nauseating headache because of Alex's British involvement. Mother remembered that later, she spotted one of the arrested teens in Parnion, following his release: his dark hair had turned pure white in his absence. Mom surmised Nazi torture was responsible.

***

On our way home, from church the Sunday Mother was questioned by Papadopoulina, we stopped at Vasili and Sophia's house. Mother wanted to tell them about her encounter with Mrs. P. My sister and I listened as Vasili arched a trim eyebrow and concurred with my mother. "It's just like Thermopylae," he said, referring to the ancient battle where the Spartans perished.

"We Greeks lost because that bastard Ephialtes told the Persians our plans." My uncle always talked about ancient history as though it happened to him personally. "There's a modern-day Ephialtes living among us here in Parnion," he went on, "and it probably is Papadopoulos." I sensed that my aunt and uncle became disturbed hearing that Papadopoulina, in her brief words with Mother, had brought my brother's name into her dubious questioning.

Alex, in the midst of underground goings-on, was ahead of the game on that Sunday morning. Unlike so many able-bodied Greek men and teenagers, my brother was still alive, not in a Nazi jail or concentration camp, and not working in a forced labor camp in distant Germany. Without delay, however, Mother, Vasili, and Alex decided that Alex had to leave Parnion.

Morose and tearful, Mother sat Nikki and me down in the *saloni* the next morning to tell us that Alex was going to Athens; she did not explain why. We asked, but she gloomily eluded our questions. All she would say was that he was going to stay with my father's brothers. Silently, all of us wondered how a lone American teenager, fleeing German surveillance in the midst of Nazi occupation, could arrive there safely. Not only were there Nazi checkpoints on all roads, but my mother had no way of letting our uncles in Athens know that Alex was on his way.

Before he took leave of us that night, she presented Alex with a small treasure to help him survive along the way. Not arms or money, because she had neither, but two thick slices of dried, brown village bread, and a handful of nuts and dried figs, all wrapped in a white handkerchief. The sparse offerings were from Sophia and Vasili's larder; the kerchief was one of Dad's that Mom had brought from Chicago. Alex solemnly took the gift and slipped it inside his threadbare sweater, one he had been wearing since our time in America.

Fear and desolation were deeply carved in Mother's face the night Alex was to take leave of us; her demeanor frightened me. My own mother, a woman I barely recognized anymore, was striving to control emotions and restrain tears. Yet as hard as she tried to remain stoic—her control finally broke. When she let out a sob, I recognized my loving mother again.

"My dear child, we may never see each other again. How can I go through life not seeing you, my son?"

Trying to sound reassuring, Alex returned her embrace. "Don't worry, Mother. I'll be fine. Nothing will happen to me. I'll be very careful and very smart. These Nazis bastards are going to lose this war. We're going to win. We will cross the ocean and join Dad in America. We will be together again, Mother. I'm sure of it. But you have to be careful too. And so do Nikki and John. All of you must stay safe!" Alex had always been sure of himself, as he was now.

Tears streaming, Mother clasped Alex to her, and couldn't let go. "I pray that we will meet again, my son. May the Holy Spirit enlighten every step you take so that you safely arrive in Athens and find your uncles. May Christ and His Holy Mother keep you healthy—safe! Survive this hell, Alex, and go home to your father in America when it is over." Mom finally managed a smile when she cautioned my brother, "Remember, no foolishness. The Phantom in American funny papers is fiction. Use the good brain God has given you."

My brother and I had never spent much time together, so it felt natural that he would not be with us for a while. But I was sad to see Alex go away; I knew I would miss him. It also upset me to see how much it hurt my mother. All of us, young and old, understood there would be much danger ahead for my brother during his journey to far-away Athens.

The night was heavy with clouds; there was no moon. Nikki, Mother, and I silently waved goodbye to Alex from the dark, second-story window. Under the shield of a dense sky, Uncle Vasili, also tearful, walked my brother to the edge of Parnion, a few hundred paces from Grandpa's house. And I sadly watched lone Alex disappear into the gloomy, black mountainside.

19 | NAZIS IN THE HOUSE

Mother spotted them from the *saloni's* window; then we heard heavy footsteps approaching the front door. "Maybe this gang is here to arrest me," she muttered facetiously under her breath. Another Greek collaborator was arriving at Grandpa's door—in the company of six German soldiers.

Alex had left town a few days before. Nikki had gone to Sophia's house to hang out with our cousin Tasia that morning; my sister knew to stay put if Germans arrived. I bravely joined Mom when the loud knock demanded a response.

Opening the heavy door, Mother was assaulted by the collaborator's harsh voice. "Let us in! These soldiers must inspect the inside of this house!" He gave no reason and Mom, tension clenching her jaw, didn't ask. She knew she had no choice.

Sticking close to Mom, I tearfully eyed a dozen shiny boots clunking from room to room on Grandpa's bare, wooden floors. Mother said later, "My soul burst with grief when Nazis violated your grandpa's noble threshold. I was afraid... they were going to take me away from you."

Impeccably uniformed, clean-shaven soldiers, smelling of stale cigarette smoke, checked nooks, crannies, and cupboards. It was plain to see that we had nothing. "What can they be looking for?" I asked myself, as my blood raced, not knowing what they would do next.

They lowered themselves into the dark, dank area of the below ground basement, with flashlights glowing, then came upstairs again. Mom and I watched them peer out windows, and share observations with each other in German. "I had no intention of asking the dirty collaborator what it was all about," Mom grumbled after they left.

A thorough military inspection completed, the collaborator informed Mother that we were about to receive the greatest of all honors: officers of the Third Reich were going to move in with us that night. She was ordered to move into the smallest room with her children, and leave the rest of the house for the officers' exclusive use. "I was so upset when I finally found out what they wanted of us, I ran outside to vomit," she admitted later.

Mother hurried to Sophia's and brought Nikki home. Visibly shaken, she directed Nikki and me to gather our sparse belongings from the *saloni*. "How much more of this hell can we take?" Mom shouted. Since Alex had left, she had taken to uttering this phrase multiple times a day. "*Panathema to patera sas*," she added. This, too—a curse on our father—was a new way of speaking for Mother. Even in all our previous hardships, I had never heard her speak ill of Dad.

"Dear children," she told us as I helped her push our trunk to the storeroom, "we're going to live under the same roof with Hitler's soldiers. Where is your father? I wish he could see us— right now—sharing my father's house with Nazi soldiers! Is this better than living out the Depression in Chicago?"

Nazis brought in dozens of kerosene lamps before the sun went down and that night Grandpa's house glowed like Vegas. Supplementary German vehicles were parked on the road outside. It must have looked like their "Führer" was in town.

Officers took over our home; lesser-ranked men camped at nearby St. Nicholas Church, acting as servants for the commissioned men living under our roof. The smell of cooking emanated from our courtyard where soldiers prepared supper under the moon and stars; I wondered if they were eating potatoes, but I didn't recognize the smells. As we were prisoners in our own home, the three of us knew only what our senses communicated; except for taste, of course, because they didn't share food with us.

Hungry, cold, and terrified—almost glued together—we three spent the night inside the storeroom wrapped in Grandma's itchy, wool, mothball-smelling blankets, and huddled around a lone, oil lamp flame for lighting.

Nikki the brave performer was gone; in the face of the Nazis, she cried. Mother attempted to soothe our fears, "Everything will be fine," she murmured as she stroked Nikki's hair. "We'll live through this too, children. They'll be gone by tomorrow night. God will protect us." My sister finally fell asleep in my mother's lap.

All night we heard the banter of a strange language. Laughter, cigarette smoke, and what sounded like angry male voices wafted into our jail cell from the slit under the closed door. Near dawn, they finally fell asleep, and we could doze, too. Mother did not sleep a wink. "How did I know what they planned to do to us during the night?" she explained in the morning when a knock on our door gave us leave to come out and go about our normal activities. Surely as long as our conquerors shared the house with us, nothing was normal.

Well, didn't we have the luck! Grandpa's venerable house received a "finest vintage" rating. The military returned to take it over, while banishing us to the storeroom, five or six more times during the war. Grandpa's house enjoyed "location, location—location" at the village's entrance, greatly assisting Nazi surveillance of everyone who entered and departed Parnion from the connecting road to Sparta and to Tripolis. To protect themselves from guerrilla revenge after dark, the Germans tripled their military force when they stayed overnight—and all of them tramped in and out of our house.

***

I crept outside one quiet morning during the Germans' third or fourth takeover of our luxurious "hotel." Peering at the village from the balcony was my typical entertainment. Below I watched a soldier enter our courtyard from the street. He led a large white sheep by a rope around its neck and deposited it in a small pen in back of our courtyard.

Watching them, I heard faint, female cries coming from the direction of St. Nick's Church. Suddenly, a gut-wrenching wail penetrated the air, typical of sounds I had heard at funerals: the pathetic keening of bereavement always gave me the willies. "Some poor mother must be remembering her dead husband or child," I thought. "But we're so far from the cemetery…"

My mind returned to the sheep. "Hey! I know the sheep the Nazi stashed in our pen. That's Martha's ewe! That soldier snatched it from Martha." Outraged, I left the balcony to tell my mother about the dastardly crime the Nazis were pulling off on poor Martha. Everyone knew Martha and her mother depended on that one sheep for survival. But, I never reached Mom.

Chilling shrieks pierced the stillness of our own courtyard. Mother came out of nowhere and we ran out onto the balcony together. Below us we viewed a scene, straight out of Euripides' tragedies. Martha was standing in the middle of our courtyard, screaming—despondent—covered in blood.

"What's happened? Don't move, Martha," Mom yelled down to her. "I'm coming!" Mother crossed herself and headed for the stairs, then uttered something to God under her breath. She flew down the steps so quickly that I had no time to tell her about the animal in our pen. Expecting to find Nazis physically attacking our neighbor, I was surprised to see Martha standing—all alone—in the middle of a bloody catastrophe.

Repeatedly bashing herself in the head with a sharp rock the size of a small melon, Martha was covered with blood. My knees buckled; every grisly smash of rock against skull and flesh made my own corpuscles crumble. Blood oozed from gouges in Martha's temple; one ear was coated with thick redness. Oozing, dark blood had matted down the brown hair on her scalp. I couldn't tell if her eyes were open or shut. Blood flowed down her brow and eyelids; red fluids trickled from her cheeks and out of her nose. Martha's signature rose-colored scarf had fallen from her shoulders and dragged on the ground beside her. I turned to look at the house behind me to see if Germans had attacked her. Two blank-faced soldiers were standing on the balcony, coldly watching the scene.

Mother sprang toward her. "Stop, Martha! My God, you'll bleed to death. Calm down! Has something happened to your mother?" Mom grabbed the bloody rock from the woman's gory hands and pitched the weapon over the courtyard wall, out toward the *perivoli*. Streams of burgundy red continued running down Martha's neck and over the bodice of her blouse.

In an instant, Mother, tenderly and firmly, took hold of Martha's bloody chin with both her hands. The woman opened her eyes, still screaming, to look at my mother who firmly grabbed her face to steady it. Martha's body shook with panic. Mine was shaking too.

Mom struggled to get the woman's attention. She seized Martha's flailing hands in mid-air, pulled them down, and clutched them, tightly, in her own hands. Distraught Martha, however, persisted in shrieking. Mother silently and calmly gazed into Martha's chaotic, red eyes, refusing to let go of her hands.

"Martha, listen to me," she said softly. "Please stop screaming. Calm down." Mom was almost whispering. "I want to help you, Martha. What is wrong?"

The rescue happened in seconds. I still hadn't told my mother what I knew and finally, in an attempt to be heard over Martha's screams, I blurted out, "Mama, the Germans stole her ewe and stashed it in our yard. I think that's why she's upset." Martha stopped.

Hearing my outburst, Mom hesitated. "Is that what happened, Martha? Is that what's wrong? Did the soldiers take your sheep?"

Martha produced a nod, but began her hopeless, catatonic wailing again.

Mother closed her eyes with disbelief, took a deep breath, then turned to look toward the house. I looked up at the balcony: the soldiers were gone.

"How dare they?" Mom exhaled. "The barbarians! The bastard barbarians!" Brown eyes ablaze, my enraged mother ordered, "Stay right here, Martha. John, you stay with her. Don't move!"

Overwhelmed with unadulterated gumption, Mother stormed into the house. Racing from room to room she finally found the senior Nazi officer; he had commandeered our house the night before. Mom angrily gestured with her blood-smeared hands that he should come outside. When they reached the courtyard, my mother pointed at bloody, pathetic Martha. "Look!" she yelled at him. "You and your damn Hitler did this! Look at that woman. Your selfish, vicious actions have created yet another Greek tragedy."

A sick feeling festered in my stomach as Mother boldly committed certain insubordination against a Nazi officer. Terrified by her behavior, I was positive the officer would either shoot her or arrest her on the spot. Wide-eyed Martha, still bleeding copiously from forehead and scalp lacerations, was as shocked as I was. She quieted down, but continued shaking.

I froze with panic dreading the tragic repercussions that were about to follow. I felt sicker when I realized that my mother wasn't finished castigating the officer. "Please God, make her stop," I prayed.

"Mama, please don't say anything more to him!" I shouted at her.

With Martha's blood sticking like glue on my mother's hands, she ignored me. Wildly gesturing more, she insisted the officer follow her to the back of the courtyard. Then flailing her arms and pointing in various directions, Mother's irate sign language communicated the connection between the ewe, Martha—and the woman's bleeding lesions.

"Give this woman her sheep," she blasted him in Greek. "This harmless woman needs it to survive. Don't you monsters understand? She needs it to survive."

I dared turn my eyes from seeing Mother in her deadly tirade to take a quick, nervous glance at the German officer. How could I save her?

Cringing while holding my breath, I expected him to draw his pistol and aim it at my mother's head in an explosion of Nazi ire. "I'll knock the gun out of his hand when he draws it," I decided.

But what I saw next left me dumbfounded. I looked over at Mom. She saw it too and looked bewildered. Mother went silent, almost seemed embarrassed.

There were tears in his eyes. An officer of the Third Reich felt and showed compassion for Martha—and for my mother. He never responded in Greek or German; he said nothing to Martha or to my mother. I never knew if the officer understood any of Mother's hot-blooded Greek rant.

In German, he shouted orders to one of his men, and unsmiling, he used his own sign language to show that Martha could take back her ewe.

Turning toward my mother and staring deeply into her quieted eyes, the officer nodded—with respect. The incident ended when, with downcast eyes, he walked back into Grandpa's house.

Trembling from head to toe, like leaves in the wind, Mother, Martha, and I were silent, but quivering. Mom sent me into the house to fetch clean rags and led Martha over to the *niftera* to wash her wounds. Then she sent me to the fountain for more water.

Even though the road was filled with Nazi soldiers, I kept my wits and scooted under the neighborhood olive tree to fetch water at St. Nick's. It took a lot of time for Mother to clean and bandage Martha, rinse the blood out of her hair, then wipe blood off Martha's dress. And while Mother tended to trembling Martha, she spoke calmly to her—Martha only shivered and sobbed.

When Mother told me that Martha was ready, I retrieved her beautiful ewe from the pen. Wordless and edgy, I accompanied them back to their home. Still shaking, Martha dragged herself along, with shoulders drooping, and eyes staring at the ground. We anxiously paused at the fountain, where the sheep drank from the culvert, innocent of the near fatal fuss wreaked over her by her devoted mistress. Nazis never again bothered Martha's vital, treasured lifeline.

***

Years later I wondered whether we would have detected an iota of humanity in German soldiers if we all had been speaking the same language. Obviously, military supremacy and the rules of the occupation set us apart. Most assuredly the language barrier kept our relationship colder, more impersonal, and on our part, chokingly fearful.

We, civilians, didn't know that armies of the Third Reich were receiving edicts from headquarters forbidding kindness toward us, the occupied. Certainly soldiers of the German army knew that disobeying proclamations from Berlin would result in severe punishment for themselves. We hated the soldiers because they were so brutal, but they, in turn, were forbidden to be humane to us. Mother, Martha, and I were lucky enough to encounter one German officer who dared to respond with compassion.

After Alex left Parnion, and after the incident with Martha, I saw Mother's drawn face grow harder. Those attractive, brown eyes took on permanent sadness. Sometimes, I caught a vacant stare in her kind eyes; it made them seem smaller and more sunken into her face. Around that time, she was verbalizing the question, which had been churning inside her for two years. She repeated it more often than she was aware of. "How much more of this hell can we take?"

And now, Nikki and I became more aware of her disparaging remarks about Dad because she proclaimed them aloud and with emphasis. "What was your father thinking when he sent us here?? Stupidities! Nonsense! We are paying with sickening fear—and maybe with our lives—for your father's foolish ideas." I didn't know what to make of Mom's flare-ups. Prior to the Nazi invasion of Grandpa's house, she had not expressed such bitterness about my father.

20 | BEBBA

Our spirits were finally lifted one sunny afternoon in the spring of 1943 when the chatter of surprise visitors entered our courtyard. Little happened to lift anyone's spirits because our Nazi occupiers made life difficult and dangerous. Relatives living outside the village rarely left their homes. But Uncle George, his wife Athanasia, and their little two-year-old boy, Fotis, had arrived and were standing in the middle of the courtyard.

Mom squealed with delight and swept Fotis into her arms. Nikki and I rushed to greet our relatives, and seconds later were pleased to find Uncle Nicholas, Mom's boisterous cousin with the big white mustache, following our visitors through the courtyard door.

Eyes sparkling amiably, with a broad smile showing below his bushy mustache, Nicholas was carrying a small brown and white goat under his arm. And when my uncle put the animal down, it stayed close to him, the way Martha's obedient ewe did with her.

The docile goat had two stubby horns on top of her head and a diamond of brown fur on her white face, just above a shiny black nose. Long ears, laying flat on either side of her head, framed her face and enhanced her charm. With some hesitation, I dared to touch the two wattles of skin hanging from her throat, like misplaced earrings. I was surprised when she didn't pull away, quite unlike skittish Agrimi, the only other goat I'd known.

"What a handsome goat, Uncle Nicholas," I remarked with a smile. The goat seemed to smile back.

"My house, up on the edge of the village, doesn't get as much German traffic as yours does, Katherine," Nicholas explained.

"The path is too narrow to accommodate their monstrous cars and trucks. Those damn soldiers haven't kidnapped any of my goats yet. But, I don't know how long my luck will last, do I?"

Then he pleasantly turned his attention toward me. "Johnny, I heard your goat died and I just happened to have an extra one in my little flock."

I was so taken with the brown-and-white nanny goat that I barely heard my uncle add, "This little goat is for you, John. But, a word of warning, before you take this nanny goat out to graze... find out which plants she should avoid eating."

Surprised and grateful that Uncle Nicholas trusted me with one of his extra special goats, I hugged him happily and he hugged me back. At that stage of the war, goats were incredibly scarce. It was hard to imagine that just two years before, Nikki and I had spied on great flocks of them drinking at St. Nick's fountain.

"Thank you, Uncle Nicholas," I shyly whispered in his ear. "Uncle Vasili and I asked an old shepherd to show us which plants are poisonous for goats. I know which ones they are. I promise we'll avoid those pastures."

I worked up the courage to pet the nanny goat, and was pleased to find she was affable and soft. Again I noticed that she appeared to smile when she looked up at me with her mouth slightly opened. I smiled too, twice as excited to have, this time, a friendly animal for a pet.

"What are you going to call this one, Johnny?" George asked.

Nikki purred, "She's such a cute baby. This one should be named 'Bebba.'" So we let Nikki be the godmother of our new goat.

Nicholas explained that Bebba wasn't like old Agrimi. Bebba was domesticated, what some called a Nubian goat, bred for her ability to produce milk. And, he said that we American kids ought to be filling our stomachs every day with nutritious goat's milk. In the midst of what would eventually be called the Greek famine, Bebba was a life-saving gift.

The visit almost resembled old times, as though the war had never happened. Mom asked me to carry the old wooden chairs outside so the adults could visit under the pleasant shade of the arbor. Nikki brought glasses of cold water for our relatives.

After a lively conversation between cousins, and additional thanks to Nicholas for his precious gift, he helped me place her in a pen at the back of the courtyard. Then he left to visit the *kafeneion*.

Nikki and I played with Fotis while our parents chatted. Our cousin was a cute little kid, too young to understand war and famine. With curly light brown hair and bright blue eyes, he delighted in the attention we lavished on him. I entertained him by acting out "Jack and Jill," a nursery rhyme I recalled from my American existence. He laughed with delight when I tumbled "down the hill." The energetic toddler helped free us, for a little while, from our doldrums. Mother appeared more relaxed, and noted my sister's happier mood.

George and Athanasia had special news: she was pregnant with their second child. It felt good to see Mother smile again. "Wonderful!" she exclaimed. "Our family can never have too many nieces and nephews to love." In retrospect, one may ask if a baby arriving during a war was actually wonderful news. But even in war, life went on with the undying hope that the enemy would soon depart and life would return to normal.

"Katherine, we have a proposal," George said, after Mother and Athanasia had hugged and smiled. "What do you think of Nikki going home with us? She can help her aunt during the pregnancy. I know you don't want to be separated from your child," my uncle told Mom. "especially while a war is going on. But Athanasia and I will keep her safe. We will treat Nikki as our own. We'll share our food and the safety of our home with her," George promised.

"Nikki, in turn will watch over Fotis and help Athanasia with chores. You'll have one less mouth to feed and hopefully by the time the new baby is born, the Germans will have lost and you will be able to return to Andrew in America."

"Perhaps it would be good for Nikki," Mother said. "Childhood fun has been scared out of her. Remember when she sang and danced all the time?" After more thought and a few private words with my sister, Mother decided to take my aunt and uncle up on their offer.

It turned out Nikki was pleased to be going "on vacation" in another village to play, non-stop, with our little cousin. She was smiling again, even as Mom reminded her that although she was traveling away from Parnion, it was not quite a vacation.

"You will have responsibilities, Nikki, and I know you will carry them out like the big and good girl you are. You are to obey your aunt and uncle, just like you would obey me." When Nikki left that afternoon she was smiling and happily waving goodbye to us. Enthusiastically clutching Fotis's little fist with one hand and Uncle George's with the other, the four walked out of the courtyard together.

But more anguish took hold of Mother when Nikki left. With Alex in Athens, living under conditions unknown to us, and Nikki gone, too, I heard more complaints regarding my father *in absentia*. And one day when Bebba and I returned to the courtyard after a long graze, I found Mother in an especially terrible mood.

"How much more of this hell can we take?" she screamed at no one in particular. "*Panathema to patera sas!*" (A curse on your father!) Her complaining words always shocked me, and I flinched again when I realized she wasn't finished with her verbal assault.

"He naïvely—no, he stupidly—sent us off to this primitive country where I have to send my children away from me—so they can survive! And you! Walking around with contaminated, bloody feet because you have no shoes! I wonder if your father has any idea of how we are forced to live. I'd like him to see me sewing homemade shoes made out of—rancid burlap for *his* hungry, skinny son.

"What have we come to?" The act of releasing her collected stresses, however, seemed to revive an iota of my mother's pleasant personality. In our hostile environment, a first-class "vent" was a good thing.

This particular rant about my shoes was a common one. I don't remember when I started going barefoot, but by this stretch of the war, I felt as if I had been walking barefoot forever. Mother was distraught about my being shoeless—*xypolitos*. "Imagine, my kid is barefoot," she lamented with a scowl. In her mind, there was only one thing was worse than being a pauper, and that was being a barefoot pauper.

Shoes endure the most punishment in a rocky, agrarian environment. During three-and-a-half years of war, when new shoes were not available, village footwear became as deteriorated as villagers' souls. Some shoeless villagers carved shoe soles from wood and attached straps to hold them on their feet. Others used discarded, flat tires that the Germans had left behind along the main road, crafting homemade shoes from cut-up, black rubber treads. Many walked barefoot, even in winter. Feet got so thick and leathery from walking barefoot all the time that villagers' soles wouldn't bleed, even if slashed with a knife.

For me, the real problem with being shoeless was that I continually stubbed and gashed my toes. Splinters and tiny pebbles found themselves inside my stinging foot wounds. Fortunately no rusty nails were scattered about. With no village hardware store, people prized and hung onto nails of every size; even bent, old nails were pounded straight again and re-used.

At the start of my barefoot days, I invariably arrived home with torn feet. Eyeing my dirty, gashed toes, Mother would immediately insist I wash my wounds using warm water and her harsh homemade soap. (Ouch!) I screamed with pain every time she pulled foreign matter out of my heels and toes, using a needle she cauterized in the oil lamp's flame. Then I heard, *"Panathema to patera sas!"* again. When her patient had quieted down, Mom bandaged my purified slashes with clean rags she had ripped into long, narrow strips.

Disgusted with the state of my feet and concerned that I'd pick up the plague or some other fatal disease walking on village paths, where dirt mixed with animal excrement, Mother had decided to make shoes for me. She wanted to keep my feet protected from rocks and animal droppings, a natural part of our environment, but perhaps, also, to soothe the embarrassment she felt of being the mother of a shoeless son.

We had no leather, and no money to buy leather, so determined Mom went hunting for "shoe makings" in the *litrivio*, the place where Vasili pressed olives to produce olive oil. She flashed me a half-hearted smile of success when she uncovered old, burlap bags. The thick, rough, smelly sacks were used to transport olive fruit to the *litrivio*, but also to filter oil after the olives had been pressed: the sacks were black, slimy, and stunk of rancid oil.

Smelly as they were, Mother lugged several of these oily bags into the house. With a sharp knife (she had no scissors) she cut foot shaped pieces, for soles, from the tough burlap, then tussled with the unwielding fabric and clumsy knife to fashion cover pieces for the top. Straining to push needle and thread through stiff, greasy burlap, she finally transformed this unlikely material into "shoes," which resembled black Donald Duck's feet. Ferragamo had nothing over my mother.

"I can't wear these things! They stink like rancid oil. They're slimy! They make me look ridiculous," I complained—a hardhearted response to such an earnest endeavor.

I wore them only when forced to. My toes oozed rancid oil when I walked; my feet froze when I wore them in snow. In rain, my designer apparel semi-soaked up water and became even more slippery—and they squished. I looked outlandish and dramatically protested every time Mother insisted I wear them. In the end, I felt guilty about my grumbling, especially when she tenderly explained, "It's all we've got, Johnny."

Of course, I felt guiltier at Mom's disappointment when the inevitable happened. The burlap, a loosely woven fabric, began unraveling under the pressure of my feet. My "duck shoes" eventually fell apart.

How easily we take wearing shoes for granted when we have factories to make them fit our feet comfortably and attractively, stores to sell myriad varieties of them, and most importantly, the means to buy them.

"When the war is over, we'll buy real shoes for you," my mother promised.

This war wouldn't go on forever, would it? I wondered about it all the time, because so many excellent things were going to happen when the war was over. We'd eat good food again. I'd wear normal new shoes. I'd finally be with my Dad in America. And people would stop dying.

But doubts poisoned my young outlook—sad questions stuck to my brain like misplaced superglue. Would we live long enough to go home? Would Mom die? Would everyone I know die? A short prayer followed those queries. "Please God," I would murmur, "keep Mom and Nikki and Alex and me alive. Keep Bebba alive, too. Keep all the people in Parnion alive! Please, God, make the bad guys lose! Make the Nazis go away!"

We waited every single day for the war to end, without an inkling that Hitler was planning to prolong our misery. Mother and I, hungry and lacking shoes, knew nothing of the proclamations and instructions Adolph Hitler issued to his officers regarding occupied Europe's innocent civilians.

Those German plans are remarkably clear today because Nazis kept good records of their atrocities, which are easily accessible to today's historians. One proclamation was specifically related to our "wellbeing," and issued about the time that Nikki, Demetri, and I were practicing our "smash hit" Christmas carol. Hitler issued it in December of 1942, by way of one of his closest henchmen, Field Marshall Wilhelm Keitel. It contained no warm and fuzzy sentiments:

"This fight has nothing to do with a soldier's chivalry nor with the decisions of the Geneva Conventions... The troops are therefore authorized and ordered in this struggle to take any measures without restriction even against women and children *if these are necessary for success. (Humanitarian) considerations of any kind are a crime against the German nation..."*

Mother had, if only temporarily, lost two of her children. Her remaining son was wearing disintegrating burlap shoes. Our only reliable food was from our goat. It wasn't going to get any better anytime soon because soldiers were going to get meaner. And Mom wrote another letter:

Dear Andrew,

It is late November of 1942, but I can't be sure of the exact day. We hope you are well when you read this letter. Since I cannot mail it, I cannot be sure you will ever see it. I apologize for the paper, but it is all we have. It is wrapping paper I found near Vasili's oil press, when I was searching for burlap to make your son some shoes.

I feel you should know of our present situation, in case we are arrested, or killed, or die of illness or starvation. I surmise you will want to know what happened to us. I plan to preserve this letter (and others previously written but not mailed to you) as best as I can. Your children and I live under extremely volatile and dangerous circumstances. For us, nothing is certain anymore. There is no way out of this hell.

As I write this, please know that Alex is in Athens. A traveler to Sparta from Athens, who contacted my brother George, brought us news that Alex arrived in Athens and is living with your brothers. I cannot attest to his safety because I do not know what conditions exist in Athens. Closed off in Parnion as we are, I am blind, deaf, and dumb about what is going on in Greece and the rest of the world. I do not see newspapers. There aren't any here. There is no radio. German soldiers occupy us. I sense that when they look at us, they do not see us as humans. It would not be safe to explain why Alex is not with us, in case this letter falls into the wrong hands. Please understand. I had no other choice but to send him away.

Nikki lives with my brother George and his wife Athanasia in their village, a few kilometers from here. Nikki is helping George's wife, who is expecting their second child. I feel relieved knowing they can feed our daughter better than I am able to do. I allowed Nikki to go with George and Athanasia because Nikki needed to escape the fear-filled environment we live in. I also felt she would be safer living in a household with a man at its head.

Johnny and I live alone in my father's house, except when Nazi soldiers move into the house with us. This may sound incredible to you but it is the truth. We have no say about it. Sometimes uniformed Nazis in menacing boots take over this house and when they do, Johnny and I stay in a storeroom at the back of the house until they go away. I pray John will survive, and I am doing everything in my power to guarantee his survival.

One of our problems, besides being stuck in an on-going war and having this house overrun with enemy soldiers, is our lack of food. We are starving. Almost everyone in Parnion is hungry. Most people here are better off than we are. The sick feeling of nausea that comes with hunger never goes away. There is little or no food to relieve empty, aching stomachs. I cannot conceal food from enemy soldiers who confiscate food, at will, when they find it—because, you see, I have no food to hide. I have no way to make a living—no crops, no livestock, no land or valuable belongings to sell. Johnny has no shoes and I am embarrassed to tell you he walks barefoot, like a waif. We live primitively.

Johnny and I subsist on wild greens we gather from fields around the village. In America they are considered weeds. When wheat was harvested last month by villagers who are better off than we are, Johnny and I waited for the villagers' donkeys, loaded down with harvested wheat, to return to the village. Then we followed behind the pack animals and gathered grains that chanced to fall and scatter to the ground. Then, at least, I would hopefully have a few handfuls of wheat to make some kind of bread. Your son and I are gleaners. We pick up odds and ends to survive.

My father was Parnion's leading citizen when he was alive. Now his daughter and grandson are the village paupers. While I was scrounging precious kernels of wheat from the ground, I couldn't help but remember buying fresh American bread, already baked, sliced, and packaged from a Chicago grocery store. I entertain John with my memories of home.

Chestnut trees grow near Vamvakou, a village higher on the mountain, about seven kilometers from here. Chestnuts mature at this time of year. Tomorrow several women and I are planning to walk there to pick as many chestnuts as we can carry back to Parnion. Hopefully, chestnuts will help sustain Johnny and me through the coldest part of winter. Walking the distance will not be easy. My shoes have worn out, it is cold, there is snow on the ground, and I have lost all my energy. I plan to leave Johnny here at my father's house to preserve the youthful strength he has left. Colder weather began earlier than usual this year. Without proper sustenance our bodies lack vigor and cold penetrates our bones.

Andrew, I confess that I have not been thinking pleasant thoughts about you. I realize that when you sent us here you did not expect us to become Hitler's prisoners. But, you did send us here. I try to erase from my mind that it was your idea for us to leave the United States. I certainly forgive you, but forgetting is difficult.

Please excuse my complaints. I have no one on whom to unload my frustrations. I don't want my black thoughts to scare the children anymore. They have already been scared enough. Everyone here suffers. I am alone, helpless, powerless, penniless, in constant danger, and overwhelmed. I don't know how much more my nerves can take. My family and some villagers have helped us. I am grateful.

All day long I pray this ungodly war will end tonight, tomorrow, or the day after. I have hope. But, under these horrific conditions, my hope often turns to despair. In case you read this and I am gone, I pray you will be in the company of our three children. Guide them in their growing up if I am not with you. Our children are stalwart in spirit and I am very proud of them. They are good children. My miserable life is dedicated to their survival. Please forgive my unpleasant thoughts of you. I know you meant well. I am just tired and devastated.

Your loving wife,
Katherine

***

"Beautiful Morning?" "Home for Christmas?"...Not for us in 1943:

- ❖ *Daylight allied bombing of Germany begins*

- ❖ *General D.D. Eisenhower named Commander of Allied Forces*

- ❖ *Allies invade Italy under General Patton*

- ❖ *Russians destroy German army at Stalingrad*

- ❖ *U.S. government and University of Pennsylvania collaborate to design world's first digital computer. Named ENIAC, it was first implemented in 1945*

- ❖ *George Washington Carver, eminent American agricultural scientist and educator, who was born in slavery in 1864, dies in Tuskegee, Alabama*

- ❖ *Meat, butter, and cheese rationed in the U.S. for the war effort*

- ❖ *Broadway opening of the musical, "Oklahoma!"*

- ❖ *Popular U.S. songs: "I'll Be Home for Christmas" and "Oh, What A Beautiful Morning" from the new musical, "Oklahoma!"*

21 | WRETCHED 1943

Frame of mind plays an essential role in determining whether we humans choose to enjoy or to ignore blessings that marvelously fill the universe around us. The beauties of nature resolutely appear according to their season, even when we're distracted, distraught, or turning a blind eye to their glorious beauty.

In autumn, wild pink cyclamen shoot up in the Spartan countryside; their restless blossoms twirl and dance with fresh breezes drifting in from some distant sea. Pristine snow, which only nature creates so perfectly, redecorates the peaks of Laconia's Mts. Parnon and Taygetos in winter, a sight as exquisite as the snowy Alps. Spring rains transform summer-browned Greek mountainsides into lush, emerald slopes; they ably challenge forty shades of Irish green. And the kind of weather Parnion enjoys in summer should make it as renowned as the Hamptons.

Yes, even during World War II, cyclamen bloomed, perfect snowfalls embellished distant mountain peaks, and undulating hillsides turned velvety green.

But lovely cyclamen can't heal fear or loneliness; flowers don't fill an empty stomach. Verdant mountainsides do not rebuild a bombed-out home. Nature's glories retain the potential to elevate saddened spirits, but oppression makes humans insensitive to them.

Some victims even turn a blind eye to God, blaming Him for "man's inhumanity to man." But God is not at fault: the responsibility for war's kind of suffering is a result of the arrogant, greedy, and diabolical ambitions of selfish human beings: man's lack of empathy—lack of love. Humanity, safety, comfort, and hope emerge where compassion exists.

Our skies were usually the bluest of blues, and Parnion's air was forever fresh and exhilarating. The noble Greek sun shining on us in World War II is still extraordinary; I think Greek light is more exquisite than it is anywhere else on Earth. High above Parnion's main street, even in awful 1943, our neighbor Artemis's red carnations reveled in glorious sunshine and tumbled over her second-story balcony to lend color and excitement to our neighborhood.

Yet, as gorgeous as those carnations were and as beautiful as a Parnion morning can be, suffering eyes viewed the village as drab, ugly, and depleted. Even if we had known the words and melody of "Oh, What a Beautiful Morning," we would not have been singing America's newest hit: in 1943, nothing seemed beautiful anymore. For Parnion and perhaps all of Europe, 1943 was the worst of many horrible years, a time when most turned a blind eye to nature's glories.

It was the year my dignified mother began humbly begging friends and relatives to feed me, her ten-year-old son, if they had food to spare. Once, she even sent me to a wedding to partake of goodies at the reception.

It was a clear Sunday afternoon when she heard the music of a fiddle gently drifting on a breeze over the courtyard wall. The violinist had come from another village to serenade the bride as she made her traditional walk from home to church on her wedding day. The fiddler's song was something rare in those times: a sound of happiness, as the bride and groom must surely have felt in that moment, despite the circumstances.

I noticed Mother listening to the tune, and could almost see the gears turning in her head—she was having an "a-ha moment." She knew some sort of food would be offered to wedding guests, and her son, John, could be one of those guests. In those days, people weren't formally invited to a village wedding: anyone who showed up was a guest, although only those close to the families attended.

Mother made sure I washed face and hands, making me as presentable as possible. Before launching me out the door, she advised me to mind my manners. "I am already embarrassed to send you out in search of free food, Johnny. Be polite. Extend your best wishes to the couple and to their parents. Say, 'Na zisete' to the bride and groom. Say 'Na zisoun' to the parents." These were typical wishes for long and happy lives that any polite wedding guest would utter.

"And, remember Johnny," she added, as she gave me one last push out the door, "don't eat like a piggy."

The evils of war saturated Parnion, but a little wedding joyfulness on that bright Sunday afternoon went a long way to touch village residents; we needed all the happiness we could snatch. And I needed to snatch a bit of food.

I caught up with the wedding party while the violinist was still playing Greek folk airs alongside the bride, en route to St. George's Church. In the simplest, home-sewn, white dress and homemade veil, she walked on the arm of her father, surrounded by the rest of her family. Villagers emerged from courtyard gates to wish the family well. Neighbors called out, "*Kala Stephana,*" to the bashful young bride, extending their personal blessings on the ritual crowns used in Orthodox wedding ceremonies.

Just as babies were born into the war-frayed world of the early 1940s, weddings took place too. Certainly, they were not elaborate affairs. In Parnion, customary Greek dancing followed the time-honored Orthodox Christian wedding rite at St. George's. If a situation was so dire that a musician could not attend, then the dancers themselves sang the melodies *a cappella.* Post-ceremony dancing was a must. Without it—why, it just wouldn't be a wedding.

Another critical component of a wedding was sweets—the necessary accompaniment to any happy event. Traditionally, the bride's family would offer luscious powdered-sugar-coated butter cookies called *kourambiedes.* Under healthier circumstances, Mom would not have wanted to fill her kid's stomach with cookies. Yet in the depths of war and starvation, Mother dispatched me to that wedding so I could eat *kourambiedes.*

After the church service, which I dutifully attended like any regular guest, I followed the party to the bride's home. And my eyes brightened and my heart jumped when I spotted the platter of luscious white goodies being extended to me. About the size of my young fist, they were rather large for cookies, but for me the bigger, the better. The host family, whether through scrounging, hoarding, or the infamous black market, was able to get their hands on the necessary ingredients to bake traditional *kourambiedes.*

Experience and technique are required to prepare and bake these light and flaky gourmet goodies; eating this delicacy takes just as much skill and experience. In order not to choke on the cloud of fragrant white powdered sugar covering the *kourambie,* I knew that I must not inhale, either with my nose or mouth, as I prepared to take that first amazing bite. Only after I had sunk my teeth into the cookie and closed my lips could I resume breathing, very carefully.

The first wonderful taste flooded my jowls with delicate sweetness and tantalized my taste buds. As the cookie softened and melted inside my anxious face, the *kourambie* deliciously stuck to the roof of my grateful mouth. What an extraordinary way to satisfy my empty stomach, elate my saddened spirits, and improve my frame of mind!

Never did any member of the bride's family announce that I was not entitled to enjoying their *kourambiedes.* Hospitality is fundamental in Greek culture; Greeks are famous for it. In Parnion, if a host snubbed a guest, he would be branded parsimonious; he and his progeny labeled "cheapskates" for eternity. Doubly unfortunate for any host—but fortunate for me—was that refusing a visitor would surely bring bad luck.

The Greek tradition dates back to earliest times when the ancients believed a guest might possibly be Zeus or some other god in disguise and on location to test a host's kindness and smarts.

You'd be in big trouble if the guest you had snubbed suddenly took off his disguise and, *voilà*, there was the frowning Zeus standing before you, deeply disappointed in his empty glass and plate, and complaining that you were ungracious and stingy. I was not Zeus or Apollo in disguise, just the hungry kid of a worried mother, who was trusting in the hosts' hospitable nature to provide something for my empty stomach.

Celebrating a joyous day in their lives, the hosts generously shared their sparse wartime wedding treats with the scrawny, bashful "American kid," and graciously treated barefoot me like a distinguished guest. I was doubly exhilarated when the mother of the bride, probably seeing the unfortunate straits I was in, offered me a second *kourambie*. I could have eaten dozens, but my mother's reminders of propriety limited me.

On my way home from the wedding, I noticed that a light dusting of powdered sugar had inadvertently landed on my chest: telltale evidence of how I had enjoyed these extra special cookies, a mark of distinction that I ravenously licked off my tattered shirt.

After I successfully crashed that wedding, Mother found other special occasions to send me to. Unfortunately, these were more often than not *mnemosina*: memorial services for the dead. Observances, praying that God's mercy will be shed on the soul of a departed family member, took place in church, following Sunday's Divine Liturgy, when the entire congregation participates in praying for the deceased. The Orthodox Church encourages the living to remember the souls of their beloved: three days after death, then seven days, forty days, and every year.

The memorial ritual includes prayers for the soul of the departed, and a dish of *kolyva*, boiled wheat, prepared by mourners. A wheat seed looks lifeless when it is planted in the ground, yet it grows and thrives. This spiritual allegory, symbolizing the Resurrection, reminds the living that good things happen to the soul after death, offering hope for the hereafter.

Those who attend the memorial express their sympathy to the bereaved by saying, "May his (or her) memory be eternal." At each *mnemosino*, at least at the ones where wheat had been procured despite shortages, I timidly murmured this in Greek—*Aionia tous i mnimi*—then enthusiastically gobbled up boiled wheat. Wealthier villagers enriched boiled wheat recipes with a rich mix of sweet and tasty additions such as powdered sugar, nuts, raisins, sesame, and pomegranate seeds. For me, it was like eating dinner and dessert all at once.

22 | SO MUCH GOING ON THAT WE DIDN'T KNOW

We were cut off from world news, so, aside from our awareness of the anonymous guerrilla fighters in the local mountains, we had no information as to who was fighting the Germans. We didn't know about, for instance, Generals Eisenhower, Bradley, Patton, and Marshall. If Germans were running Parnion, we thought they were running the rest of the world as well. For all we knew, they were occupying Chicago. It didn't seem possible that the Germans could ever lose a battle.

What I have read in more recent histories of World War II is that Hitler's strategy had weaknesses. For instance, the Nazis delayed their attack on the U.S.S.R. by six weeks because they had found it necessary to divert some of the forces into Greece to help Hitler's Italian ally, Mussolini, in April of 1941.

One theory purports that because German forces did not enter the Soviet Union until June, rather than April, the whole timeline was thrown off, and Russia's infamous winter weather eventually caught up with the Nazis. Harsh weather was aided by tenacious Soviet counterattacks.

The number of Nazi losses during the Battle of Stalingrad, between July 1942 and February 1943, were staggering—historians estimate 200,000 Nazi troops died, and 91,000 German soldiers surrendered. Some experts consider it the turning point of the war.

Greek resistance inflicted frustrating setbacks on German forces. Germans found themselves caught up with the Greek resistance like a grizzly bear fighting off a swarm of unrelenting bees. Guerrilla fighters slowed down and stalled the Nazis enough to play a vital role in Hitler's loss of the war.

Georgy Constaninovich Zhoukov, Field Marshal of the Soviet Army, wrote in his memoirs that "If the Russian people managed to raise, resist, and at the doors of Moscow to halt and reverse the German torrent, they owe it to the Greek people who delayed the German divisions during the time they (the Nazis) could bring us to our knees."

However, back in Parnion in 1943, there was no way for us to know that any powerful Nazi ever surrendered. German soldiers who came to Parnion bullied and overpowered us. We had no inkling that the Nazis had begun to *lose* their pursuit of world conquest.

More than two very long years had passed since we'd had contact with my father in the United States. He didn't know of our existence and we didn't know of his. Mother constantly brought him up in her remarks and conversations, perhaps to keep him alive in our thoughts. But when 1942 slowly advanced into 1943, her comments about Dad grew even more negative. "After all," she reminded me again, "it was your father's idea that we come to Greece."

Mother may have bad-mouthed my father for our wretched circumstances, but she couldn't praise Bebba enough. Mom's hopes for outliving and surviving our misery were tied up in our nanny goat. "Thank God for that beautiful little animal," she would say nearly every day. "As long as we keep her safe from Germans, and fed, she'll provide you with precious milk, Johnny. Our beloved Bebba is keeping you alive."

After Nikki went to live with George and Athanasia, I was alone. So I began spending more time with my cousin Demetri. Uncle Paul, Demetri's father, worked long hours at his little grist mill near the Oinountas River. When Paul stayed at the mill overnight, his wife Anastasia often sent Demetri to deliver his evening meal.

One summer evening, Demetri asked me to go with him. The sun was still high in the sky and the Germans had not come into Parnion that particular day. With plenty of time before nightfall, I tagged along without letting Mother know where I was going.

Hiking toward the Oinountas River, we spotted a bearded, blond man, in the distance, taking water from one of the springs near the village. "Who's that?" Dimitri asked.

"I've never seen him before," I answered. "Maybe Uncle Paul knows him."

When we arrived at the mill and shared our news of the stranger, Uncle Paul told us our eyes must have played tricks on us. He assured us that if the man was not wearing a German uniform (and we knew he hadn't been) there was no possibility of a stranger hanging around the village.

"It makes no sense for someone new to come to live in Parnion now with Nazis all around us." Then Paul laughed and made a joke out of our sighting. "Maybe it was a ghost. Or maybe an authentic, mythological nymph—maybe a centaur."

Demetri and I were sure we had seen a real, flesh and blood man. Rejecting his father's teasing, Demetri assured his father, "Don't kid around, Papa. This guy wasn't ancient or mythological. He was real."

"Don't be making fools of yourselves in the village with this ridiculous story, boys. You were seeing things that weren't there. When the sun goes down at this time of day, changing light can play tricks on your eyes. Get some good sleep tonight and forget about this silly apparition."

After the war, I learned that Demetri's father was secretly feeding concealed British soldiers. Paul, who had lived in Boston and spoke English, regularly provided his wife's meals to these hungry men. The bearded stranger we saw at the well was, no doubt, a Brit. Paul denied his existence to protect him. That "apparition" was the closest contact we kids had to Greek resistance at the time.

A few weeks later, Demetri invited me to go along with him to the mill again, but Mom reminded me I had chores to do. She said I needed to gather leaves for Bebba to eat. This, it turned out, was just an excuse.

Mother was completely aware of Paul's involvement with the hidden British, and she didn't want me, inadvertently, getting involved in any covert actions, having stressed enough with my brother Alex's underground secrets.

Demetri typically passed the house of the woman we called "Aunt Maria" when he delivered meals to his father. The older woman had introduced herself to us, early on, when we first returned to Parnion. Maria was not a blood relation; we children called her "Aunt" out of respect and affection.

After more drop-in visits with Maria in our courtyard, Mother learned that Maria was widowed and lived alone; her daughters had married and left Parnion to live in their husbands' villages. Dressed in black, of course, her traditional scarf had a habit of slipping off her head to reveal white hair, pulled into a large, silvery bun at the back of her head. Framed by the black scarf draped on her bent shoulders, her grandmotherly face smiled when she stopped to talk to me.

When I asked how she was feeling, she'd mention arthritis in her joints, but always asked about Mother. It was hard to live in the village without a man in the house, she would say, and then remind me, "Of course you, Mr. John, are the man of your grandfather's house now."

The day I was out collecting leaves for Bebba, and Demetri was delivering food to his father, Demetri passed Maria's courtyard wall, as usual. But, as he walked by her gate, it suddenly flung open and the old woman darted out at him. Wildly waving her arms, she screamed, "Turn around! Go back home!"

Stunned, Demetri explained, "I'm taking food to my father, Aunt Maria."

"I know," she said. "Go back home! Germans are watching you—from up there." The frantic, winded, old woman pointed toward the direction he was heading. "Germans—with a huge gun—are hiding in the underbrush. I saw them from my window. They're going to kill you. Turn around, Demetri! Go home! Now."

Shaken, he quickly obeyed. Still hanging on to the sack of food, Demetri dashed home. Aunt Maria had saved his life that evening. What my cousin didn't know was that on the previous night, the guerrillas had killed eight Germans outside Parnion's village limits. And that morning, Nazis had moved extra men and a huge cannon into the outskirts of the village. They were prepared to shoot anything that moved: man, woman, or child—in retaliation.

The Germans suspected *antartes* were receiving aid from Parnion villagers. But in fact, these resistance fighters usually stuck to themselves, up in the hills. They were from other parts of Greece, so they didn't feel compelled to visit people in our town. Uncle Vasili told us that as far as he knew the majority of villagers had the same experience as we did: minimum or no contact with *antartes*. Even so, the Germans suspected much more.

Mother had warned me to be wary of strangers in the village; and I knew, by then, that *antartes* fighting the Germans lived in the mountains around Parnion. The sole contact I can remember with a guerrilla took place on a moonless night.

A knock sounded on our door, and when Mother opened it a crack, she found herself peering at a stranger. The young man, camouflaged in black with dirt smeared on his face, asked, "I'm sorry to disturb you, Ma'am. I'm so hungry. Might you have some food to spare?"

I heard her say, "Son, we have little to eat in this house. There are a few walnuts I can spare but I really have nothing else to offer you." She handed him some walnuts and he politely thanked her before saying, "Good night."

"I was afraid for a second," Mother confessed to me after she shut the door, "but he was quite courteous."

The Third Reich worked hard to demoralize locals and turn them against the guerrillas. But it worked against them. When

Nazis' unjustly attacked innocent citizens in Parnion, the villagers' anti-Nazi resolve strengthened; townsfolk became more sympathetic to the resistance's actions against the Nazis. This caused the German army to become more viciously punishing.

One mystery piqued my curiosity during the war. I didn't understand how village men knew that Nazi soldiers were on their way into town before distant motor sounds could be heard. I often wondered how our men had enough time before German convoys arrived to flee the village and find hiding places in the mountains.

When I visited Greece decades later, I learned the secret from Uncle Vasili. Men and older boys had devised a clandestine system for alerting each other when Nazis were on their way to Parnion— before the rest of us heard German cars, motorcycles and trucks approaching.

Vasili told me that he and other male villagers regularly took turns at stationing themselves along the main road from Sparta. The first "station" was at the fork of the road where it split toward the neighboring village of Vasara or toward Parnion.

When the German convoy turned toward Parnion, the first villager in the clandestine chain would set a match to a dry *aphana* plant, something like tumbleweed. After the plant blazed up, he immediately snuffed it out.

This sent a signal to the next man up the road, who set a second *aphana* on fire and extinguished it. This action, in turn, signaled the next villager in the chain to ignite and snuff out yet another *aphana*.

When the last fire was set at ground level, a man stationed high above the village at the Byzantine monastery, far across the ravine but visible from Parnion, ignited a final fiery signal.

At that moment, the last assigned villager in the chain, who was stationed near the Church of Saint George on the main square, rang the church bell with a predetermined chime that meant, "Able-bodied men, get out of town. The Germans are coming!"

***

More of what was going on that we didn't know about in 1943:

- ❖ *Japanese driven off Guadalcanal*

- ❖ *Cost of a gallon of gas in the U.S.: 15 cents*

- ❖ *American journalist Ernie Pyle, writing sympathetically of the American GI war experiences, is most widely read war correspondent in U.S.*

- ❖ *February: Greek Jews are ordered to wear yellow star with label "Jude" and "Hevraios" written in German and Greek*

- ❖ *March: Most of Thessaloniki's Jews are deported*

- ❖ *September: Adolph Eichmann orders all Jews in Athens and all of Greece to be taken into custody and immediately sent to Auschwitz*

- ❖ *Incarceration in Haidari, SS run prison near Athens with horrific reputation for torture and firing squads, is part of Nazi solution to break down the will of the Greek population*

23 | OMENS

Uncle George received a distressing message from Aunt Joanna's daughter and sent it to Uncle Vasili: Joanna was missing. Neither daughter nor son knew their mother's whereabouts. Mom's sister had been last seen departing on a ship from the port in Lemnos. And it was impossible, under the occupying Nazi regime, to trace the progress of her journey after leaving Lemnos. The crushing news instantly brought on Mother's and my aunts' inconsolable grieving.

Anguished cries, like those of Sophocles' choruses, filled Grandpa's fireplace room that terrible, cloudy, and gray afternoon. Our women were articulating their heart-breaking sorrow with scary keening.

I knew sticking my fingers in my ears or disappearing from the scene would be heartless, a hollow escape at a moment of family sorrow, so I reluctantly stayed put. But my aunts' laments alarmed me, as did the pained sorrow on my mother's face. For them, the devastating news was synonymous with hearing of their beloved sister's death. I stood by, sad and helpless.

"Joanna is dead! We curse you *Charos* because our Joanna has been taken away from us—forever!" Sophia wailed. My aunt addressed Death as though he were in the same room with us. "*Charos*, you went behind our backs to rob us of our sweet sister. My soul aches because you are gone, dear Joanna! Precious sister, we will never again laugh together. Never—forever!"

Aunt Stella, pulling her hair, chimed in with, "My God! What a catastrophe! Damned, devil Nazis murdered our worthy and loving sister. Damn Hitler! Damn his henchmen! *Charos*, come and take me, too, so I can be with my blessed Joanna!"

Sophia continued, "*Christos kai Panagia!* (Christ and Holy Mary). Black torment breaks my heart! Our sweet Joanna is dead and we don't know where her body rests. Joanna is unburied! Where are you, Joanna? Our family is lost without you!"

Unrestrained emotions accompanied their fixations on a string of imagined and horrible scenarios, baseless presumptions for Joanna's disappearance. A horrendous nightmare of unrestrained grief sent my aunts and even my usually even-tempered mother out of control.

I was relieved when Uncle Vasili's logic, mixed with optimism and his understanding of the village female psyche, was able to calm them.

"Listen to me, please, ladies. Quiet down and listen!" he said, flailing his arms to get the women's attention. "We don't know that Joanna has died. The news tells us that she is missing! That does not mean she is dead. In fact, Joanna may be safer than we are. Perhaps she got off the ship at the wrong port. Perhaps Joanna is being well-cared for until she comes home."

Big sister Stella, loudest member of the chorus, paid no attention to brother-in-law Vasili. Stella carried on with her keening, "Why did she travel half way around the earth to visit an island we know nothing about? I told her that she should have stayed... sitting on her eggs... and not budge from Parnion."

Here, Aunt Stella puffed herself up like a broody hen and shook her head with dismay. "But she wouldn't heed my sage advice. My heart bleeds with sorrow because my beloved sister is gone from me forever."

Vasili persisted in being the voice of reason. To get the women's attention, he threw in powerful words like "sin" and "omen."

"Crying, wailing, and mourning are not options," he chided them. "It's plainly wrong—a destructive omen—to mourn someone who is probably alive. Yes, we're powerless to inquire about her whereabouts.

"Yet, I assure you! Joanna is only temporarily lost—misplaced. My dear ladies, we must not mourn Joanna—who is probably as alive as I am. Ask Father Haralambos and he'll tell you it is a sin to mourn the living."

Bringing displeasure to God's eyes was not an option for our women. They eventually calmed themselves, prayed, and waited for more hopeful news. They knew that mourning Joanna foreshadowed her death—a horrific prophecy to unleash on a cherished sister.

And while women in our family prayed for missing Joanna, belligerent Nazi investigations and destructive home searches for weapons and ammunition escalated.

Enemy soldiers again reached into rubble, empty chicken coops, and already robbed homes. Nazi looting free-for-alls plagued Parnion; soldiers took every bit of valuable personal property and food they discovered under the guise of searching for suspected firearms.

We had no guns and there was no hidden food supply at our house. Still, after one Nazi search, Mom discovered her few pieces of simple but precious jewelry were missing. She had brought them with us from Chicago and stashed them away in some obscure nook of Grandpa's house that even I had never found.

Mother lamented losing the delicate gold chain Dad had given her as a wedding present. The small, gold, baptismal crosses and chains Alex, Nikki, and I had received from our godparents were gone too. The theft increased her melancholy, but after a few hours she threw her hands up in an air of concession.

"Perhaps three German children will, one day, wear souvenir, gold crosses their daddies brought to them from a trip to Parnion. Thank God, it wasn't any worse, Johnny. We have a roof over our heads—and we're still alive."

She had in mind the mysterious disappearance, a month earlier, of white-haired Aunt Maria. Maria had been the kind old woman who saved my cousin Demetri from German gunfire when he was delivering dinner to his father at the mill. News reached us that the old woman went missing after German soldiers invaded and searched her house.

When Nazis, led by a reprehensible collaborator, combed Aunt Maria's house for weapons, they found her late husband's hunting gun buried in the basement. Too crippled with arthritis to manage the difficult ladder maneuver necessary to climb down into the below ground area of her old house, she had ignored her basement for years and had no idea a weapon was there. Maria had explained this to the Nazis, but her logic made no difference to them. They arrested her, and we anxiously waited for her to return home—it never happened.

Eventually, her daughters, who lived away from the village, sent word to relatives in Parnion that Nazis had shot a group of prisoners, including elderly Maria, at German headquarters in Sparta. With this revolting news, village hatred for the Germans intensified. How could they have killed a kindly, innocent old woman?

I can't say who was hated more when this brutal transgression became known: the Nazis or their Greek collaborators who had directed needless military attention on a blameless, arthritic old lady.

Overwhelmed with adversity by mid-1943, while watching me grow taller, undernourished, emaciated, and shoeless, Mother had sensed that I was falling into ongoing gloom. She had already witnessed the fear Nazi occupation had instilled in my sister, and Mom couldn't bear to watch it reoccur with her youngest child.

I noticed that she had stopped complaining about Dad. And to sidetrack me from thoughts of war and hunger, as well as to build up hope in me for a life in America after the war ended, she spoke to me of our lives in Chicago before 1937, recalling places where our family had lived.

Mother reminisced about Logan Square, a Northwest Side Chicago neighborhood where she and my father had lived before Alex was born. Melancholy peppered her thoughts as she described street medians, beautifully planted with trees and flowering bushes.

Medians, she explained, for I had forgotten this word, if I had ever known it, were patches that ran down the middle of wide boulevards in big cities.

She recalled for me that the two-flat building where they lived on Springfield Avenue had a grass lawn in front and in back, "by the alley." An alley, Mom explained, was a minor city-owned passageway behind the house, "as wide as Parnion's main street."

"How wide are boulevards in America, then," I asked, "if minor passageways are as wide as the street in front of Grandpa's house?"

"America is blessed with marvelous wonders, Johnny. You will be amazed! One of these days, we'll go back—and you will be amazed."

She reminded me of the neighborhood on the West Side where we had lived after moving from Geneva, Illinois. Mother referred to it as "Crawford and Madison," near Chicago's immense and gorgeous Garfield Park. That great green space, dotted with thousands of trees, included a gold-domed building, a glass enclosed "flower house" (conservatory), and a lagoon large enough to accommodate row-boating: the lagoon's water froze over in winter and became an outdoor rink for ice skaters. Mother remembered walking us tots to Garfield Park for our daily airings.

There, in the "grandest" of parks, she met other Greek immigrant mothers who had brought their children to play. Mothers chatted, peacefully, while children swooshed down slides and played together on swings and teeter-totters. Such things were American wonders, she told me, built especially for kids to play on.

She recalled that during the Depression, when Alex was ten years old, he had sold newspapers in front of the huge and distinctive Marlboro Theater on Madison Street, a few blocks from the park. Tall buildings and elegant shops lined Madison because, Mom told me, there were still people around with money to spend during the 1930s. She remembered large, well-appointed, food-fragrant restaurants where my father had been employed as a substitute cook during "hard times." I had forgotten my Chicago life prior to coming to Greece and the places my mother described for me were unreal visions: American fairy tales.

"My memories may seem like impossibilities to you, Johnny. But they are real. You'll see them—when we finally go home. That's when you'll begin your new American life." When I looked doubtful, Mom reiterated, "We will go home to America, Johnny! We definitely will!"

Mother also worked at inventing distractions to help me survive overpowering catastrophes. Making an effort to be cheerful, under the direst of circumstances, she found things we could laugh about together and forced herself to smile to save me from falling into depression. Before retiring at night, Mom issued an assignment. In the morning I was to announce five good things in my life for which I was thankful, assuring her that I had thanked God for them in my nightly prayers.

It didn't take much deliberation to put Mom first on my thankful list; she remained there permanently. Bebba, my pet goat, came in second. Alex and Nikki tied for third place. Uncles Vasili and Nicholas, two of my favorite Parnion people, scored high. And even though I couldn't remember my father, he was on my list because I was thankful to have a father in the U.S. who we could return to when the tribulations were over.

Had I grown up in Chicago or Geneva, Illinois, my inventory may have listed a bike, a favorite ice cream flavor, a little red wagon, or a baseball mitt. Instead, my Parnion list revolved around beloved human beings and a goat. I was a very lucky kid.

Unlike Agrimi, my first goat, docile Bebba followed me wherever I walked. She enjoyed being cuddled and fondly looked into my eyes when I doted over her. Like me, what my goat took most pleasure in was eating. Due to the increased presence of Nazis, I could no longer take Bebba out to graze. So Mom made sure that I faithfully gathered greens and leaves for Bebba; dry ones worked, too. The goat ate more regularly than we did.

When I got lazy about going out to gather food for Bebba, which had to be done every day, Mother's impatience surfaced. "Who do you think is going to feed that goat, Johnny? Your father's servants?"

When I dawdled at the door, not wanting to go out in the cold to fetch water for Bebba to drink, I'd hear, "Are you afraid you'll sever your roots if you walk a little faster, John? Move. You're not a tree!"

Mother constantly reminded me, "Without eating, Bebba cannot make milk, Johnny. I've told you over and over again that Bebba is keeping you alive, so you must make sure she has food to eat. Every day!" On days when Germans did not show up, I did take Bebba grazing to parts of the village less familiar to me, tying a rope around her neck, like a leash, to keep her safe beside me.

One quiet spring morning, I took Bebba to a nearby hillside, bright green with newly sprouted holm oaks—an all-you-can-eat salad buffet for goats. Bebba instantly became oblivious to the world around her and, intent on munching her way through her own private Eden, immersed herself in lusciously green but barbed shrubbery. And when I mindlessly loosened my grip on her leash to pull a stinging barb out of my elbow, she got away from me so quickly that I lost sight of her in the tall, thorny shrubs. I got no response calling her name, and the worst came to mind. "What if some unseen goat predator dragged her away from me?"

I screamed "Bebba! Bebba!" She usually replied with a bleat when I called—but I heard nothing. With *pournaria* tearing my skin at every turn, I promised my anxious self, "I'll never take her near *pournaria* again—if I ever find her." Desperate, half angry, and feeling totally empty that I had lost my little pal for good, I waded further into a sea of flesh-cutting shrubs.

Panicked, and stabbed with every movement, I finally spotted something moving in a patch of bright green leaves. I gingerly surged further into the sharp branches and was relieved to encounter the back of a little white head with long floppy ears intently tugging and pulling down new sprouts. Munching blissfully away on tender shoots, Bebba casually looked at me, as if she were saying, "Choice location, John! This is gourmet stuff."

I spotted the end of her rope, grabbed it, pulled her away from her sumptuous salad, and took her home. Torn and bleeding, I reported my adventure to my mother who nursed my scratches, while explaining that goatherds and shepherds put bells around their animals' necks to keep track of them as they graze. "Where am I going to find a bell for her?" I sighed.

"Try Uncle Vasili's *litrivio*. There are odds and ends out there—if the Germans haven't taken Grandpa's scraps too." My day turned luckier when I uncovered a small bell among smelly, oily burlap sacks. And good luck held out when I uncovered a heavy string to tie the bell around my Bebba's neck. I was now officially a goatherd, with one lone nanny in my flock; I could hear her every movement.

Another morning, we heard the hum of engines soaring high above Parnion, a sound we had not experienced since the bombing of Kalamata. "What now?" Mother asked, as she searched the skies through the windows. "That's all we need now—falling bombs."

The dreadful destruction we had experienced in Kalamata flashed behind my eyes. We held our breaths, ready to drop and cover our heads, and waited for disastrous whistling sounds... but none came. So we cautiously went outdoors to investigate the source of distant humming. White wisps of "something" were drifting down on Uncle Nicholas, out on the street in front of our house.

"It's snowing messages," he laughed. His relaxed demeanor prompted me to run into the street to catch one of the white tufts. "These are from the good guys," Nicholas assured me, already having read one. The planes had buzzed on past Parnion but were still dropping thousands of pieces of paper. They scattered like snow, on roofs, hillsides, roads, courtyards—all the village's nooks and crannies. Neighbors gathered on the street, craning their necks to search the sky. A passing woman crossed herself.

Heaven-sent, very welcome communications informed us, in Greek, that our Allies were resolutely fighting on land, sea, and in the air to defeat Germany. The bottom line of the note, dropped by either British or American airplanes, was: "Resist!"

"All we have left in us is resistance," Nicholas remarked as he stuffed one in his coat pocket and started on his daily stroll toward the *kafeneion*. "Do those pilots know we're living through hell down here? But I'm sure good times will come again, Katherine. Any news about Joanna?"

"Nothing," Mother replied sadly, as she gathered up some of the white wisps.

"She'll turn up. Worry doesn't help find her. You've got enough on your mind," he called back as he neared St. Nick's Church.

By 1943, in spite of, or because of, the horrendous misery Greek people were suffering, the great majority *lived* resistance. And several more airdrops of paper "encouragement" descended on Parnion. Each time leaflets fell, neighbors ran around to collect as many as possible. Villagers, who lacked just about everything but resistance, found a very practical use for the feather light sheets. Neatly stacked, pristine piles of airborne paper could be found close to every primitive Parnion toilet.

If I had been in the U.S. during the early 1940s, I probably would have been memorizing baseball statistics for fun, as most American boys my age were doing. But I had no idea what baseball was about. I had not even heard of the great Babe Ruth. Instead of baseball cards, books, Hollywood movies, or popular radio programs to occupy my ten-year-old brain, I was immersed in a primeval village environment of omens, superstitions, gloom, and occupation. Mother didn't put much credence in omens, but she didn't preach against them either. Villagers, however, searched for meaning in signs that I took as ordinary, everyday happenings.

"There's enough bad news around us without my going to look for more trouble because a crow flies over the house, Johnny," Mom said. "Crows fly anywhere they like. They fly over millions of houses in America—with no resulting catastrophes. Remember that crows, even though they are not as cute as swallows, are just big black birds scrounging for food to stay alive—just like you and I are doing.

"You know what I consider a bad omen, Johnny?" Mom answered her own question. "Dirty hands!" And she would shoo me toward the *niftera* to wash up for the tenth time that day. In spite of what Mom said, I continually heard from villagers their analyses of omens as predictors of the future; none of them involved dirty hands. I still remember a few.

When a butterfly flutters into the house, it means residents are going to receive a letter announcing death.

Bad news is on its way if a bird flies into your window or a crow flies over your house.

Three crows flying over a house predict certain death.

When two bad things happen, a third catastrophe will certainly follow.

Three crows croaking together foretell disaster.

One distinct element regarding these omens was that villagers always saw evil about to befall someone else: never themselves. Mother's explanation: "The camel sees the funny looking thing on another camel's back but cannot see his own ridiculous hump."

Sayings existed in the culture to dispel negative omens. The one I remember: "If you are bringing good to us, may good things happen to you. But if you are bringing evil, may blackness and evil envelope you."

These magically dispelling words were to be directed at the crow, butterfly, or bird bumping into your window, while making the sign of the cross—three times. With all our frantic prayers and gestures at nature, which was just doing its thing, we must have been giving God a few laughs.

Then violence assaulted Parnion's stillness yet again, one November afternoon. The village abruptly reverberated with exploding machine gun barrages. This was hard not to interpret as a bad omen. Sharp, pulsating blasts bounced off mountainsides and could be heard by every living thing. When the horrific assault ended, a deadly quiet paralyzed us; even birds suspended their songs and flight.

Villagers were adept at judging sounds traveling from a distance and immediately knew the blasts, as powerful as they were, took place beyond Parnion. Yet they recognized the blasts were too close for comfort. Everyone knew that distressing news— more catastrophic than usual—would soon arrive in the village. A few hours later, St. George's Church bell tolled the sickening two slow rings, which signified a death in the village. The ensuing silence was interrupted by two additional slow clangs.

Mother and I cautiously stepped into the street to find out what catastrophe required two separate death knells. Looking toward St. Nick's, we spotted a short procession of Parnion men slowly approaching the village from the ravine, instead of the main road. Gasping for breath from the rough climb, the men were struggling to scale the steep gorge.

I immediately recognized *Kyrios* Kostas, one of our neighbors, at the head of the group. Although his gait and attire were familiar to me, I noticed a significant change in Kostas's expression. His cheerful eyes were frozen into a defiant gaze; despair was evident in his face.

Weeping, and struggling to catch his breath, Kostas led a cluster of six disheveled young and old village men. They were carrying a sight that has remained with me all my life: two bloody and shattered young bodies on makeshift stretchers.

I clamped my eyes shut, hoping the scene of human meat, bone, blood, gaping mouths, and vacant eyes would disappear by the time I cautiously opened them again. But it didn't work: the certain death foretold by the machine guns blasts was passing in front of me. Worse yet, I recognized the victims.

Nauseating panic jolted my child-spirit: I could identify violently disfigured features. Bloodied, distorted but familiar boyish faces were attached to ripped-apart, bleeding bodies. Flailing arms and limp legs swung to and fro with the motion of the walking men. The dead bodies, dangling over two parallel sets of wooden poles held together with ragged white sheets were... Kostas's only sons.

Tears streamed down *Kyrios* Kostas's slim face, but he boldly kept his head and torso erect in leading the procession to his home. Just as we had, neighbors had emerged into the street when they heard the church's dreaded knells, then bowed their heads, crossed themselves, and wept at the appalling sight that inched toward them.

Kostas's wife, waiting for him in their courtyard doorway extended her arms toward her returning husband, not expecting to see the ghastly sight behind him. I heard her breathless sob before she let out the piercing scream that flooded the glum silence. Recognizing her sons atop the stretchers, she fell into a dead swoon, and passed out in the village street.

I had played with the two fun-loving, friendly teenage boys when we first arrived in the village. They were the first kids, other than our own cousins, to befriend Nikki and me. Now they were bloody, motionless, dead bodies hanging over stretchers. Like my neighbors, I mourned the loss of two amazing, innocent kids— gunned down in a mean, senseless, retaliatory Nazi murder.

Glancing up at my mother, I saw her face had, again, evolved into a stiff, tragic mask. She was making the sign of the cross over her heart. Then she placed her arm around my shoulder, and held me so tight that it hurt. Every witness of this procession made the sign of the cross, praying God had already received the decent and amiable boys in heaven, yet grieving that these happy boys were gone from us forever. Women's screams and wailing continued in a sound wave as the wretched news traveled toward the far end of the village.

Kosta's boys were just two of 118 innocent men, most of them teenagers, who had been rounded up near the main road that led from Tripolis to Sparta. The Nazis had gunned them down, execution style, in retaliation for a guerrilla attack on German soldiers.

Decades later, a white marble monument in memory of the November 1943 victims was erected at the isolated place along the road where the massacre had taken place. One hundred eighteen names are carved into the marble: two of them are *Kyrios* Kostas's sons, the brothers from Parnion. The marble monument commemorates the worst day of omens in Parnion, up until then, the village's darkest hour.

Aionia tous i mnimi. (May their memories be eternal.)

***

Nazi atrocities in Peloponnesos, 1943:

- ❖ *October: Guerrillas in N. Peloponnesos area of Kalavryta abduct and kill 78 Nazis*

- ❖ *November: 118 Greek men and boys taken hostage and shot on the Tripolis-Sparta road as retaliation for guerrilla attack on Germans along that road*

- ❖ *December: 50 Greek hostages hanged by Germans for guerrilla attack on railroad east of Tripolis in Peloponnesos*

- ❖ *December: Nazis burn down 25 villages in mountains near Kalavryta, and Kalavryta itself, executing 696 Greeks, including almost the entire male population of Kalavryta*

24 | DEATH KNELLS—1943

One morning in the autumn of 1943, a loud knock on our door brought a report of more tragedy. Artemis entered, crying. "*Kyra* Katherine, Phillip brought me some very tragic news this morning."

We never got used to hearing bad news, even though a litany of it developed daily. Mother braced herself. "God help us, what's happened, Artemis?" Our neighbor drew closer to Mom, took and squeezed her hand. "Our dear Margarita has died."

The unexpected news stunned Mother. "I just spoke to her yesterday afternoon. She was going out to gather wood for her fire. Margarita was as able as ever... My God, did Nazis shoot her?"

"No," Artemis replied. "She was found dead in the woods after sunrise this morning. Some men, out early, hunting for birds, came across her body. It was an accident."

Margarita had been my mother's support, even her role model, for surviving in the village as a lone woman in charge of a household. But Mother's dear friend was suddenly dead. The unexpected news shocked everyone, but was particularly devastating to my mother, especially after she heard details of the horrible accident.

The evening before, the feisty octogenarian had gone into the wooded area adjacent to the village, alone, as she always had, to gather dry branches to build the daily fire in her home. She neatly tied the branches she had collected into a bundle to carry on her back, her customary way of transporting kindling back to her house.

But, when Margarita bent over to hoist the branches onto her back, the rope caught her around the neck. Too weak to struggle with the load, and with no one around to help her, the rope choked her: asphyxiation caused Margarita's premature end.

Mother was shaken. She cried inconsolably that morning, praying that God would bring rest to her dear friend's soul. I tried to be especially obedient and helpful, hoping to soothe Mom's sudden grief. But sadness wouldn't go away. Tearfully, she told me that we would attend the memorial service at Margarita's home that night, and we would attend her funeral the next day.

Tradition held that it was unacceptable to mourn someone who might still be alive, as my mother and her sisters resolved to do when Joanna went missing. Tradition also frowned on pre-building coffins. According to old Greek lore, the worst of all omens was to build a coffin in advance of a death. So an immediate order was placed with the village carpenter, Uncle Vasili, to build a casket for Margarita.

During the war, coffins were the mainstay of his carpentry business; he provided them even when he couldn't be reimbursed. Fascinated by my uncle's skill with wood, I often watched him construct his projects. I felt gloomy, though, watching him building *Kyra* Margarita's final resting place.

Vasili began constructing the coffin by putting together slats of lumber to form the bottom of the box; he connected the slats with pieces of wood to build-up the sides. Even in this time of desperate need, Vasili was a master carpenter; he sanded and used his plane along the grain of the wood to smooth its finish.

A casket, by tradition, was hexagonally shaped. Instead of being a simple rectangular box, it slightly flared out at the shoulder requiring six boards of varying lengths instead of four. Work completed, my uncle stuffed hay into the casket, and covered the hay with a clean white bed sheet before delivering the box to the home of the deceased. By tradition, the bereaved provided the sheet.

Older village ladies arrived that morning to help prepare Margarita's body for burial. Her nephews came, too. There were no morticians; families prepared remains for burial. As the women performed their duties, and throughout the evening of the visitation in Margarita's home, they sang *myrologia*: wrenching dirges intoned in her honor. The funeral chants respected traditional folk practices, but were unrelated to Orthodox Christian burial rites.

After washing the deceased, the body, except for the head, was wrapped in a clean white bed sheet. The women clothed Margarita in her best attire, carefully fitting her Sunday-dress over the shroud. Then she was laid atop the white sheet in the casket. If wild flowers were blooming in the fields around Parnion, they were placed in the coffin and decoratively arranged around the body, along with stems of fresh sweet basil and bay leaves. But Margarita died in late autumn and the village ladies and the nephews regretted the lack of flowers. But by now people had gotten used to shortages of everything in Parnion.

I remember viewing Margarita's beloved, distinguished, but motionless old face bathed in yellow candlelight, as she rested in her house—inside the coffin. It was weird to see her still and lifeless.

Village crones, swathed in black from head to toe, sat around her body and took turns chanting heartrending lamentations that brought mourners to tears, wailing, and sobbing. I couldn't completely understand all the words but I sensed they were sad and creepy. Since then, I have learned that some of the words in the *myrologia* were made up as the singers went along, somewhat like modern rap music.

The darkish, spooky atmosphere freaked me out; I shuddered and begged in a whispered, "Isn't it over yet? Let's go, Mama!" But just then, Father Haralambos arrived. I was relieved to see him enter the dimly lit house because his arrival halted the awful wailing.

He wore the *epitrachleion* around his neck and over the front of his black cassock. The vestment, a long narrow, blue stole embroidered with small Greek crosses, signaled he was there to lead us in prayer. The stole is the visible symbol of an Orthodox cleric's priesthood; he wears it only when conducting prayer services. Father had lugged an icon under his arm and carried a smoking censer in hand to perform the Orthodox *Trisagion* service: traditional prayers for the repose of Margarita's good soul in eternity.

Vasili was present to chant responses to the cleric's prayers. I relaxed a little hearing the familiar and comforting baritone chant of our village priest and my uncle's clear tenor voice, as clouds of fragrant, white smoke billowed from the silvery incense burner. Mom had explained that rising incense smoke symbolizes prayers ascending to heaven. But as Margarita's house filled with incense smoke, I noticed the sad, emaciated faces chanting prayers along with the priest.

The service was a comfortable distraction because the living mourners, packed into Margarita' small house to pay their respects that night—looked ghostly to me. Instead of staring at the body in the coffin, my eyes wandered around the room and surveyed the skinny lot of villagers. Dark crescents underscored sullen, cheerless eyes inside emaciated and sallow faces. Clothing, sparse in home wardrobes before the war, now hung on Parnion's citizens, worn, faded, and patched. Darkness mingled with murky candlelight, portraying the good people I personally knew as—eerie.

So, my eyes glued on Father Haralambos and his white beard, tinged yellow in the candle-glow. After prayers, he took a seat next to the icon of Jesus he had placed next to the casket. A woman popped out of the darkness to serve him a demitasse of thick Greek coffee; taking his first sip, he wished Margarita's bereaved nephews, "*Aionia tis i mnimi.*" (May her memory be eternal.) Feeling relief that the ordeal was finally over, I was sorely disappointed when the women started chanting *myrologia* again.

"Please God, make them stop." I prayed, silently.

As an experienced death chanter got into her groove again, she recalled incidents from Margarita's life, and blamed a personification of death for her fatal accident. *Charos* himself, she wailed, had sought out our neighbor during the ill-fated evening and finally found her in the shady woods.

Charos always wins in the end, another elderly woman in black sang, to no one in particular. With only her sallow face showing in the blackness, she chanted that Death had taken Margarita away from our world and into his own after our neighbor had bundled the branches that eventually killed her.

Frightened by the ghostly cadence, I couldn't wait to get out of the spookiness. I wanted no more stories of *Charos's* weird tactics. At that point of the evening, Haralambos rose from his chair, reminded us of the funeral the next morning, and left.

"If it's all right for the priest to leave, why can't we go home?" I whispered in my mother's ear.

She ignored me, but I persisted. Desperately tugging on Mom's sleeve, I begged, "Let's go now."

Twenty long minutes later, Mother finally complied with my anxiety. We respectfully crossed ourselves in front of our dear friend's wooden casket and left her house. Outside, on the dark village street, Mother explained it would have been disrespectful to leave earlier. "After all, *Kyra* Margarita was like a member of our family." Mom had lost a mother figure: a bereavement that evoked more loneliness.

My memories of Margarita's passing also call up recollections of Parnion's elderly and handicapped citizens. Many were senior citizens who had no close family in the village to care for them during the war. While dear Margarita, at eighty-eight, had been capable of gathering and transporting her own firewood, other old folks in the village suffered with immobility.

Many had adult children who lived and worked in Greek cities. Some were parents of adults who had immigrated to America. Prior to the war, those parents regularly received dollars from their American offspring to relieve long-established pre-war poverty. The war stopped mail from abroad and the elderly lost vital financial support; deprivation was severe and it was worsened by terror.

Now that I am a senior citizen, I reflect back to the aged and frail in Parnion who lived alone. Like the rest of us, they felt the pain and heard the growling of their own empty stomachs, but grew less physically capable of caring for themselves. Our friend Margarita had died while collecting the firewood necessary to keep her household functioning; she was physically independent.

What about the others? How did they make it to their outdoor toilets? Mother and I could escape to a goat corral when necessary; many of the elderly could not. Who soothed the old people who lived alone? Surely, kind neighbors and relatives lent assistance, but probably not often enough. My mother consoled me in the war, but who comforted Mother? No one. Her magnanimous soul bore our entire burden.

Too belatedly, my heart goes out to the elderly and chronically ill of WWII: the poor who had barely eked out a living before the war began, and frail citizens who fared the worst. Wealthier citizens, with more land and sturdy hands to work the land, did much better. They counted on rations of wheat, corn, olives, and walnuts, harvested pre-war, for sustenance. Nazis confiscated from them too, but they had successfully hidden enough food in caves and in the woods to survive more easily.

Funerals filled Father Haralambos's ecclesiastical schedule; we attended too many of them. During his funeral homilies, he explained that the church teaches us, the living, to rejoice when our loved ones leave us to enjoy a better life with God in paradise. It was a difficult lesson to absorb with the plethora of Nazi murders and atrocious deaths overtaking us, especially those of children and young people.

One of the hymns in the funeral service encourages rejoicing, but there was no joy among us, no matter what good-intentioned Father Haralambos preached. I had heard the exquisite funeral hymn, integral to the service, so often that it would unpredictably go through my head, like a popular song that one struggles to forget as it mentally plays over and over again. While kids in America were humming Count Basie's "One O'clock Jump," I had a funeral hymn popping in and out of my head.

"*Makaria i odos i porevei simeron...*" (Ever blessed be the way, the way on which you walk this day, for there is prepared for you a place of everlasting rest.)

The hymn would come to mind at unpredictable moments as I walked Bebba to graze, or while I took water at St. Nick's fountain. Then I'd work hard at shaking the words and melody out of my head.

I also recall how wartime deprivation brought mourners into church—shoeless. They walked barefoot in the procession of Margarita's casket to the cemetery as tattered clothing hung on their gaunt bodies. I heard the mourning women's final wails when Father Haralambos blessed and anointed Margarita's body for the last time, sprinkling a handful of dirt into the casket, a symbol of the substance used to create Adam, the very first of God's children.

I'll never forget the jarring, blood-curdling cries that multiplied in the moments before the coffin lid was reverently set in place over our dear Margarita. Before it was sorrowfully lowered into the ground, the casket lid echoed a final, gloomy thud, forever sealing up the body of our energetic, now lifeless, neighbor. That final thump sent chills through my own young, barefoot, and skinny body—also attired in tattered clothes. May beloved *Kyra* Margarita rest in God's eternal peace.

Panagiota—of the Shipping Magnates—got sick during the prolonged outbreak of illness in Parnion during the winter of 1943. Neighbors noticed that it had been almost a week since she had warmed her shoulders in the sun at her usual bench by St. Nick's Church. Mother heated up a cup of Bebba's precious milk and dropped in to visit, but the poor woman needed more than milk.

"It's a pitiable situation. Panagiota has a high fever, but no one knows what's causing it." Mom sadly reported. "Panagiota needs a good doctor and hospitalization. But neither is available in

Parnion." The only help the village had to treat Panagiota's fever was ice, harvested from the mountaintop, packed in hay, and carried to the village on donkey-back.

A few days later, the church's death knell chimed for Panagiota, and we attended her funeral. Neighbors, who had looked after her while she lived, took care of burial preparations. Uncle Vasili donated a coffin. When the subject of informing her well-heeled relatives came up, someone said, "We'll have to wait until the war ends." But another neighbor asked, "Do they care? If they weren't concerned about her in life, why would they care about her death?"

In life, Panagiota hadn't always understood what was going on, but she had whispered a shy *"Euharisto"* (thank you) in appreciation for the goodness of those around her. We missed harmless, shy Panagiota when she was gone. When I walked by "Panagiota's Bench," I always remembered how her bashful smile had taught me the lesson of kindness and consideration for others, especially in a world at war. *Aionia tis i mnimi.* (May her memory be eternal.)

Each family in Parnion owned its own graveyard plot. Land is scarce in Greece: a family plot is used over and over again, to make room for more dead people.

This necessity explains the need in Greece to remove the remains of the deceased three years after the funeral. In that amount of time, the body has usually decomposed and only the bones remain. Villagers considered it a bad omen to dig up a body and find that it had not yet decayed: it meant the deceased must have been a serious sinner.

Under the best or worst of circumstances family members intoned ritual prayers as they cleansed the remains with wine. Skull and bones were then placed in a special metal box and stored in the ossuary: a building constructed at the edge of the village cemetery to respectfully store the human remains of village residents.

I clearly remember the words carved into the outer wall of Parnion's ossuary. The old proverb still looms over the village as a constant reminder to the living of what the future has in store, from the generations of departed whose bones lay within:

"Ekei pou eisai eimouna. Edo pou eimai erhesai."
(Where you are, I have been. Where I am, you are coming.)

In spite of the death and misery surrounding us during miserable 1943, we still had hope that the barbarian hordes from the north would be defeated. I heard an old man express his thoughts on the subject: "Perhaps, our neighbors and loved ones are not dying in vain. Maybe they have died for a cause that will finally bring liberation to the Greek people who—having invented democracy—have spent thousands of years fighting and dying to achieve it."

"When?" I asked myself.

Two, slow resonances, the death knell toll by St. George's bell, became a familiar and too frequent sound. Anxiety sickened my empty stomach when I heard the two determined clangs. "Is it someone we know?" I'd ask my mother. Then, worse yet, I'd ask myself, "Who will be next?" Ninety percent of Parnion's women wore black, not for style, but for mourning.

We lived with danger even when Nazis were not directly threatening us; Hitler's soldiers capably brought on inadvertent demise. One unintentional disaster followed the Nazi theft, slaughter, and butchering of a goat. Soldiers stored fresh goat meat in the frigid, clean waters of the village reservoir—to chill it. After they filled their stomachs, the soldiers forgot about the leftover raw meat they had left behind in the reservoir. When the abandoned meat began to decay, it contaminated the water.

Villagers who drew water from the reservoir got terribly sick. Already weakened children drank the contaminated water and died. One victim was a boy from Athens who had been sent to Parnion to live with his grandparents. His loving mom and dad intended to save their adored child from Athens's ravaging famine. Instead they tragically lost him in death to contaminated water in a village that took pride in its fresh, clean, and abundant water supply.

Typhus also became a major problem. Typhus, a bacterial disease spread by ticks, fleas, and lice, was prevalent during the war in villages, like Parnion, where hygiene was poor and temperatures were cold. The distressing symptoms included extremely high fever, nausea, a hacking cough, and frightening rash.

Villagers feared the disease because they had no medicine to treat it. (Now antibiotics can be administered.) Typhus broke out all over the village, and many children died as a result, compounded by malnutrition. Lower and warmer elevations in Greece suffered with wartime malaria, but Parnion's scourge was typhus.

One morning, I watched two village men loading bales of hay onto a donkey and heading into the higher mountains. Curious, I asked Mother about them. "They're climbing to the top of Mt. Parnon," she said, "to chop ice, up at snow level. They'll cool down the high fevers of their sick children with it. And hopefully save their lives."

"Won't ice melt?"

"Hay acts as insulation." Mom explained. "It keeps the ice frozen until they return home." Prior to the development of aspirin, acetaminophen, and antibiotics, the old time remedy to alleviate high fevers was to bring down feverish patients' temperatures in icy, cold baths.

With only one doctor in Parnion—who had no medicine—not even quinine pills, there wasn't much that could be done for the sick. When our loved ones became ill, we harbored the mortal dread that they would die, accompanied by fear for our own mortality.

The specter of *Charos*, the villagers' personification of death, invisibly harangued us. Some famine victims were transported to their native villages to be buried in long-established family plots, because there was no money to bury them in city cemeteries. I remember the frightful sight of a shrouded corpse being transported to the village on the back of a donkey. The deceased was a villager who had moved away from Parnion, before the war, to work in Sparta.

Our family endured many hardships during the war, but we never came down with typhus. Even as we starved, we incredibly stayed relatively free of disease. I surmise that Mother's determined "clean hands" hygiene policy, along with Bebba's milk, and wild leafy greens (containing myriad vitamins and minerals) that we scratched out of the ground, helped. Walnuts with their healthy oils and filling protein played their part in our survival, too.

Deaths mounted in Parnion. Dozens of funerals took place, yet fewer memorial services were held; most households lacked the wheat necessary to make *kolyva* for the *mnemosino*. The priest depended on donations for church rituals: olive oil, wine, whole-wheat berries, and bread were donated for use in blessings and sacraments.

It was understood that the leftover-surplus was intended for the priest's family: part of his meager salary. Father Haralambos needed a minimum amount of bread for consecration and to bless for distribution after the Liturgy as *antidoron* (literally translated as "instead of the gift"). Bread for the sacrament of Communion was the one constant; Haralambos had it available until the war ended.

I eventually became an altar boy, assisting the priest during the Liturgy. It was an honor that brought relief to my mother who knew Haralambos would share leftover *antidoron* with me, after services, before he took home the sparse, surplus bread for his family.

I have a memory of devouring my pieces of blessed bread while sitting down at an old church table. Weak from accumulated hunger and not knowing if I would ever see another piece of bread again, I felt no embarrassment about sticking out my tongue to lick up and finish every infinitesimal crumb off a rough tabletop that generously meted out painful wood slivers.

Services for the dead were commemorated so often while I was an altar boy that I learned the prayers by heart. I still remember, *"... to the soul of Thy servant who hath fallen asleep, O Lord, give rest in a place of light, in a place of green pasture, in a place of refreshment whence pain and sorrow and sighing have fled away..."*

25 | HANGING ON—1943

By autumn of 1943, we had been living hand to mouth for two-and-a-half years and it seemed as though war was a horribly permanent condition. One morning, Mom announced that the two of us were going to hike to an abandoned olive grove that Grandpa had owned in the village boondocks.

"If we cultivate Grandpa's old olive trees, Johnny," she said, "then at least we'll have olives to eat and precious olive oil. We'll survive on olives and use them for barter." When I asked Uncle Vasili why the grove had been abandoned, he replied, "That decision must have been made before I married your aunt and I really don't know why."

Lugging a shovel and a hoe with us for four miles, Mother and I dragged our weakened, hungry selves to the small grove: fifteen scarcely subsisting olive trees. Dead, brittle branches outnumbered the few limbs, which had survived in a state of shriveled existence. Sick, mostly dry, grayish-green leaves hinted that life might stubbornly be hanging on somewhere inside elderly, woody plants.

The trees looked dead to me, but Mom knew that olive trees are noted for their longevity. The grove had not been cared for in decades and was overrun with grasses, weeds, and shrubs. Mom understood her father's grove begged for intensive care to survive. "The only way to start our job here, Johnny, is—to start," she sighed. "I think the reason this grove was ignored is that no one was desperate enough to do all this work. It was easier to let it go."

Working for a month, everyday but Sunday, my muscles throbbed. With no work gloves, stinging blisters formed on my fingers; when blisters broke and split wide-open, a yucky fluid oozed out of them. Tingling with pain, my eleven-year-old hands cramped with soreness. Surely my mother ached more than I did, but she never complained.

Exposed to the unrelenting Greek mid-day sun, we strained and perspired while we pulled clusters of superfluous roots and immovable rocks out of the merciless ground. Sweat poured down our foreheads and seared our eyes. When I complained, Mom tied a white handkerchief around my head to soak up running perspiration; I was a kid farmer/pirate.

We broke our backs in our effort to penetrate the marble-hard ground. Knocking clumps of petrified earth to smithereens with hoe and shovel, we freed precious soil from decades of vegetation and mineral aggregate, which had prevented the trees from thriving. For four weeks, we broke up clumps of obstinate dirt mixed with more weeds and more rocks, both appearing to multiply before us like a relentless skin rash. Then our emaciated week bodies struggled to clear them away.

For days and days, we pulled out uncountable grasses and tossed them onto a mounting pile of discarded greenery. We finally pulverized the dirt into the unbreakable ground by pounding, pounding, and pounding obstinate, stony clumps, while sweating lakes of perspiration and enduring unbearable muscle pain.

Mother said we had to make sure we cultivated the soil all the way out to the drip line, the edge of the outside branches, for each one of the fifteen trees—otherwise our labors would be for naught. When our month of working was finally over, she announced we weren't finished yet.

"We still have to prune out the dead branches on each tree. After that we need to trim and clip living limbs to stimulate new growth. We'll borrow Vasili's giant clippers before we come back tomorrow."

I was a helper; Mother, using village-born expertise, did most of the crushing labor. It took us a never-ending thirty days of excavating the earth around the sick grove, but we finally cleared it and beautifully transformed rocky, root-bound dirt into fertile, hospitable loam. Proud of our efforts, Mother stood back to admire our accomplishment.

"We have created a work of natural art, Johnny. Grandpa would be proud." Then she related a proverb to me. "The old Greeks of Grandpa's generation used to say, 'when you plant an olive tree, you plant it for your grandchildren.'

"Several generations of patience and hard work are necessary to finally see fruit on olive trees, John. And you and I will have to wait until next autumn to pick olives. Eating comes later."

Mom was taking the long view. If the trees produced ripe fruit the following fall, we couldn't just grab olives off the tree and eat them like cherries. Raw olives are bitter. If they ripened, we'd have to shake them off the trees, collect every single olive, and lug our harvest back to Grandpa's house to process and cure, before we could eat them: an additional six to eight weeks.

"Next fall?" I said, aghast, as Mother explained the process. "And then another six weeks? I'm hungry right now, Mama."

"*To kalo argei na erthei, to kako erhete amesos*," Mother said. (Good things take their time in coming, but bad things happen immediately.) "Isn't that the truth?" I remarked, hoisting the shovel, and tramping back down the road toward home, behind her. I had already waited too long for the war to end.

Cultivating that orchard with my mother, when I was a hungry kid in the middle of the war, contributed to one of the unique lessons I learned during the long German occupation and accompanying famine: grueling agricultural labor does not produce immediate results, the way popping corn does. Instant gratification does not follow backbreaking labor.

Rainfall in that part of the world comes in late fall and winter. So after we worked the orchard, we had to sit back and wait, hoping for adequate rain to stimulate the newly cultivated trees. Would we find blossoms on the trees in spring? Were we the ones, among Grandpa's progeny, who would finally eat olives from his grove? I hoped so because I was so very hungry.

It took a world war and ensuing starvation to shine attention and significance on a deserted olive grove that Grandpa, or perhaps his father, had planted in the ground.

While we waited out the cold winter of 1943-1944, hoping for rain, the Germans installed a mounted machine gun on the main road leading into Parnion, at the village "doorway." On the first day of setting up the reviled weapon, an old woman, who lived at the entrance of the village, walked from her courtyard out into the street, unaware that a new weapon had been positioned near her house.

Perhaps she heard soldiers milling around and went outside to check on strange noises, but her neighbors observed that when she spotted the Nazi with his ominous, steel machine gun mounted on its pedestal out in the middle of the road, the old woman panicked and ran back toward her house.

Traumatized neighbors tragically witnessed a startling spray of machine gun bullets brutally cut down and murder the old woman before she reached her door. The bloody atrocity created more sleepless nights and more unmitigated fear. As a result, the senseless killing of another innocent old woman instigated deeper hatred of the Germans.

The trigger-happy Nazi gunner went on to spray intermittent barrages toward trees, hillsides, and the upper reaches of the village—toward anything that moved—whenever the spirit moved him. The first few times we heard the sudden release of bullets, many of us dropped everything and silently scattered away from the village to our usual hiding places; Mom and I ran to the smelly goat corral again.

***

And as we didn't even know about all the events going on in the village during the war, we surely couldn't fathom what was happening in the United States. However, in 1943, a secret mission had begun its training program stateside, in Colorado. The military assignment, known as "Co. 2671 Special Reconnaissance Battalion," was primarily composed of U.S. Army, undercover Greek-American commandos—soldiers who were going to be dropped behind enemy lines in Greece from April to November of 1944.

Volunteers for this mission had to be in top physical and mental condition and able to speak Greek fluently. A predicted casualty rate for the group was astronomical: 90-95%. One hundred sixty men made up the final company, which was divided into autonomous groups. They were parachuted behind German lines in Greece to operate in the area of Epirus, various sections of Macedonia, Roumeli, Thessaly, and Northern Peloponnesos.

Their task was to weaken the German offensive in Greece and to pin the Germans down in Greece to prevent them from joining their fellow Nazi soldiers in Western Europe at a time when the Allied invasion of Europe was taking place—the invasion of France at Normandy, in June of 1944.

The U.S. Army commandos, working in cooperation with Greek guerrillas, destroyed German-run locomotives and thousands of miles of railroad lines to impede Nazi transportation inside Greece; they blew up bridges and German convoys. When Nazis realized that clandestine Americans were fighting them in Greece, they instructed that captured Americans were to be shot on the spot.

German soldiers, who surrendered to the Americans in Greece during these 1944 events, were turned over to guerrillas. The U.S. government's official record estimated 1,794 Germans were killed and wounded; 105 Germans were taken as prisoners. In spite of the predicted high casualty rate, only thirteen Greek-Americans were injured.

This account is not fiction, but only came to light in the 1980s when the CIA declassified these files. Had these courageous men of the 122nd Infantry Battalion dared to break the CIA's stringent rules to share their wartime successes, they would have been disciplined. They were required to keep secret that as American soldiers they fought Nazis in Greece, the land of their forebears, by working in tandem with the Greek resistance.

Because the mission was undercover and covert, if they had leaked participation of their dangerous assignment, they not only would have gotten into trouble with the American government, they also would have been suspected by friends, family, and the general public of inventing preposterous stories.

Along with the rest of the world, Mom and I didn't know that fellow Greek-American "boys," trained by the U.S. Army and sent by the OSS to Greece in 1944, were fighting to end the hell we were stuck in. Some of these valiant warriors fought less than 100 miles away from Parnion.

***

The Germans were well on their way to losing the war in 1944, but we didn't know it. We were actually seeing more Nazi soldiers in 1944 than at the beginning of the occupation. In fact, Germans began spending more time in the village when they came to wipe out guerrillas. They passed a whole week at Grandpa's house on one very long, miserable incursion.

And when I wondered to Mom about why I hadn't seen my cousin Demetri during a fortnight of continuing German presence (soldiers weren't spending the nights at our house), I learned from Mother, who had received an update from Stella, that the Germans had set up camp at Anastasia and Paul's house. Demetri was staying close to home because the Nazis were based there. When the military finally left town, my cousin shared his hellish two weeks with me.

"My father never came home," Demetri reported. "He stayed hidden near the mill the whole time, while Mother and I stayed close to our house. We spent nights in our smallest room, hungry, while Nazis barbequed stolen lambs out on our terrace. They pilfered the lambs from some village that they had terrorized before coming to Parnion.

"But, before the Germans left our house," Demetri whispered confidentially, "one soldier offered me a few sweet, spicy cookies and hard candy wrapped in colorful paper."

Assuming that my cousin had refused because the goodies might be loaded with poison, I hesitated to say, "Of course, you didn't take them... "

"Of course I did!" he replied. "I'm hungry! They melted in my mouth—and I didn't die. I'm still hungry, though. And I didn't tell my mother that I took the goodies. She would have freaked out.

"The Nazis have big maps, John. So huge... that they had to spread them on the floor to look at them," he continued. "I watched from a distance while they huddled over their maps. They were studying a road. On paper, the route must have appeared to extend past Parnion's cemetery. So, pleased with themselves, two Nazis ran outside, jumped on their motorcycles, and 'vroomed' away, satisfied that they had found new access to guerrilla territory. But Mother and I knew they'd be back.

"Sure enough, within a few minutes, the motorcycles 'vroomed' right back into our courtyard," Demetri reported with satisfaction. "Everyone in the village knows you can't go past the cemetery. There is no road past the cemetery—it's a dead end. Their fancy maps aren't as good as they think they are."

Demetri laughed about faulty Germans maps, and I laughed too. Returning home, I fantasized about spicy cookies and candy melting in my mouth. Then, I felt my stomach growl.

Persistent hunger motivates serious thinking about acquiring food. During the first year of Nazi occupation, when Mom had allowed fruit on the trees in the *pervoli* to ripen, as one would normally do, she found she had nothing to harvest. Like locusts, hungry soldiers had raided our trees.

Having learned her lesson, during the following seasons Mother picked fruit while it was still green and sour. Then she cooked apples, cherries, pears, and figs in a kind of meatless stew, as if they were vegetables. And previous Nazi food thefts did not discourage Mother from planting another garden. She sowed winter squash and wheat in the field where the potatoes had thrived.

I continued ensuring that our personal and essential link to nourishment, Bebba, was hidden from soldiers. Our little goat was far too precious to wind up in a Nazi barbecue. When it looked like Germans were going to stay overnight, I removed Bebba's bell and snuck her into the ravine, near the Oinountas River. Tethered, she could nibble vegetation and drink water. Tied down, I felt sure she'd stay put while German soldiers occupied our house.

Sometimes, I hid Bebba in the nearby woods, beyond the edge of town, a place Germans avoided because they feared furtive guerrilla attacks. When I showed up to retrieve her, Bebba greeted me by wagging her little tail like a happy puppy.

A message from the International Red Cross finally arrived in the village in late 1943 or early 1944. Through global appeals and much negotiation, the Red Cross had finally received permission from the Germans to deliver medicine to village doctors in Greece, in the form of quinine pills. There was a notion among villagers that quinine was good for everything that ailed us; research in later years proved differently.

As if we weren't scared enough—Mom got sick.

News that our local doctor had received Red Cross medication arrived the day after Mother came down with a high fever and severe headache, her first illness of the occupation. Her infirmity, whatever it was, scared me. Aunts Sophia and Stella were anxious too. After witnessing so many deaths, we couldn't help but think the worst about illness in the family.

My aunts, who said Mother did not appear to have typhus symptoms, worked at easing her discomfort with cold compresses and what seemed like gallons of chamomile tea. Tiny white, chamomile flowers grew wild in the village; we had plenty of tea. And Parnion, of course, was famous for its plentiful water. When Mother heard that gratis Red Cross medicine had arrived in town, she sent me to the village doctor to ask him for a few quinine pills, hoping they would speed her recovery.

Shivering under several heavy blankets that my aunts had stacked over her in bed, she whispered, "Johnny, there's no money to pay the doctor. They say that Red Cross medicine is free. If he asks for payment for his services, say nothing. I'm too sick to think about it now."

"Terrified" doesn't come close to the anxiety that overwhelmed me. I had never seen this kind of weakness in her before. Mother asking for medicine was the worst of all omens. After all she had been through, she never complained about not feeling well and never was she not well enough—to think.

"How sick is she?" I asked myself, more afraid of her illness than I was of the crazy gunner behind the machine gun, down the road.

I immediately took off for the doctor's house. Parnion's doctor lived with his mother, a well-respected, elderly woman who I now realize probably suffered with Parkinson's disease. Shaking uncontrollably, she was a permanent daytime fixture out on their balcony in good weather. A kid like me didn't know anything about Parkinson's. For me, the elderly woman in black was a fearsome sight; I was afraid of standing too close to her. She smiled and kindly welcomed me as I waited to go inside. But insensitive, ignorant me merely nodded. I managed to flash a fast grin at her, but kept as far away as possible.

"Next!" the doctor called from inside his house/office. When he turned and saw me, he said, "Oh, the American kid!" A little embarrassed by his remark, I took a deep breath and explained my mother's symptoms; then I pleaded for medication. Surely he noticed the frightened "*Americanaki*" had arrived empty-handed. But, as Mother advised, I said nothing more.

The doctor's response was abrupt: "I don't have any more pills. Red Cross did not provide enough."

The short, pudgy, gray-haired physician, who stared frostily at me through thick glasses, dispensed no medical advice, showed no compassion, and gave no counsel. Cold as the snows up on Mt. Parnon, he dismissed me without uttering another word. I was more distressed about Mother's condition when I left the doctor than when I had arrived.

"Maybe her sickness is fatal," I thought to myself as I grappled with the unthinkable. The doctor's silence and aloofness unnerved me. I recalled Margarita, Panagiota, and all the people who had died around me since war and its cohort, disease, invaded the village with the Nazis.

"Please God, please, please, please don't let my mother die," I prayed. "She's too good—in every way. You know her, God. You know my mama. Help her get better. Please make her live!"

Caught up in entreating God for my mother's survival, I started away from the doctor's house, dejected and crying. At the same time, my empty stomach began churning; nausea was setting in again. I felt sick. But then I spotted a boy I had shared a desk with at school in the early days of the war. He too was arriving to see the doctor.

Embarrassed to have him see my tears, I quickly wiped my eyes with my sleeve. He said nothing; he only nodded his head to indicate recognition. The kid, who carried a small bag, looked as distracted and worried as I was. We didn't exchange words. And I decided to wait for my contemporary. When the kid emerged from the doctor's house without the bag, I greeted him and asked, "Did you get any medicine?"

He showed me four pills the doctor had wrapped up in one of the white pieces of paper from the Allied airdrop. "The doctor says they're quinine tablets," he explained. His eyes filled with tears when he added, "They're for my mother. She's so sick, I'm afraid she's going to die." When I asked about her symptoms, he described the same signs we had seen in Mom.

"There's no charge for quinine pills," I commented, wondering about the bag the boy no longer carried. He replied, "We heard that too, but my mother sent a bag of beans to the doctor, just in case, and he kept them." Before we parted, the kid shared some medical insight with me that I greatly appreciated since both our mothers shared the same symptoms. He said, "The doctor says my mother should be better in a few days."

Stella, Sophia, and I watched Mom's condition improve after a week of my aunts' vigilant and loving attention to her unknown illness. Without a doctor's care, quinine, or Red Cross intervention, my mother was well again.

Yet on the day I visited the doctor on Mother's behalf, I learned an important lesson from the other kid's bag of beans: there are rules for the "haves" and different rules for the "have nots." In war, as in peace, some people (like Parnion's doctor) break rules to benefit themselves. So much for health care in Parnion.

Bartering, as the kid had done for quinine, was commonplace in Greek villages of that era; it was an accepted method of acquiring services and necessities. We had nothing to barter, so I had no personal experience with exchanging goods until one evening in the winter of wretched 1943 when I fortuitously and unexpectedly came upon a large sack.

The Nazis had been in the village all day. When they finally pulled out of town, we exhaled our typical great sigh of relief that the "barbarians" were gone and we went about our daily activities. I went outside to the street and spotted a sack filled with "something" that German soldiers had thrown into a patch of prickly weeds on the street side of Grandpa's courtyard. Foreign letters printed on the bag formed German words; I couldn't read them.

"Should I touch it?" I asked myself as I eyeballed the mystery sack. Mentally reviewing my mother's warnings about keeping my distance from unknown entities in wartime, I dared lay my index finger on the sack in defiance of maternal orders. Nothing happened.

I studied the sack for a while. Then I concluded, "I can't just leave it outside for someone else to take. Maybe it's something

Mama can use." Ignoring her admonitions, I dragged it safely into the courtyard.

"Haven't I warned you about strange stuff that comes from Germans?" Mother shouted in a frantic voice. "What good are my warnings if you don't pay attention to them, Johnny? This could be a bomb!"

"It's just a sack of something. See, I didn't blow up. Maybe you can use it," I replied. Waving me out of the way, she turned it over, kicked it, and using her finger, she carefully poked a small hole into one end of the bag; a white granular substance began pouring out.

"If I die, Johnny, you'll know it's from what I'm going to do right now." Before I could stop her, she put her finger on the white stuff and gently transferred the substance to her tongue.

"What are you doing, Mama?" I screamed. "You don't want me to touch it but you go right ahead and stick it in your mouth?? Maybe it's poison!"

"It's salt!" she declared, smiling. Mother was thrilled with my curious discovery, even though I had broken her rule. She took a few minutes to study the sack and the salt pouring out of it. And in no time, she came up with a plan. "That's more salt than we can use, John. What we need is olive oil and wheat—and I know how we're going to get it. Tomorrow, we're going to visit a shepherd."

I didn't connect olive oil or wheat with sheep herding. But what did I know? She knew shepherds require salt, which had become very scarce, to make cheese from sheep's milk. She also knew that the shepherd would be willing to make a deal with her for the salt.

The next day, I witnessed my mother skillfully trade salt for precious olive oil and a small bag of wheat that villagers with olive trees and wheat had previously traded for the shepherd's cheese. Through Mother's skillful bartering, he threw some *mizithra* cheese and yogurt into the deal.

During the most wretched year of the war for us, the abandoned sack of German salt probably saved us from the final stages of starvation.

26 | THE CURFEW

Our occupiers declared a curfew in the village. Their collaborator posted a scribbled notice, in Greek, at the top of the lion fountain in Parnion's main square. The sign proclaimed the limited hours villagers were allowed to be outside their homes. Only the German army was permitted out on the streets past 5 P.M., even though the sun would continue to light up village nooks and crannies for another hour.

The Nazis who declared the curfew wore watches and knew the exact time, probably to a millisecond. But, clocks and watches were extremely rare in Parnion. Villagers told time by the church bell on Sunday morning or the shadow the sun cast on the ravine. The shadow was in a different location in winter than in spring, summer, or fall: it gave approximations, not exact minutes. Whoever read the posted curfew sign or heard about the clampdown law was informed and obeyed. Many in the village were completely unaware of it.

Before she left Parnion with Uncle George's family, my sister Nikki had built up the courage to climb the fig tree in the *perivoli* to watch Germans when they arrived in town; after spotting them, she'd run into the house for safety. I had my own special spot for surveillance: an elevated place in the side yard of Grandpa's house. There, I believed, I could spy undetected on Nazi activities in our neighborhood. Lying flat on my stomach, I clandestinely observed Germans come and go. Ten or eleven year old me was sure he was putting something over on the Nazis because they didn't know a "mole" was studying their movements.

I boldly assumed they were oblivious to being watched. But, were they?

One afternoon, during my "undercover work," I watched a soldier snatch a hidden, baby goat from a neighboring courtyard. The kid's helpless bleating in the rough hands of the German made me uneasy. It quadrupled my resolve to keep Bebba safe.

From previous spying, I knew the snatcher/soldier would slay the animal. Then he would hang its lifeless body from a tree and, with a super sharp German knife, slash his victim's underside from throat to tail. After that he would pull out and toss away its internal organs. The skinned goat was usually left hanging until the blood drained out. A soldier always returned to butcher the animal and prepare it for cooking. Previous observations indicated that the Germans threw away the innards.

Disturbed by the small goat's bleating call for help, I knew there was nothing I could do to save the kid, and still stay alive myself. But, at the same time, I was starving. I couldn't remember the last time I had consumed a mini-morsel of meat. Watching the soldier butcher the goat, I decided to salvage the innards. As man of the house, I would "bring home the bacon" and deliver the goat's liver, heart, stomach, and intestines for Mother to cook. My mouth began watering in anticipation of eating goat's liver fried to a crisp in olive oil, with a dash of oregano.

I slipped down from my secret vantage point to spring into action. I stealthily crept down the road toward the place, near home, where the animal had been killed, all the while dreaming about eating something flavorful, something I could really chew with gusto: a change from our usual diet of boiled greens washed down with Bebba's milk.

Hidden from view, I loitered in the area where the goat hung. I lingered there for a long time. But no soldiers came to take the carcass away. Bolder and bolder, I inched myself closer and closer to my prize: shiny red entrails. Meanwhile, my deprived, aching stomach had brought on nausea. When I decided I could wait no longer, I attacked.

Lunging at my new fortune of fresh viscera, I grabbed the liver and all the guts I could carry. Leaky, sticky entrails squished between my fingers, and I stretched my hands out to the sides of my skinny body to keep my ragged clothes from getting soiled. A real mess, I started running home; slimy intestines dribbled blood all over the road and splashed on to my bare feet.

And just then, a powerful thrust, like the end of a broom handle, shot deeply and painfully into my ribs. "Aagh!!" I gasped. Unable to breathe, I caught my skinny self from falling over. Straining to take a breath, I spun around to see what had stabbed me.

My eyes found themselves centimeters away from the barrel of an immense, silvery German gun—pointing directly at my forehead. My face had turned into a grayish, wool Nazi uniform, smelling of cigarette smoke and body odor; it was studded with shiny military buttons. I slowly glanced upward. A monstrous, iron-faced soldier glared down at me. The helmeted, armed grizzly bear in full uniform was not smiling. With my eyelashes scant inches away from the weapon in my face, my empty stomach nose-dived. I was sure it had dropped onto the road.

"He's going to shoot me. I'm going to die—right now!" I was sure of it. Barking German words at me that I could not understand, the dour Nazi finally turned his gun away from my head; my body shuddered with instantaneous relief. But, to my regret, he started waving the cold, steel, Nazi firearm in front of my face again. Then he used it to point to his fancy wristwatch. He continued his barrage of German and flung his arm westward, with gun firmly in hand, to make me look at the setting sun.

I was always a shy kid who didn't say much, especially to people I didn't know. I instinctively knew this was not the time to be chatty—especially with a ferocious Nazi soldier waving a revolver in my face. Petrified and confused, I desperately yearned to spare my short life and clarify my motives for acquiring Nazi butchered, goat entrails. I longed to say, "But you guys don't eat the guts." Worse yet, I couldn't speak German.

I ached to defend my crime. But we had no common language to communicate. So I kept my thoughts to myself. "I'm taking the goat's guts... that they were going to leave on the ground to rot and stink up the neighborhood. Is he going to kill me because I took the guts? Or does my crime have something to do with his watch?"

Whichever it was, I knew innocence didn't make a difference during occupation. Blameless people, I knew personally, died when Germans and their collaborators started showing up.

Later, I understood he was referring to the curfew. At the time, I didn't know what a curfew was, let alone that there was one. I didn't know what crime I had committed, aside from taking goat innards. With the end of my life so imminent, Mom came to mind—and I felt worse.

What would Mama's grief be like when my dead, bullet-ridden body was carried into Grandpa's courtyard? At once, I recalled the mother of the two innocent boys murdered in retaliation for guerrilla activity. They were carried home—dead—on makeshift stretchers.

Somewhere in my head I saw my mother screaming and fainting with grief in Grandpa's doorway. The grisly picture pained me. She had gone through too much already without having to attend my funeral and bury me in Parnion.

"I can't run away because he'll shoot me for escaping. And I can't explain why I took the guts because he doesn't understand Greek. There's nothing I can do to stay alive right now," I silently announced to myself.

Tears ran down my face when I looked up at the German again. Employing wholly unpredictable movements with his daunting weapon, he grabbed me by the shoulders. Then he forced me around and made me stand with my back to him. He jabbed me, again, with his gun. I tensed my shoulders, clenched my teary eyelids, held my breath, and waited to blow up in a bloody explosion. Swallowing hard, I was still not breathing when I felt another sharp thrust to my ribs.

"No blast yet. I'm still whole. But, here it comes!" I told myself, as I drew my limbs together and cringed. Would I hear the gun going off when I exploded? Or would I be dead—and deaf to sound? Nothing happened.

Laughing contemptuously, the Nazi grizzly bear removed the gun from my back and waved it in front of my nose. "What's so funny? Does he want me to leave?"

I didn't want to run away without his permission because he might shoot me for fleeing. What was I supposed to do? I dared to glance up at him again. For a second time he made motions with his gun that communicated, "Go!"

Boldly staring into stern German eyes, I needed to make sure I correctly understood his message. Again he waved his silvery revolver in front of my nose and motioned for me to continue on my way. So I took off, speeding away faster than I ever had run in my life. I never looked back.

Nearing home, I heard Artemis's distressed voice calling out to me; she had watched my interaction with the German from her open window. "Get yourself home as quickly as possible, Johnny! It is forbidden for you to be out on the street at this hour."

When I finally got inside Grandpa's courtyard, breathless and shaking, I looked down at my bloody, trembling hands. My fingers were still clasped around the slippery goat's liver.

Those terrifying childhood experiences in Parnion come back to me when I watch dramas about the Second World War on TV or at the movies. Portrayed by handsome, dynamic, robust heroes, and co-starring beautiful, well-dressed, healthy-looking women, some accounts offend me. They are completely implausible to those of us who lived through real war. Life-threatening pyrotechnics are not thrilling when you actually hear their gut-wrenching blasts; they are never accompanied by musical sound tracks.

In Parnion and environs, Nazis were shooting real bullets that ended precious life—forever. Because I lived through it, I could never again see war as something funny or amusing. You wish you could be Superman or the Phantom, but in the face of great military power, the little guy rarely gets to be the hero. You did what you were told to do by ruthless Nazis—with no exception. Otherwise, you could be eradicated. They were masters at eradicating.

Even now, almost seventy years later, I stiffen with dread when someone unexpectedly pats me on the back.

27 | NO SMARTPHONE OR CENTRAL HEATING: A WINTER'S TALE

In my WWII experience, cracking and cleaning a walnut was entertainment. I had no basis for comparison to feel deprived. My childhood was jammed with unique but tragic experiences that I, along with millions of other kids, gratefully survived. I sorrowfully acknowledge that many children died. My recollections are not complaints; I never felt deprived. Hungry? Yes. Deprived? Never.

Mom carried on the best she could, except for spurts of anger aimed at Dad, who was so very far away. She silently endured the unending fears that plagued her, the sleepless nights, her own empty stomach, and the daily, backbreaking efforts to grow something for us to eat. Mom cried resentful, anxious tears alone, away from my presence.

Gratefully, neighbors and relatives had been generous in sharing seeds with us. Burpee's famous American seed catalogue was unknown in Parnion. Seeds for the next season were collected from plants left to mature and dry at summer's end; villagers saved more than needed.

Donated seeds, which Mother had planted, grew into cabbages under the protection of wild shrubs at the edge of our looted potato garden. She stretched cooked cabbage leaves out over multiple mealtimes for our sustenance during the winter of 1943.

Gardening had actually become a pleasant diversion for me. But, winters were harsh: too cold for fruits and vegetables to grow. We spent most winter days indoors except for the glorious ones, when clouds cleared and sunshine warmed our chills.

I watched the outside world from the balcony and second-story window. The old olive tree, between Grandpa's house and St. Nick's, did not lose its leaves in winter, but drooped when exquisite snow weighed it down. Mom observed, "She resembles a bride on her wedding day."

I reminisce as I sit in my office crammed with books, recalling that in winter there wasn't a copy of one single book to read over and over again so its spine could fall apart and its pages erode in tatters. Instead, I watched over Bebba and scrounged up dry leaves for her to eat; finding them in winter was almost impossible; the search led to finger-numbing cold. Mother made sure we built up a supply of goat fodder in autumn when dry leaves and grasses were plentiful; we stored silage in the lower front room of the house. On the coldest days and nights Bebba stayed indoors too, in the lower back room.

My memory still summons up Bebba on a winter day, cuddled into the deep windowsill, chewing her cud. Mother spared a thick piece of old cloth (everything we owned was old) for our goat to recline on for added comfort. The niche fit Bebba perfectly. She enjoyed basking in the window's warm sunshine, and she contentedly chewed her cud while observing the world outdoors. My little goat had no wartime worries. She ate less in winter, perhaps because she was not as active; Bebba preferred mulberry leaves to cornhusks and dry grasses. Goats have a more discerning palate than they are given credit for.

Winter brought rain to Parnion; sometimes it was cold enough for rain to turn to snow and hailstones. They drifted down from darkened skies on everything in sight: hailstones stung, but snow was fun.

We kids ran outside to catch snowflakes on our tongues and throw snowballs. But skinny, starving young bodies chilled to the bone, especially when we were barefoot and threadbare. Of course, we were hungrier in winter. Dandelion greens did not grow, wild or cultivated. Mother's homegrown cabbage leaves aided our survival.

Central heating was unknown: there were no radiators or portable electric heaters. Our only source for warmth was the fireplace in the living room. For at least a century, it had kept previous generations of Grandpa's family fairly cozy, and provided a place to cook family meals. Mom and I moved our beds to the room with the fireplace in winter; it was the warmest place in the house.

Most occasions for togetherness with local relatives took place during those frigid days. We gathered near Grandpa's fireplace, all of us wearing multiple layers of clothes to retain body heat. Mother wore her heavy, black wool "Chicago coat" like a uniform, donning it inside and outside the house: it was several sizes too big for her now. As nightfall came early, we procured light from the hearth and the one and only oil lamp. I remember leaning in toward Grandpa's blazing fireside to absorb heat, but while warming my face and chest, it left my backside chilled.

In a world without books, radio, movies, and the like, our elders told us stories, both ancient and modern, to amuse us. Vasili specialized in ancient Greek mythology, as well as Aesop's fables. His favorite was the one about the grasshopper and the ant, explaining that while the grasshopper lounged around and sang during summer, the ant worked hard at storing up ears of corn for winter. "The grasshopper," Vasili continued, "told the ant to relax, take it easy, and sing-along with him because plenty of summer-time food was available. But the ant continued working. Yet during the following winter, when the grasshopper was dying of hunger, the ant had corn to eat." Vasili ended with a simple moral: "Planning ahead for winter is vital, for insects and humans alike."

Vasili also told riveting accounts of being a soldier and prisoner of war during the Greek war with Turkey in 1921. He tearfully recalled his soldier buddies from Parnion who were imprisoned in Asia Minor by the Turks, and reported that they were never heard from again. Aunt Stella told tearful stories too, about her husband going off to America and never coming back. Aunt Joanna usually came up in the conversation: Vasili kept insisting that Joanna would be found. I began to wonder if he believed it himself.

As for Mom, she entertained us with the story of Katherine, her patron saint, a brilliant young woman who lived 300 years after Christ. Denying ancient gods, Katherine was arrested and tried for being a Christian. Mother had read that after Katherine's convincing trial oratory, fifty philosophers converted to Christianity. The bad guys still put her to death; being Christian was against the law in those days.

Mother also took pleasure in recalling glorious American holidays—Thanksgiving (a holiday completely unknown to our Greek family), Christmas, and Easter. She described luscious holiday foods that made my mouth water: Thanksgiving's roasted turkey with chestnut dressing and American sweet potatoes; roast beef and delectable Christmas sweets; succulent Easter lamb, savory potatoes, and buttery *koulourakia* cookies. These dinner "stories" didn't have a plot, but I was riveted to them because I was hungry. The foods she spoke of were strange and exotic to me, but even though they were absent and unavailable, I loved hearing about them.

The treats I hankered for were local. I dreamed of filling my stomach with dried figs, sweet *petimezi* (a thick syrup made of unfermented grape juice), walnuts, almonds, and raisins. Crispy fresh bread just out of the oven, honey, roasted chestnuts, and sweet fruit preserves made of apricots and sour cherries extended my list. They were the food delicacies of my young years in Parnion. I didn't know anything about this mysterious pumpkin pie Mother described. I had never heard of a Hershey Bar.

Cousin Mary's college graduation photo, hanging on the wall of Grandpa's house, brought memories of our loved ones in Chicago. Sitting around the fireplace in abject poverty, we were not only impressed our American cousin could play the piano, but also that her family actually owned a real piano. And Mom had no problem repeating that Mary was the first person—a woman—in the history of Grandpa's family to graduate from college.

The three sisters, Mother, Stella, and Sophia, also spoke of Ellie, Mary's mother in Chicago. Married in Greece, Ellie and her husband George, parents of five children, had immigrated to the U.S. early in the 20th century and never returned to their homeland. In the 1930s they endured the loss of their twenty-five-year-old-son to heart disease. Sophia nodded, sadly noting, "There's tragedy and death in America too."

We heard stories about John, Mom's oldest brother, who left Greece in 1898 to immigrate to Salt Lake City, Utah. He eventually owned a successful café and made several journeys between the U.S. and Greece. John accompanied my mother to America on a ship named *King Alexander* in 1920 and they settled in Chicago. He gave Mother away at her wedding to Dad in 1924. When John became incurably ill, he returned to Parnion, and died in Grandma's arms; she never recovered from burying her oldest son. They said John died of cancer. But in 1925, medicine in Parnion was primitive: it was only a guess.

Mom always spoke of Dad; she missed him. She may have cursed him in hours of distress, but she usually remembered him warmly. When the two of us were alone, she took special care to tell me stories about Dad. It saddened her that I couldn't remember my father, so she took extra time on the details. Mother reminded me that he was a kind and good man who had made a mistake in sending us away, adding, "We all make mistakes, Johnny."

Recalling Dad's restaurant in Geneva, Illinois, Mother told me how the landlord cheated my father out of the store's equipment that he had paid for during the Depression. The subject of Dad's hot beef sandwiches partnered with creamy mashed potatoes, and gloriously topped with his special recipe for gravy made us drool. She said that when Dad bought eggs for his restaurant, he purchased them by the case. In contrast, when we had one egg, way back at the beginning of the war, Alex, Mom, Nikki, and I had shared it four ways. Eggs were an unattainable, wartime opulence.

"Remember, Johnny, how when we first got here, you kids would pretend the chicken ribs you were eating were lamb chops?

249

Oh, to have even one of those little bones now. But when we get back home to America—we will never be hungry again. And someday, we will finally sink our teeth into your father's hot beef sandwiches with gravy and mashed potatoes."

After my aunts and uncles went home, it would be time to go to sleep. To take the chill off sheets and blankets, Mom heated two roof tiles in the fireplace. When they were warm enough, we carefully removed them from the fire with a shovel, wrapped each in a blanket, and slipped each one between our bedcovers. Even though we were hungry, a condition that tends to keep one awake, warmed bedding brought comfort and helped sleep come sooner.

Hiking into the woods, almost every day, we had to gather dried twigs and branches to sustain a fire in the fireplace. Scrounging for firewood, dry tree limbs, and dry, prickly *aphanes* was labor, not fun. *Aphanes* are tumbleweed-like plants: the same ones village scouts lit as signals. They burn brightly, but too quickly.

Mother explained to me that children in Chicago wore heavy woolen coats, leggings, scarves, hats, and mittens in winter. We didn't own coats like Chicago kids, so we layered on itchy, wool sweaters, whether they fit us or not. Smelling of mothballs, hand knit, old sweaters emerged from Grandma's old trunk, as did lifesaving, heavy, bright red and blue wool blankets, which Grandmother had woven.

Before retiring for the night, we lit one glorious *aphana*, enjoyed its brilliant flame, felt its momentary warmth and climbed into a bed warmed by a wrapped, hot roof tile. On those winter nights, Mom swathed me in as many layers of clothing as possible, and placed Grandma's thick, itchy, wool blankets on top of me. I could hardly turn over from the weight of the bedding.

Lying there in a completely dark house, pinned in bed by blankets, after a night of stories, I wondered: Will we ever see Dad again? Will we be reunited with Alex? We hadn't heard anything else about my brother since the news that he'd arrived in Athens.

Could we actually survive hunger, disease, and killings thrust on us by Hitler's all-powerful German army?

These were the questions our family pondered while we hunkered by the fireplace all winter. Perhaps spring thaw would bring some cheer, and some answers.

28 | INFERNO

When villagers heard the Nazi convoy approaching our road on a chilly March morning in 1944, we reacted in the way that was now a habit. Able-bodied men scattered to the hills; the rest of us sought safety inside our homes. But this invasion was hideously unique. The Germans didn't slowly and menacingly drive through town in one intimidating cluster. This time individual soldiers jumped off the convoy as it sped through the village. Each soldier then took command of two or three houses.

When they were all in position, couriers from Hitler's hell began setting fires. And that's when women, children, and old people rushed outdoors to investigate a stench of "something burning." Spotting fiery columns of smoke quickly rising over familiar red roofs all around the village, they realized, with hearts stopping, that the "something" that was burning was—Parnion.

On that cool March morning Mom had kept warm in her black "Chicago coat" when she ventured outside, after sunrise, to tackle courtyard chores. She was still wearing her black coat when I found her sitting by the window, intently sewing buttons on my ragged shirt. When we heard Germans arriving, Mom decided to quietly tackle indoor jobs; I was assigned to sweep the old wooden floor.

As I was cleaning out ashes from the cold fireplace, with broom in hand, I noticed Mother glance up from mending to sniff the air. In an instant, she was dashing downstairs, crying out, "Do you smell smoke, Johnny?" I dropped the broom and followed.

A sickening spectacle glared at us in the courtyard— Grandpa's house was on fire. My blood turned to ice when I spotted mammoth flames rapidly enveloping the interior walls of the front room, at courtyard level. A dazzling orange blaze had ignited the ancient, combustible bamboo, used a century before to construct interior walls.

A few days before, I had found an abandoned load of tinder-dry cornhusks and had lugged them to the ground floor, front room to replenish Bebba's larder. To our horror, Nazis had set those cornhusks ablaze, along with the exposed bamboo visible through a huge hole in the previously damaged wall. Ferocious, bright yellow flames were devouring the helpless partition.

Mother, motionless and silent, stood gawking at the swiftly proliferating fire in a kind of stupor: scary, strange behavior for this woman. Her face and coat reflected intense orange light from a treacherously close blaze. But her only reaction was to stare into the unbearable heat, without moving. Gasping for air, I approached to pull her away. But in an attempt to breathe, I turned my face away from the fire for a second. What I heard next melted my core—Mom's horrifying scream.

A piercing, desperate noise exploded out of my mother. Never before had I heard her make a horrific sound like that. Her chilling screech triggered an odd reaction in me—my teeth were chattering and my body quivered nonstop. Her ghastly cry abruptly stopped when she spotted my thunderstruck expression. "My God, what is happening to us, Johnny? Our house is burning down…"

But worse than her shriek and the threatening fire dancing dangerously around us, Mother abruptly fell to the ground. The bizarre movement turned eleven-year-old me into mush. Powerless, I watched her collapse to the earth on her knees. And then, even more strangely she proceeded to pull her black coat up over the back of her head, like she was trying to bury herself in the fire—but she stopped moving.

"Mama!" I screamed. She was slumped over lifeless—no movement at all. The unthinkable came to mind. "Is she dead??"

My body shivered as I fiercely yanked her arm in an attempt to get her up and away from the fire. Teeth chattering wildly, I yelled, "Mama! Get up! What's wrong? What's the matter with you, Mama? Get up! Get away from the fire! Don't die, Mama! Please God, don't let Mama die!"

When I heard her muffled wail of grief begin again, I was grateful for it. She slowly began rising to her feet. I saw her back straighten underneath the black coat. Forcing herself to defeat overpowering sorrow and despair, my mother regally attained her full height again. Then she stared at me, and lovingly touched the side of my trembling face.

And in a blink, Mother's compassion turned to anger. Twisting her torso to take a good look around us, she spotted the Nazi soldier who had, no doubt, lit the blaze; he was standing outside the courtyard door, admiring his handiwork. My brief moment of relief passed when I saw Mother's scowl. It told me that she was determined to do something out of the ordinary. I feared it was going to be something life threatening.

First, she motioned for me to move away and I backed off, still shaking. But I didn't take my eyes off my fully enraged mother. She was drilling her eyes into those of the young, well-armed Nazi soldier, out on the street, mere yards away from us. Burning torch in hand, he was on his way to set another fire. But, catching sight of the two of us, he flashed a smirking, foul, deceitful smile.

The defiance in Mother's face told me she was going to act quickly. So I was relieved when the Nazi rushed on, intent on more torching. Mother was, most certainly, not going to stand by, motionless, and watch her father's house burn down. It was our sole sanctuary.

She tore around to the house's side yard and confidently returned with an immense, unwieldy metal can filled with at least fifteen gallons of water. With her arms around its mid-section, Mother single-handedly unloaded it on the flames inside the wall with a direct hit.

Just that morning, before the Nazis arrived, I had attempted to knock over the same can, with a thoughtless, boyish, but painful, whack with my foot. I thought it had turned over and spilled. Now it miraculously contained water again. And my mother was carrying it as if it were a feather pillow; I still can't explain why or how. It was our "Miracle of Parnion."

I grabbed a smaller container of standing water from the place in the yard where Mother had recently done laundry and tossed its contents on the cornhusks' lingering blaze. Then, Mom came at the glowing ashes with the courtyard *niftera.* Of course, she filled it to the brim for washing our hands and faces that very morning.

Simultaneously, I darted into the courtyard, fetched a shallow drinking trough and splashed Bebba's water on glowing embers. Passing Mom in the doorway on my way out, she was rushing inside again with another clumsy water can that had filled after a recent March rain. Frantically searching for more standing water in the yard, I uncovered a discarded pot filled with rainwater. Lugging it inside, I spilled it on smoldering scraps. White steam rose up at us from charred, black residue.

After we had used all available water, Mother grabbed a shovel and ran out to the *perivoli.* She ran in and out spreading shovels of garden dirt on anything that appeared to smolder. I searched around for additional flames and smoke but, most incredibly, the fire was extinguished. We ran in all directions checking and double-checking the entire house and property to make sure there were no fiery remnants. Bebba was safe, too. Grandpa's old house appeared to be out of danger for the time being.

Then, we ran out to the street. Mother held her head in her hands and wept when she observed Parnion—burning from village entrance all the way to the cemetery. Deadly yellows, flaming oranges, and smoky blacks painted themselves onto trees, houses, stucco, courtyard walls, and people. And if flames and smoke weren't sufficient to bring village-wide panic, the fire terrified us with its voice: strident and crackling.

Alarming female screams and eerie keening filled the smoky air. Women shrieked and pulled their hair in grief; others kneeled down and covered their heads with their scarves. With soldiers in close proximity, none of them dared to douse flames damaging their homes. Armed Nazis were still more deadly than the inferno that was overtaking us.

Children cried at the spectacle and, like me, were frightened and confused by their mothers' reactions to the devastation. Some women had done as my mother had, attacking the fires with whatever water or dirt they could find, but only after soldiers had turned their backs.

Then, out of nowhere, the earth shuddered under our feet. The rumble felt like an earthquake, but Mom suspected Nazi-set explosions. She grabbed me and held me tight. That's when she sensed my continued shivering. Holding me even tighter, she crossed herself. "This is living hell, Johnny. Pray to God that we survive." Hanging on to each other, we braced ourselves for the next tremor.

Soldiers were not only setting fires, they also had transported dynamite to the village. They were blowing up buildings. Six newer, two-story structures near the main square, buildings that had been the pride of the village (one used as a kind of village hall), were completely leveled to the ground with dynamite. It was surmised the Nazis had blown them to smithereens because they suspected the structures were guerrilla headquarters. They weren't.

Later, my cousin Demetri told me how, over on his side of the village, he had watched, mesmerized, when an elderly neighbor yanked at a lighted stick of dynamite. The Germans had forced the explosive into a large crack on the outer wall of her house. As its fuse sparked and hissed, the white-haired woman tugged and pulled at the stick. Noticing Demetri, she had screamed, "Run! You're going to get hurt! Run away!"

Dashing toward home, Demetri had looked back and witnessed the plucky octogenarian finally remove the dynamite from the wall. Running with stick and sizzling fuse in hand, she plunged it into a nearby watery ditch. She had saved herself and her home.

Running and coughing, while inhaling heavy smoke from multiplying fires, Demetri finally reached his house and found his mother, our Aunt Anastasia, defiantly barring German soldiers from entering. Screaming, *"Ohi! Ohi!"* (No! No!) with arms outstretched, she was blocking the path at their front gate.

Demetri's body went limp when a Nazi pulled a pistol from his holster and pushed its barrel, hard, against his mother's head. Demetri was positive the German was going to kill her. So he ran to her and pulled at his mother's apron and the hem of her dress—anything to get her away from the soldier. But Anastasia stayed defiant. Crying and gasping for breath, Demetri begged her to move. Whether it was her son's desperation, or the gun at her head—Anastasia finally relented. The Nazis retaliated the defense of her home by burning it to the ground.

The nightmare of the firestorm lasted until almost sunset. The atmosphere was smeared with choking smoke when the Nazi convoy revved up to leave the village. Hanging on to moving military trucks, some soldiers were still brandishing blazing torches. We were thankful to be alive. They hadn't come to kill us that day. Their purpose was to scare the hell out of us, and they had succeeded.

Mother and I watched the trucks pass from our open courtyard gate. We spotted the same young soldier who had set Grandpa's house on fire earlier in the day. He spotted us too, and noticed that our house was still standing. The devil incarnate jumped off the truck and, torch in hand, ignited a new blaze near the courtyard wall. He leaped back up onto the moving vehicle as quickly as he had come, rejoining his laughing fellow conquerors. Then the whole monstrous lot of them sped out of Parnion. Mother hurriedly grabbed a hoe and furiously hacked away at the fire, burying flames with dirt before embers had a chance to spread.

The hellish scene of blazing orange fire and gray smoke, like something out of *Dante's Inferno*, continued all night. Embers floated up in the dark, illuminated the sky like fireworks, then landed to ignite an outbuilding or unburned corner of a roof. The men were still hiding in the distant hills.

Courageous women sacrificed their own safety, working hard all day and night to valiantly save their children, their homes, and their property. Too many found no success in extinguishing overpowering fires. Homeless, bewildered, frightened children wandered the streets, not knowing what to do or where to go. The day seared our souls as well as our properties.

Sixty of Parnion's houses had been torched. Some were leveled to the ground by the monstrous conflagration. Others were half gone and a number remained whole, not because it had been the Nazi's intent to save them, but because, as villagers said, *tychi* (luck) had played a part.

Dear departed *Kyra* Margarita's house was a lucky one, untouched by evil fires. Nor did soldiers approach the late Panagiota's inaccessible location, situated on an obscure path. Vasili and Sophia's house, located on the main road, was severely damaged but repairable, as was Artemis and Phillip's. Refugees for a second time, Demetri and his parents took residence in his deceased, second grandfather's vacant house, on Parnion's northern outskirts.

Old Uncle Nicholas's dwelling on the village's eastern periphery was seriously damaged because German foot soldiers made a point of setting fire to houses on the edge of town, closest to places in the mountains where guerrillas hid.

We learned that the dynamited building, which had been used as a kind of village hall, had contained baptismal and marriage records for village families, which went back for generations, even before the Turkish occupation. Vital records were reduced to carbon smithereens and lost forever in the explosion and fire.

Aunt Stella's house suffered damages, but she declared it was still habitable and insisted on staying in it, even though Mother and Aunt Sophia encouraged her to move into Grandpa's house with us. She supposed that Germans knew Grandpa's house was still livable and officers would return for overnight stays. Stella wanted no part of sharing any roof with Nazis. Period. Uncle Vasili, Parnion's carpenter, immediately began repairs at his own house and then at Stella's.

Acrid, bitter smoke odors would infuse Parnion for months. Homeless villagers immediately started piecing together needed shelters. Rusty pieces of corrugated metal gleaned from empty chicken coops became the roofs of lean-to, makeshift houses. Resolute men and women labored to clean up residue from the catastrophic inferno. For the rest of the war, Parnion's citizens worked at getting lives and property in order again, suffering setbacks every time the Germans returned to town. Rebuilding would have to wait until the day the war ended.

Mr. and Mrs. Papadopoulos's house was never touched by German fire during the holocaust. But, in this case, villagers did not attribute the omission to *tychi*. In fact, observant, neighboring women said it was thanks to the several German soldiers stationed around the Papadopoulos home during the fire.

However, one dark night, a week after the German pyrotechnic attack on Parnion, the Greek resistance burned the house of Parnion's only shopkeeper to the ground. No one was injured.

29 | PILGRIMAGE

In April 1944, after the fire and near the end of the rainy season, Mother and I trudged four miles to check on the progress of the olive trees we had cultivated the previous fall. What we saw was the first good omen in months: each and every tree was loaded with tiny white blossoms. "Flowers are good signs of future fruit, Johnny," Mother assured me as we walked between the gnarled trees. "If nothing goes wrong we'll have olives by December."

Good news continued that spring. We received a message from Uncle George that his wife, Athanasia, had given birth to a healthy little girl; mother and child were doing well. The family planned to come to Parnion to return Nikki to us after the forty-day period following the child's birth and traditional church blessing. But stepped-up Nazi hostilities made it too dangerous; the plan was delayed. Uncle George finally brought Nikki back to us in late spring. We greeted them with hugs and kisses while George admired new leaves and tiny, green grape clusters on the overhead vines in Grandpa's courtyard. Nikki was excited to tell us about the new baby girl and how much fun she'd had with little Fotis.

My sister reported that there were mean Nazi soldiers in Uncle George's village too, although at least they had not set it on fire. George cried as he examined the horrible catastrophe that Nazi-set fires had inflicted on his birth village. "Thank God no one was killed," he remarked, wiping away tears. "Good things can only happen in our dear Parnion after these barbarians lose. There's nothing else to say." When he went down the road to visit Vasili and Sophia, Nikki shared with us that she was relieved to be back with Mom and me in Parnion. She protested that Aunt Athanasia had kept her too busy with household chores.

During George's visit, I overheard Mom tell my uncle that she was arranging for Bebba to be mated again so baby goats could be born and Bebba could continue to give milk. George agreed with her plan. He also advised Mom that we could either slaughter Bebba's kids for food, or barter with them to ease our dire situation. His advice left me horrified.

"That's barbaric," I shuddered. "How could we ever eat Bebba's *children*?"

Mother tried to explain that the purpose of having goats as livestock was not only to have milk, but also to produce meat. "Johnny, people here do not make goats into pets."

"That's the purpose of a stranger's livestock," I protested. "Bebba is a member of our family. You say, yourself, she's keeping us alive. Every single day, Bebba rescues us with her delicious milk! I could never eat a member of Bebba's family."

In time, Bebba gave birth to two endearing kids. The little ones had inherited Bebba's friendly disposition and were fun to play with and Nikki and I were assigned to hide three animals from the Germans. When Vasili or Sophia brought up the "future" of Bebba's kids, I continued my verbal campaign to protect Bebba's "children." Mother remained silent on the subject.

The ugly war grind continued on through the summer of 1944, but at least olives were ripening. Perhaps in gratitude that we were still alive, Mother initiated a pilgrimage to an *exokklisi* (outlying church) a few miles away. The night before, Mom explained we were going to hike to a tiny country church on its feast day, September 14, with aunts Sophia, Anastasia, and our good neighbor Artemis. Our purpose was to pray for war's end and for our Aunt Joanna's safe return.

Each woman in our devout, ragged party carried a small bunch of freshly cut, small-leafed basil gathered from sparse wartime gardens. Every summer, housewives in Parnion took pride in growing the fragrant herb in small flowerpots. Taking fresh, green basil to church on September 14 is a time-honored tradition on the Feast of the Holy Cross.

In Greece, the herb is grown for its fragrance and religious significance. Greeks don't usually cook with basil and neither did Nazis, so it was plentiful. It is believed that basil plants were found where Christ's cross was uncovered, three hundred years after the Crucifixion, when Helen, mother of Emperor Constantine, found "the true Cross" in the Holy Land.

The six of us hiked several miles into an even more remote region of Mt. Parnon. Greek villages, now as in the distant past, support a main church, like St. George's in Parnion, with a permanent priest. But, small *exokklisia*—in the boondocks—only schedule services on their feasts: days decreed by church calendar to celebrate the saint or spiritual concept for which the church is named.

Outlying country chapels were perched into hillsides, on mountaintops, and inside caves. Worshipers from near and far traveled arduous mountain paths on foot to arrive at these bucolic settings, most inaccessible to main roads. And local priests, sometimes even the bishop, all garbed in colorful vestments, led liturgical rites on special holidays.

During the Ottoman Turkish occupation of Greece, from the 15th to the 19th centuries, believers had purposely implemented narrow and precarious access paths to these isolated churches to discourage wrongdoers from robbing or desecrating them. Many tiny chapels were designed with extremely small entry doors, forcing worshipers to bend over or squeeze down to get inside. Uncle Vasili told me that when the Turks invaded Greece in the 1400s, they made a concerted effort to destroy Christian churches, so they brutally rode their horses into church buildings, brandishing scimitars to smash whatever stood in their way. Too often they desecrated sacred altars and gouged out the eyes and faces of Christ and the saints on wall frescoes.

Many *exokklisia* were little jewels of architecture and art, with interior walls covered with exquisite Byzantine frescoes. Most had been consecrated so far in the past that the local old people could not remember which generation of their ancestors lived when the church had been built. Typically, they held scant interior space for the faithful. No pews, chairs, or prayer books helped worshipers focus on the liturgy, though most senior citizens knew all the words by heart. Worshipers accompanied the priest's supplications and chanters' responses in well-remembered Byzantine chant. No one departed until the last "Amen."

We departed Grandpa's house in the coolness of dawn to hike rocky, narrow footpaths, through scratchy brush. Along the way, people from other villages joined our procession to the *exokklisi* where we remained from early Matins' first prayer until the Liturgy's final blessing. With no room inside to fit everyone, late arrivals would stand outdoors for four or five hours in early September's blistering heat. Eleven-year-old boys, like me, were especially vulnerable to distraction.

The church was already full when we arrived. The crowds would grow even larger as the morning wore on. But it was early enough for Mother and our other companions to find places inside. Nikki and I dragged behind Mom through the crowd to a back wall. That was a good thing: we could lean back to support ourselves, and extend the stamina we needed for the very long service.

I instantly found myself face to face with a tall, elderly, white-bearded priest. He was blazing his trail through the tight throng with a gold, vigorously swinging, incense censer to bless the faithful. Worshipers jumped away from the determined priest's smoking vessel, but at the same time they devoutly crossed themselves. The experienced cleric's gnarled hand masterfully commanded the censer; he flung it back and forth, like a nimble farmer spreading seeds. Billows of fragrant, white, incense smoke drifted up into the church's small dome.

I looked around and spotted old artwork: the *exokklisi* was an artistic gem. Darkened, wall-to-wall frescoes of ancient holy people spiritually wrapped the packed-in crowd like an heirloom, patchwork quilt. Paintings darkened by centuries of incense smoke, had portrayed centuries-old, near-life-size figures of church heroes. Every square inch of surface was covered with icons of the revered faithful who lived at the beginning of Christianity.

Stern holy eyes stared directly down at distracted boys leaning against the church wall. Ignorant of guidelines integral to Byzantine art, I scanned walls and dome. Then I decided that the grim-faced saints should be smiling instead of scowling. After all, they were in paradise, enjoying heavenly rewards, not trapped in World War II like we were.

More worshipers squeezed into the tiny church as the priest began his homily. But all of a sudden, a woman let out a scream. The crowd stirred and buzzed, and only quieted down when another woman loudly clarified that two of the faithful, standing near her, had passed out. All eyes focused on two drawn, wrinkled old grandmothers being carried out of the church; they were so swathed in sweltering black that only their reddened faces showed.

A younger woman, dressed in black, advised that exhaustion, coupled with hunger and heat, brought on fainting and that we should expect more people to pass out before the day was over. The frail, ascetic priest hesitated when the commotion interrupted his sermon. But as soon as the ailing women were out the door and being cared for outside, where there was more air to breathe, he picked up where he left off and continued preaching.

The priest stood a few steps above the faithful on stairs leading up to a carved, wooden *eikonostasion* (altar screen). It spanned the width of the chapel and was divided in the center with an archway that led to the altar. An icon of Christ was positioned on the right of the arch; another, of the Holy Mother, was on the left. Paintings depicting Christ on the cross, angels Michael and Gabriel, and a Byzantine version of the Last Supper were installed in niches on the ornate altar screen.

Most in the exhausted, gaunt congregation stood barefoot, but they were focused on the cleric's message. Now, as a senior citizen myself, I'm able to appreciate that those adults in the crowded *exokklisi,* when I was eleven years old, were, like my mother, hungry and severely weakened by the brutalities of occupation. Yet, they nobly, steadfastly, and voluntarily endured hours of a never-ending homily and slowly chanted liturgy to pray for an end to vicious war.

In the eternity it took the old priest to deliver his sermon, I had ample time to study his elongated white mustache and stare at the way it blended into his very long, white beard. His fascinating whiskers had been cultivated, through decades of priesthood, into a long point, which reached well below his very skinny waist. When the priest turned sideways to address worshipers, his emaciated frame showed through the openings of fraying, but beautifully embroidered, light blue vestments. Typical of priests in Greece, his snowy white, long hair had been neatly pulled into a simple knot at the back of his head. I wondered how long it had taken his hair and beard to grow to such astonishing lengths.

I tried to follow and understand his sermon, but the homily outlasted my short attention span. Unfortunately, his spiritual message never penetrated my boyish brain. And I lapsed again into my little world of invented juvenile entertainment.

Something about the ancient priest reminded me of one of the icons I had spotted earlier on an upper wall. Where had I seen it? While he droned on I scanned the primordial surfaces, the arched niches, and tiny dome, clouded with trapped incense smoke. I finally spotted the singular likeness I had been searching. I had lost it in the crowd of painted saints. The image, piquing my curiosity, had been created a thousand years before, by an unsung iconographer with talents matching Michelangelo's.

My discovery, blackened with centuries of soot from smoke and burning candles, stared down on the faithful from the wall to the right of the altar. An elderly, bearded Byzantine male with penetrating eyes was an exact replica of the aged, wrinkled cleric, with long white beard and penetrating eyes, delivering the unending sermon. I nudged Nikki with my shoulder. My eyes urged her to notice the connection between the austere icon and the austere in-person priest.

"You know why the priest is so old?" I murmured. Nikki nodded that she didn't know. So I whispered my facetious answer in her ear. "He's the surviving twin of that saint up there." Nikki's giggle got Mother's attention, and Mom flashed us her "get serious because we're in church" look. My game was over for the day.

Faith is challenged during wartime, but it does not completely evaporate. From the time of Homer's writings, world literature reveals human petitions to a Higher Being in times of peril. From my own experience, I tend to agree with the adage: "There are no atheists in foxholes."

My focus again turned to the old priest. He was petitioning for "peace in the world," a prayer built into the Divine Liturgy and repeated multiple times every single day in Christian Orthodox churches throughout the world. Personally participating in war as a victim makes the familiar prayer urgent and more meaningful. And I joined the others in another prayer led by the priest: "For our deliverance from all affliction, wrath, danger and distress, let us pray to the Lord." Focusing on my own special petition, I asked God to protect Mom, my siblings, Bebba, Dad, and all our family. I hoped that, like incense smoke, my own prayers were ascending.

The interior of the tiny church overflowed with people when services ended: more crowds covered the hillside around the *exokklisi*. The white-bearded priest announced he was taking the liberty to add one more, very special petition to the multitude of prayers. Then priest and chanters led barefoot, ragged, hungry, and bedraggled pilgrims in an extraordinary petition to God for urgent, heavenly assistance, a prayer traditionally chanted in springtime Lenten services.

"Lord of the Powers, be with us, for when we are in distress, we have no other help but you. Deliver us from every sorrow, evil and distress…"

The burst of communal Byzantine chant emerging from within the treasured country church joined with the voices of the throngs standing on the arid, straw-colored Laconian hillside. Harmonious voices praying for the end to a brutal and devastating world war echoed into the canyons and against the surrounding summer-scorched foothills of Mt. Parnon. Those melodious sounds singularly transformed normally silent hillsides into an extraordinary patch of the planet. A little bit of heaven had caressed our war-torn portion of earth on that sunny September day.

***

DNA? Never heard of it in 1944:

- ❖ *Oswald Avery, at the Rockefeller Institute, isolates DNA*

- ❖ *Howard Aiken and IBM engineers at Harvard University began developing Mark I, an electro-mechanical calculator*

- ❖ *January: Allies land at Anzio, Italy*

- ❖ *Allies inflict round the clock mass air raids on Berlin*

- ❖ *April-November: Greek-American soldiers of the U.S. Army deployed by the OSS are dropped behind German lines in Greece to disrupt German wartime operations*

- ❖ *June: D-Day Allies invade beaches of Normandy: 160,000 allied troops were transported to the coast of France by 5,000 ships and supported by 13,000 aircraft in their campaign to liberate Europe*

30 | SURPRISES

On a certain, long-remembered, autumn afternoon in 1944, the sun shined amber gold, in the unique way that late September, October, and November solemnly color sunlight. I was outside, playing with a few pals, when I spotted Uncle Vasili and Barba Lambros chatting beside a stone wall, between our neighborhood's old olive tree and St. Nick's fountain. Their grave faces revealed that they were assessing Parnion's unfortunate condition, the usual topic of conversation among adults.

During their powwow, Lambros nodded to Vasili to take notice of an unfamiliar man approaching the village on foot. The mysterious figure, dressed in somewhat familiar attire, was pulling a donkey by a rope. The apparition slowly neared Parnion from the road leading to Sparta and Tripolis. Vasili and Lambros adjusted their eyes in the thick autumn light to clearly view the hazy vision. Instantly suspicious of the oncoming specter, they quickly stepped behind the wall, out of the newcomer's sight.

The weird sight belonged to a lone, disheveled German soldier who was trudging toward St. Nicholas's Church. Nazis never trudged. They were never disheveled. Vasili suspected a satanical trick. "It's a diabolical disguise. This Nazi devil is a decoy," he whispered to Lambros. "A surprise attack on Parnion may be in the works."

"Entrapment!" Lambros concurred. "There were no fire signals today. The church bell rang no alarm. We're in danger. Is there time to alert everyone?"

Adrenaline pumping, Vasili disclosed dreadful suspicions. "I pray our signalers haven't been discovered and slaughtered in... cold blood. How do we alert villagers?"

Donkey and soldier had already advanced as far as Grandpa's property. At the same time Uncle Nicholas, on his way to the *kafeneion*, stepped out into the street from the path at the side of Grandpa's house.

"*Guten tag*," the strangely attired Nazi said to Nicholas. "*Guten tag*." And my old uncle nearly jumped out of his skin. "*Guten tag*," the German repeated, smiling. "It was all too bizarre," Nicholas explained later.

Kicking our usual stuffed sock around, the other boys and I heard rough-sounding German words from behind us. Pausing our game, we were startled to see the peculiar Nazi with the donkey. The German, who appeared unarmed, looked harmless enough for us to get closer and study him. So we approached.

Old Nicholas glanced in our direction and shrugged his shoulders, "I don't know what the Nazi is saying. He keeps repeating the same words in German."

Lambros and Vasili quickly came into view from their hiding place behind the wall. They waved their arms and flashed stern looks at us. "Shoo away from here, boys. You know better than to approach a German soldier," scowling Vasili scolded.

"It's only one soldier, Father... He looks more pitiful than we do," my cousin Kosta said.

"What are you thinking, Kosta? German machine guns may be closing in on us right now," his distraught father warned. "Go home!"

Counseling us calmly, Lambros whispered, "With no warning to alarm us today, all of us are vulnerable. Germans could pop out of nowhere to kill us—right here in the street. Horrific massacres have taken place that you boys probably don't know about..."

Vasili interrupted, "Get away from here, boys. But, don't draw attention to yourselves. Casually move away. Go! Hide!"

The soldier turned his head to look at us boys, and then he spoke different sounding words. *"Der Krieg ist zu Ende."* We didn't understand German either.

"What's he saying?" Vasili's son, Kosta asked. Shrugging shoulders answered my cousin's question.

Curious neighbors, overhearing the fuss outside, began emerging from courtyard gates. Puzzled, they gawked with judgmental, suspicious eyes at the dirty-faced German with tousled hair and unbuttoned, wrinkled uniform. And Vasili became jumpier when additional innocent bystanders, vulnerable to furtive attack, appeared on the scene. He trained his eyes on the Sparta road to spot the Nazi convoy he suspected was primed to assault the village.

"I didn't know a German could look like this," one man scoffed, gesturing to the German's mud-splattered boots and missing buttons. The soldier's soiled jacket hung open, revealing a grimy T-shirt. His military cap was stripped of insignias, and his bluish, grayish, greenish pants were ripped at the knees. The soldier didn't seem to mind the crowd's scrutiny, even though he in no way exuded the perfect spit and polish the Third Reich demanded of its men.

As more people gathered, Vasili frantically blurted out, "It's a charade—a despicable Nazi trick!" He was remembering news he had learned of the massacre at Kalavryta in northern Peloponnesos the year before. Nazis had, on a sunny day like this one, killed the entire male population in one day. It was dangerous for so many people to be out in the street together, so close to a German—so off guard. When Vasili spotted Aunt Sophia, Tasia, my mother, and Nikki joining the group on the street, he removed his cap and frantically waved it at them. "Go back home, Sophia! Katherine! Take the children and go back inside. Immediately!"

Observing my uncle's panic, the soldier calmly repeated, *"Der Krieg ist zu Ende."*

Then Lambros got an idea. Turning to the soldier, he asked, "You speak English?"

With his eyes showing relief, the German earnestly nodded, "Yes! Yes... a little."

"What are you saying?" Uncle Nicholas prodded. He had learned to speak English in America too.

The soldier paused to think before putting his words together. "The... war... is... ended."

"What?" Lambros and Nicholas said, in stunned unison. "Say that again."

"The war is ended."

Mom told us later that her heart pumped harder when she heard the soldier's words, but she remained silent. "It was too good to be true," she said. "Would a Nazi soldier tell the truth?"

Lambros grilled the German with arched eyebrow, suspecting foul play. "How do you know... war is ended? Maybe you lie."

"I speak truth. The German army was ordered by Berlin to leave Greece. War is ended in Greece. Berlin commands all German soldiers to leave your country. But I hide in a cave."

"Why didn't you go with them?" Nicholas questioned suspiciously.

"I want—no more war! Germans lose. I don't want to fight anyplace else with German army. I hide to stay behind. I hate being soldier. I hate war."

Barba Lambros took a deep breath, looked at Vasili, and then turned to the crowd. "I don't know if this bastard is telling us the truth because... he may be the devil incarnate. He says the war has ended. The German army was ordered by Berlin to leave Greece."

There were no hurrahs. We stared at the men, numb and silent.

Nicholas doubted the report. "We really don't know... if what he says is true. This idiot may be a lunatic." Parnion had gone so many years cut off from the world that no one knew who could be trusted. There was no way to verify what the soldier was saying.

Vasili did not believe the soldier. My uncle, on the verge of tears, anticipated the German army's descent on us from hidden spots all over Parnion. "Don't be naïve," he cried out. "Did

Germans notify us in advance that they were coming to torch our village?

"Nazis have always taken us by surprise. They are ruthless murderers! Are we next? Is Parnion the next *Kalavryta?*"

No one could answer. Like Vasili, we suspected both the messenger and the message. Silence mixed with murmured questions, mumbled doubts, female prayers. Women made the sign of the cross over themselves.

One man finally spoke up. "Tell this German," he shouted from behind the crowd, "that if he is telling us the truth, we will have him gilded with gold."

Just then, we heard shouts explode in the main square, at the other end of the village. Adrenaline pulsed; heads turned. Women crossed themselves, and tearful Uncle Vasili bowed his head, resigned to abject defeat. "The final catastrophe approaches," he moaned, to no one in particular. "Why didn't we run and hide? This dirty Nazi decoy purposely delayed us from hiding. God help us all."

Screaming voices from an erupting ruckus distracted the lot of us. A horrific thought quickly agonized me, "Is this the surprise attack Uncle Vasili predicted? What do we do now?" But I spotted familiar young men racing at us, shouting, with a half dozen older men on their heels. They were approaching us from the direction of St. George's Church. All were screaming words I couldn't make out. The jittery crowd strained to understand indistinguishable outcries shouted by a pack of recognizable villagers. I finally made out mind-boggling words—but did I hear them correctly?

"The war is over! The war has ended! The Germans are leaving Greece!"

"How do they know?" I asked myself. "They haven't seen this dirty soldier yet."

Curious about the uproar, more villagers emerged from courtyards to congregate in the street by St. Nick's fountain; the crowd grew even larger. Two black-garbed, elderly women arrived at St. Nick's, huffing and puffing, relieved to sit and catch their breaths on Panagiota's bench. The taller *yiayia* (grandmother) aimed a reproachful stare at the Nazi, then posed a question to one of the young men. "Son, how do you know the war is over?"

Exhilarated, he replied, "We heard it on the radio!"

"Radio? What radio?" our neighbor Artemis questioned.

I was baffled. "Radio? We don't even have electricity."

"A radio the English soldiers turned over to us before they made their escape from Mt. Parnon," the young, dark-haired man answered with assurance. Smiling, he added, "Father Haralambos kept it hidden at St. George's."

"I don't understand," Artemis interrupted. "How can you operate a radio with no electricity?" At that, the mystified, buzzing crowd came alive with animated questions and commentary. Curiously, most men, including Nicholas, Lambros, nervous Vasili, and Artemis's husband Phillip, showed no surprise when a radio was mentioned.

The *yiayia* wrapped in black and sitting on the bench suspiciously raised one eyebrow. "With all the searching and stealing the Nazis have wreaked on Parnion in almost four years, they didn't find a radio?" she asked the young man. "Who is lying to us, son, you or the unwashed German with the donkey?"

"Dear *Yiayia*, for months there has been a radio hidden underneath St. George's sacred altar!" Faces in the crowd, including mine, showed confusion hearing about an unknown radio working, under a revered altar—in a village with no electricity.

Throwing his hands in the air, a white-haired grandfather yelled out in frustration, "What do you mean by a radio? We have no electricity to power a radio in this village!"

"It works with a battery." The young man explained. "Thanks to Barba Lambros's American know-how we can generate power to renew the battery."

"Battery? What's a battery?" I silently wondered to myself.

The dark-haired, young man continued his explanation of clandestine village activities. "Every time Germans approached to search the church, the radio was quickly removed and hidden someplace else. When the Germans left St. George's, good Father Haralambos delivered the radio to its hiding place under the altar." The crowd now turned to look at the priest who had joined the crowd.

Father Haralambos began explaining, "With our own village lookouts guarding us during the times we were able to listen to the radio, and for obvious reasons—under complete secrecy—we have heard the BBC, a British radio station from London."

With pity on her wrinkled, black-framed face, another old woman turned toward our village priest. "Father Haralambos, how on God's earth can you hear something said in London when you are standing in Parnion? Have you all lost your senses? Has this damned war damaged your minds?"

The younger man patiently explained, "The radio is a new device, *Yiayia*. It helps us hear from places all over the world. That is, we can hear when the signal is strong enough. And now that we know that Greece is no longer occupied by the Nazis, we can tell you about the radio and the speeches we heard by Roosevelt, the American president… and by Churchill."

"Of course, we didn't understand their English," the priest explained to the crowd. "Their speeches were translated into Greek by an organization called 'The Voice of America.'"

Now Barba Lambros gave recent details about the war: details that he had never divulged and that the majority of us did not know.

"We can also tell you that in recent months we learned the Germans have been losing ground. The Americans and the rest of our Allies invaded the beachheads of France this past June. They are fighting to liberate Europe from Germany. As we speak, Americans airplanes are dropping bombs on Berlin."

"However, be warned," the young man added. "There is no victory over the Nazis yet. This war has not ended for all of Europe—or in Asia. I repeat, my friends, the war is not over yet."

Villagers now focused on the German. He had said the war was over. But radio reports differed—the war was still going on.

Then the young villager finished his remarks to the crowd, "But the Nazis have left Greece. Perhaps we can breathe again."

It was the day I never forgot. I can still see the unkempt soldier with the humble donkey walking at his side. I can still hear the villager's offer to have him covered in gold, if he was telling the truth. Regrettably, there was no gold around to carry out the promise.

But there was no dancing in Parnion's square to celebrate the Nazis' withdrawal; no champagne corks popped. The good news did not instantly restore happiness and wellbeing. We were so annihilated by hunger, disease, and fear that we had forgotten how to feel joy and relief. It took time to soak in the reality that the Germans were gone—an unfathomable amount of time.

For Mom, my sister, and me, the war ended as abruptly as it had started for us in Kalamata. But, gone forever was the peaceful, sylvan environment Parnion enjoyed in 1937 when we had first climbed out of Sophocles's truck. With German withdrawal in late 1944, we may have been able to breathe more freely, but wartime misery stuck like bug-infested flypaper.

A month later, we still held our breaths with dread, listening for the roar of Nazi cars, trucks, and motorcycles, though none came. Eliminating deep-rooted terror is kind of like having a wart removed from your finger. You intuitively check to feel the bump, even after you know it's gone.

More practically, with no food supply—we were still hungry. Homes damaged by fire and dynamite had to be rebuilt. Government was in disarray. Inflation had destroyed the Greek economy. Families yearned to be reunited. Aunt Joanna had to be found.

***

The beginning of the end—1944:

- ❖ *Olympic Games cancelled because of the war*

- ❖ *June: Distomo, Greece: Killing everyone they could find, more than 200 people are massacred in their homes by German soldiers. Red Cross team arriving several days later finds bodies dangling from trees as they entered the village of Distomo*

- ❖ *United Nations is established*

- ❖ *Paris is liberated*

- ❖ *October: Greece liberated from German occupation; 325,000 Greek civilian deaths occurred between 1940 and 1944*

- ❖ *December: German counterattack at the "Battle of the Bulge" on the German/Belgium border is finally defeated when Patton's U.S. 3rd Army brings relief*

- ❖ *19,000 American casualties among the 77,000 total allies killed at the Battle of the Bulge, the largest, bloodiest land battle of WWII in which Americans had participated*

31 | LEAVING PARNION

The day after the disheveled German soldier and his donkey appeared out of nowhere, Parnion's hottest news involved the war's end—and the disappearance of Mr. and Mrs. Papadopoulos. That morning, the town woke to find a huge padlock installed on the front door of the village's only store; its shelves were almost bare. No one knew where the couple went. One villager's remarks regarding their disappearance did not favor turning the other cheek. "Good riddance!" I heard him say. "Those damned collaborators helped Nazis make life a living hell for us. I hope they went to Berlin, so American bombs can fall on them. It's time for collaborators to feel the same terror and death they helped the damned Nazis wreak on innocent, fellow countrymen."

"Normalcy" would finally return to Parnion—slowly—bit by infinitesimal bit. On the other hand, what's "normal?" For kids like Nikki and me, an empty, growling stomach and soul-twisting fear had been "normal." Yes, there were a few positive changes; we were finally seeing new people, who weren't Nazis, come to our charred, war-disfigured hamlet. Men, traveling through Parnion to reach the road going to Sparta, began passing through town again from villages north and east of Parnion. They shared their own stories of death, fires, and terror when they paused to refresh themselves at St. Nick's fountain or the *kafeneion* on the main square.

Mom's focus was pulling her family together and returning to America as soon as possible. She finally received communication from Athens; we learned that Alex was safe, living with our uncles Tassos, Petros, and Speros. She thanked God, over and over again, that her oldest child survived the war, physically unharmed. Right away she sent word to Alex, then eighteen, to contact the American Embassy and begin the process for returning to the U.S.

"I thank God that all of us in your grandparents' family here have survived this hell, " she shared with Nikki and me. "And your uncles assure us Joanna will be found now that the Germans are gone." Aunt Joanna's children had already started investigating her disappearance, but it was still too early to know anything. Hundreds, maybe thousands of people were lost; the government was in shambles. Millions of unspeakable tragedies had taken place all over the world, and of course, the war was still going on in Asia and the rest of Europe. "So far," Mother said, "*tychi* (luck) has been with us." Even though Mom knew that God was with us, she believed *tychi* had played a vital part in our survival.

Mom received another message from Petros, our Athenian, lawyer/uncle, informing us that other Greek Americans, like us, had been trapped in Greece. American embassy bureaucracy was clogged with requests to return home to the United States. Petros urged her to wait in Parnion.

"Other Americans were trapped in Greece? Who knew?" Mother was shaken by the news. "I have loaded so much guilt on myself for the past four years because I thought I was the only clueless one who couldn't get my American children out in time."

When hostilities ended in Greece in late 1944, food did not miraculously float down on us like manna from heaven. Widespread hunger continued. Mom was rightly fearful that some permanently debilitating or even fatal illness would hit Nikki or me as we waited in Parnion. And Nikki and I worried that Mom would get sick.

Mother jotted a return note to Petros to stress that we urgently needed to leave because sickness, death, and starvation were solidly ensconced in the village. For all we knew, this was just a short window of opportunity to get out—before some other catastrophe detained us and permanently sealed our entrapment in Parnion.

Our "war story" wasn't a screenplay devised by Louis B. Mayer. When I watched Hollywood movies about WWII in Ann Arbor's Michigan Theater during the late 1940s, the endings were always polished, optimistic and happy. MGM's celluloid wars were almost pretty; every hair on Gable's coifed head stayed in place.

No aviator, resembling Gary Cooper in a custom-made uniform with white, silk scarf blowing in the breeze, dropped out of the sky over Parnion. No Gary, Clark, or gutsy Spencer Tracy look-alikes arrived to make it all better for us. We were stuck in a village where people were ragged, barefoot, hungry, sick, and dying. But at the end of 1944, we had one advantage—and only one advantage—enemy soldiers weren't shooting real bullets at us anymore.

Too often, we had allowed hope to wane, but for almost four years the desire to return to America had sustained us. Mother was tremendously eager to begin our return journey, except that stubborn old "time" didn't cooperate. It never fails, when you're in a hurry, time frustrates by slowing to a snail's pace. With no phone in Parnion and postwar mail services gravely lacking efficiency, it took forever to communicate with Athens. Mother finally received another note.

Petros wrote that he had received a communication from Dad—this was extraordinary news that made us feel like we were hearing from God himself. My father had sent money to Petros for us via the Red Cross. We were informed that Dad no longer lived in Illinois; he was the owner of a small restaurant in Michigan. My father wrote that he had purchased a home for all of us in Ann Arbor, and anxiously looked forward to our return. The last words of advice from Petros were: "Continue waiting in Parnion."

"Thank God your father is alive." Directing her remarks at Nikki and me, Mom crossed herself. "I was so afraid that during these black years something might have happened to him. I never said anything. You already had too many reasons to be afraid." This was a startling thought. As frightened as I had been for years,

279

of things real and imagined, it had never crossed my mind that my father might have died while we lived. I had something else to be grateful for.

After giving thought to my uncle's communication, Mother asked, "Is it impossible for your father to directly communicate with us? I don't need Petros as a middleman, do I?"

Certainly, she was grateful for the safety, food, and shelter my uncles had provided Alex in Athens after his escape from the Nazis in Parnion. Yet, she still harbored negative feelings about Dad's brothers in Athens. Mom felt their refusal to help when she had been forced to go to court before the war had delayed our return to the U.S. More than once I had heard Mother say, "That detestable lawsuit was the hellish glue that stuck us to this damn war."

***

New Year's Day, 1945, found us still in Parnion. We knew more about world events now that village men openly kept track of the war on the radio, which had been relocated from the church to the *kafeneion*. The lone coffee house, which had briefly closed, was reopened because Parnion men believed a Greek village without a *kafeneion* was a village without a heart.

Yet Nazis were still waging war in the rest of Europe. Our Allied soldiers were nobly fighting the Battle of the Bulge in severely frigid weather somewhere between snow-clogged Belgium and Germany. It was a clash the Germans initiated in mid-December and had been winning until allied command sent General George Patton and the U.S. Third Army into the demoralizing bloody combat. Tragically more than 20,000 allied soldiers died before the battle turned into an allied victory in late January of 1945. Petros's communications from Athens continued to advise us to "Wait."

While I fervently desired to leave the war behind and go back to the U.S., I was also concerned about leaving the village:

Bebba's future was at the top of my worry list. Mom made it very clear to me that no goat, not even lovable Bebba, would accompany us to America. When I asked, "What will happen to Bebba?" Mother explained we'd have to turn ownership of our goat over to someone in the village.

"Who can take care of her in the way she deserves to be cared for?" I countered. "Bebba is no ordinary goat. She's a part of this family. I'm afraid she'll wind up in a flock. Some ignorant goatherd will grab her and stick her into an immense herd of anonymous—even wild—goats! Mama, that's like having you plunk me into an orphanage."

"Who do you trust most in Parnion, John?" Mother asked, trying to ease my tears and anxiety. The answer was easy. "Uncle Vasili!" I trusted him with all my heart. Still, even knowing my goat would be in the care of my favorite uncle, I couldn't shake off my apprehensions about leaving Bebba behind.

Days and nights dragged on—like months. Mother's patience ran out at the start of February 1945. "I cannot wait another week. It's time to leave," she announced one day.

"We own nothing. Packing is simple. We're leaving before we get stuck here for another five miserable years." Mom decided that all she would pack into Buddy were our two heavy, bright red and blue, woolen blankets, the ones personally woven by Grandma. She hoped the money Dad sent to Petros would cover buying new shoes and clothes, if any were available in Athens, so we wouldn't arrive in America like barefoot, ragged urchins, if we ever got that far.

Sophocles, who had initially transported us to Parnion when we first arrived in 1937 and had his truck confiscated by the Germans, was already behind the wheel of a "new" one. It was a German "jeep like" Kübelwagen. Nazis had abandoned the inoperable vehicle during their rapid exit from the Mt. Parnon area. Sophocles had spotted it at the side of a road outside the village and rescued it. He said he felt no qualms about keeping the vehicle in exchange for the beloved truck the Nazis had stolen. Proud that

281

he was capable of repairing the "jeep" himself, Sophocles, the only one in town who knew how to drive, was jubilant to have "wheels" again.

Mother asked him to drive us to Athens in his "new machine," promising to pay him for his services after we arrived. Sophocles said he looked forward to the adventure and a date was set to depart: in two days.

"I prefer to leave immediately, children," she told us, "because I don't want a catastrophe to strike us while we linger. But I want to leave Grandpa's house in good order. And we need time to say goodbye to our family and the other kind people who helped us through this nightmare. I don't want villagers to say of us that we disappeared, like Papadopoulos, in the middle of the night."

Nikki was effervescent and couldn't wait for our next adventure. She had no difficulty leaving Parnion. She told everyone who would listen that she looked forward to wearing pretty dresses, going to an American school, and living in an American city with bright lights. Without question, Nikki planned to indulge in all the luxuries accompanying life in the U.S.

Preparing to depart, Mother meted cleaning assignments to Nikki and me; the next two days were spent cleaning the house from top to bottom. My fingers were numb from the cold, as I swept the nooks and crannies of Grandpa's courtyard. But, unlike Nikki, I was sad.

Of course, I wanted to go to America too; it was all we spoke of. Yet, I wasn't comfortable leaving the only family I knew in my short life. My recollections of America were sparse; I had forgotten English and only spoke Greek. Parnion was the only home I knew, even if I had lived there under such primitive, hellish circumstances. For me, parting from Parnion was difficult.

For starters, we were going to live in a place I had never heard of. "A Narbor?" I couldn't even understand the word. "What is a narbor?" I asked Mom. She explained the town's name was composed of two words: "Ann" was a woman's name and an "arbor" was a trellis like the one supporting the courtyard grapevine. "It's Ann Arbor," she told me. "Two words, Johnny." I didn't get it; why was a woman's name linked with a trellis?

"Michigan? That's an odd word, too," I said.

I remembered Chicago a little. At least Chicago had an aunt, an uncle, and cousins—I loved having cousins. The ones in Parnion had been my playmates, my buddies. "I wish we could take Demetri, Kosta, and Tasia with us to Michigan," I said to my mother. She smiled, "I wish we could too."

We had no relatives in this Ann Arbor place we were going to in Michigan. We always knew that when the war was over we could go back to the U.S., but now I realized that the loved ones we were leaving behind did not have that luxury. We had done a lot of adjusting to changing conditions in Greece, from 1937 on. Now I'd need to adjust to living in a town of bizarre names in America where there were no cousins.

Except—yes, I appreciated the special blessing of having an authentic father waiting for me in the U.S.A. During the occupation I had learned that good fathers were scarce; they died in war. But I couldn't remember my own father's face. We had not brought a photo of him when we left America in 1937.

On our last morning in Parnion, Artemis and Phillip brought over their new donkey for me to ride. Phillip had purchased the new animal to replace the one seized by the Nazis; he described it as a little too feisty, not tame like his previous donkey. And Phillip explained the reason he brought the donkey over for me to ride.

"I think life is going to change for all of us... even here in Parnion, now that the war is over, Johnny. I doubt you'll ride a donkey in America. And someday, donkeys will be gone from Greek villages because we'll be driving cars or trucks, just like Sophocles." Phillip's face brightened up, "I'd love to own and drive a truck. And, when that day comes, John, you can tell your children, 'I rode a donkey through Parnion, just for fun, when I was a boy.'"

Phillip helped me mount the animal, and as I started down the main street, it was hard for me to imagine the village with cars, instead of donkeys. Right away, I noticed the donkey was moving too fast; it was hard to slow him down. Very quickly, we had arrived at the main square.

I paused the donkey long enough to admire the bubbling lion fountain and peaceful St. George's Church. Familiar men at two or three *kafeneion* tables were focused, waving their hands about, no doubt discussing politics. Starting up again, we turned onto a minor road, passed our still shuttered, one-story schoolhouse, and quickly arrived at the cemetery. As was usual during those tragic years, black-clad women lingered between the white marble gravestones, lighting candles and igniting incense. With heads bowed, mourning wives, mothers, and sisters crossed themselves, as fragrant, white smoke drifted up into the gray, winter sky.

Having reached the dead end, I forced the difficult donkey to turn around so we could return to Grandpa's house. Passing St. Nick's fountain, I found Martha resting on Panagiota's bench; her splendid white ewe was nestled by her side. Martha smiled and called out, *"Kalo sas taxidi"* (A good journey). I returned her gracious wish with *"Kali antamosi"* (May we meet again). My quick, farewell tour of Parnion was over. Indeed, Phillip's stubborn, fast-moving donkey had been hard to manage.

Looking back, I wish that on that last day in Parnion, riding around on the donkey, I could have appreciated the place as I do now. During the time I lived there, I took its natural beauty for granted, and assumed emerald ravines and starry nights were commonplace. I expected that the world outside my rural cocoon was, more or less, similar to Parnion. After leaving the village, I came to understand that flocks of goats and sheep crowding St. Nick's fountain, and even the racket roosters make at sunrise, were extraordinary phenomena. When I dismounted the unruly donkey on that last day and went back inside Grandpa's house, I was unaware that the place I would soon be leaving was a singularly beautiful patch of earth.

Departure time had arrived: filled with teary farewells, unending embraces, and Greek style kisses, on both cheeks. Adults brought verbal messages for us to deliver to friends and family in the U.S. Each sensed the need to communicate personal survival to loved ones in America. Mother promised to make the contacts in-person, or by letter.

The family gathered in the sunny courtyard, under the bare grapevine. Aunt Anastasia, Uncle Paul, and Demetri came early to exchange farewells, and they left before the others arrived. Paul reported that he was working on rebuilding their burned-down home. During their short visit, Anastasia handed Mother a small piece of crocheted lace: her own exquisite handiwork. She said she had been working on it and had kept it in her apron pocket on the day the Germans burned Parnion. "Take it to America, dear cousin, to remember us by," she said, as the two women embraced and shed tears together. It was hard for me to say goodbye to Demetri; I didn't cry but I wanted to take him with us.

Miraculously, our Parnion family was intact: Vasili, Sophia, Kosta and Tasia; elderly Aunt Stella; our good neighbors Artemis and Phillip; Anastasia, Paul, and my best friend, Demetri. We were emaciated and ragged, but not one of us had died from executions, random shootings, famine, or disease.

However, Mom and her sister Sophia were no longer robust, bright-eyed, and blessed with rosy-cheeks. Standing around in Grandpa's chilly courtyard under the leafless vine, preparing to take our first steps back to America, it was evident that my mother and aunts were physically and mentally aged beyond their numerical years. All three were hollow cheeked, haggard, sallow, and skinny.

During the course of war, the sisters' beautiful, bright brown eyes took on permanent sadness. Deep wrinkles were now etched into their grayish complexions, and Nazi occupation had gradually eroded the tendency of all three sisters to smile. As we said our farewells, well-worn, patched, and faded dresses hung on their bodies, three sizes too big. White-haired Aunt Stella had looked old to me when we first came to Greece, but by 1945, both of her younger siblings were silver-haired and drawn, appearing as old as Stella.

Uncle Vasili looked skinny and old too; his movie star mustache and mane of thick hair were mostly gray. Though much thinner, he was still incredibly strong. And essence of wine, Vasili's signature fragrance, had never faded. Yet in all the time I spent with my dear uncle, he never, even once, showed signs of intoxication.

The sisters wept copious farewell tears. Mother promised to write and asked them to do the same. "Tell Joanna that my heart aches because I missed her. Beloved sisters, we must and will stay connected." With unbounded appreciation we thanked my aunts with our warmest embraces for their compassion, their charity, and openhanded assistance. "There is no way on earth I can thank you enough for helping my children survive," Mom sobbed.

Sophia, choking on tears, moaned, "I will miss you more than I can say, Katherine. Who knows if we will ever be together again?"

And as the eldest, Stella gave the final, emotion-filled blessing. "This turned out to be a complicated and hellish reunion, dear Katherine. May God watch over you and your dear children as you finally return to your Andrew, and to America. *Kali antamosi,* my beloved sister." (May we meet again under good circumstances.)

A few minutes before climbing into Sophocles's *Kübelwagen,* I whispered to Mom that I had one more thing to do before we left the village. "I need to say one more goodbye." Rushing into the back of Grandpa's courtyard I found Bebba and her two kids.

I had spent sleepless nights before departure day agonizing over the future of my goat. Even after sunrise on my last morning in Parnion, uncertainty plagued me, wondering if Bebba would be well cared for. Would she miss me? She loved the forest. Would Uncle Vasili have time in his day of busy carpentry to take her into the forest? Would he be too occupied to pet her?

And the worst question of all had popped into my head. "What if Uncle Vasili needed money? Would he sell our little Bebba to strangers?" What would happen to my dear pet if outsiders got a hold of her? Would she wind up—anonymous—herded from one place to another—in a flock of unfriendly goats who would be aloof and oblivious to her sweet personality and exceptional importance? But there was no closure for my questions. I had no choice: I had to say goodbye.

"I'm going to miss you, my little friend," I whispered as I hugged her neck. "You are the best pet in the world. You saved us, Bebba." Sobbing, I ran my hands along her back for my last touch. My gentle goat looked me in the eyes, as if she knew something was different. The little bell I had once tied around her neck chimed again when she lifted her head to look at me.

"You are going to be living with Uncle Vasili now," I explained. "You know, I wouldn't give you to just anybody. Uncle is a very good man and will take good care of you. He knows you are very special and he appreciates you—like I do," I promised.

Struggling to catch my breath, I held my little pet close, and Bebba looked into my eyes. Then she slightly opened her mouth— I was positive it was a smile. When she bleated her farewell, I squeezed her tightly around the middle again, and kissed the top of her head, for the last time.

Vasili spotted me hugging my treasured Bebba and watched me wiping my eyes on my sleeve as I inched my way back toward the jeep. Touched by the parting, my uncle instantly made a decision. At the last minute, he urged Mother to take one of Bebba's kids with us to Athens.

"Are you joking? That's ridiculous, Vasili. Transport a goat? Impossible! Where will we put it? And where will we keep it in Athens? That's an absurd idea! We are not traveling to Athens with a goat!" Mother was quite agitated with her brother-in-law's last minute, impractical, very inconvenient offer.

"John will care for the animal and Andrew's brothers in the big city will be happy you brought him. Believe me," Vasili reassured her. Anticipating that Bebba's kid would distract me from my unhappiness, and before Mother could stop him, he hurried back into the courtyard to fetch one of the baby goats. Unlike me, Vasili understood the real reason Dad's brothers would be glad to welcome a goat in their midst. Citizens of the big city endured terrible food shortages.

Our family had gathered on the street in front of Grandpa's house for final embraces and tears while Vasili and Sophocles loaded almost empty Buddy into the back of the vehicle. By then, Uncle Nicholas and Barba Lambros had joined the group. Nicholas approached Mom to hug her. And as he did, he pulled a sprig of green basil out of his shirt pocket and silently presented it to her.

"Fresh basil? In February? Are you a magician, Nicholas? Where did you find basil in the middle of winter?" Mother asked, finally smiling through her tears.

"I keep it as a house plant in winter, Katherine. Hopefully, someday in the very near future, when you enjoy the fragrance of basil in your own American backyard, it will bring pleasant memories of your old, white-haired Cousin Nicholas. Dear Katherine, when I am alone in my house or sometimes when I work my fields I sing to myself. I even sing songs I learned in Boston, when I lived in America. This morning, a song popped into my head that's appropriate to your departure. Perhaps you know it, too."

Then, most unpredictably, the kind old man with the noble head and big white mustache began crooning, "Give my regards to—Broadway. Remember me to Herald Square..." After a few more lines my dear old uncle, like George M. Cohan, added a line he composed himself, "Give my regards to—Andrew. You'll see him soon in grand New York." Mom quietly hugged him, smiled, and cried some more.

And for the first time in memory, Barba Lambros was silent. He merely embraced each of us and wished, "*Kalo sas taxidi*" (Safe travels). But tears rolled from his eyes when, in English, he softly added, "God Bless America."

Nikki eagerly jumped into the jeep first. Carefully maneuvering the open door, Mom followed. Hesitating before I joined them in the magnificently polished *Kübelwagen*, I reached out again to Uncle Vasili who, on closer inspection, had tears in his eyes. My uncle managed a parting smile as he handed me the small goat. For a second time, we hugged each other tightly, the small goat trapped between us, but said nothing; words weren't necessary. I knew that along with my cousins, I would miss all the adults who had gathered to say goodbye.

I was downhearted when I climbed into the transport. But the three of us, and the unnamed little goat, successfully squeezed into the open vehicle with Sophocles, who didn't mind the presence of an animal in his "new" and very crowded "machine." More hugging and crying ensued over the doors of the open car. Wishes for a good reunion, someday, were repeated until the jeep's engine spurted and a rough shifting of gears put us in motion.

I stole a final glance up at my porthole on Parnion's world—the second floor window of Grandpa's house. When the jeep backfired, Mother made the sign of the cross over herself. In that instant, Sophocles pulled away with a jerking action which made all of us gasp. The jolt startled the little brown and white kid on my lap, and he called out his own farewell bleat to Parnion.

Bumping and lurching, we commenced riding toward the highway connecting Sparta and Tripolis. Our loved ones and other villagers were still shouting, "Safe journeys to you!" from behind us and we turned around to wave back. Still visible through the cloud of dust left in the jeep's wake, I saw them crossing themselves. But when we reached the final curve in the road, they were gone from view, and I heaved an extra deep, cheerless sigh when I lost sight of them.

Passing the fringes of Parnion, I spotted a familiar clump of trees. "Look!" I shouted to my mother over the jeep's noisy engine. "Those are Grandpa's olive trees! But something's wrong, Mom. What happened? The branches are drooping."

Mother managed another rare smile. "Johnny, the limbs are touching the ground because they're loaded with new olives! We did a good job, you and I. And—thank God—we won't be here to eat them."

***

No tears for Hitler—1945:

- ❖ *January 28: Battle of the Bulge ends*

- ❖ *February 11: President Roosevelt, Winston Churchill, and Joseph Stalin meet in Yalta to decide how Germany will be divided and governed after its defeat*

- ❖ *March 7: Troops of the U.S. 1st Army cross the Rhine at Remagen and push into Germany*

- ❖ *April 11: Soldiers from the 6th Armored Division of General George S. Patton's Third Army discover and liberate the Buchenwald Concentration Camp near Weimar, Germany*

- ❖ *April 12: Franklin Delano Roosevelt dies and Harry S. Truman becomes President of the United States*

- ❖ *April 30: Hitler commits suicide*

- ❖ *May 7: War ends in Europe with formal German surrender*

- ❖ *August 15: South Korea liberated from Japanese colonial rule*

32 | GOING HOME, SLOWLY

We spent almost a year in Athens. Our uncles' apartment was too tiny to accommodate seven people, plus a small goat. So Mother's first business in the big city was to rent a room for the four of us, using funds Dad had sent: the goat remained with my uncles. Our very basic shelter, inside a private home, enjoyed a plus side: indoor running water and electricity. We shared the kitchen with our landlords. Our room's single, vertical window opened onto a tiny balcony and overlooked white, marble city sidewalks, crowded with pedestrians.

Alex was still translating for the British in Athens. My brother told us he had met a *New York Times* journalist, reporting about Greece's post-war problems. Alex had sent the first message to Dad in the U.S. about our survival via that *Times* reporter.

One evening when we were gathered in our little room, Alex explained to the three of us how he avoided arrest during his impossible journey to Athens from Parnion, a few years before. We listened, transfixed, while he described his travels. "The German military machine had been guarding all passable roads throughout the Peloponnesian peninsula—all the way to Athens," he reminded us. "To avoid getting captured, I knew I had to outsmart German sentries.

"I scraped my way to Athens along obscure mule and goat paths… so no one could spot me. The countryside was crawling with Nazis and I didn't know which Greeks were damned collaborators. I couldn't trust anyone."

He described bloody gashes he suffered walking through wild, impenetrable brush in the mountain wilderness, and remembered how hungry he had felt. "During the day, I found shelter in remote churches, shepherds' huts, and abandoned caves. I climbed mountains at night." Steep mountainous hikes through impassable terrain took their toll on him as he scaled craggy heights in darkness and cold. But Alex finally reached northeastern Peloponnesos. He had arrived at the Isthmus of Corinth, a severely narrow, and profoundly steep canal flooded at its base by waters of the Corinthian Gulf mingling with those of the Aegean Sea.

A narrow neck of land, an isthmus, had always connected the Greek mainland, at the north, with Peloponnesos, in the south. The isthmus separated the western Ionian Sea from the Aegean, on Greece's eastern side. Newer technology in the 1890s finally allowed a four-mile marine passageway to be dug through the isthmus. The resulting canal permitted a shortcut for ships, which previously needed to sail around the entire Peloponnesian peninsula to travel from one sea to the other.

To facilitate land travelers, construction of two crucial bridges over the canal vitally relinked the two landmasses: one bridge for pedestrians and motor vehicles, the other for the railroad.

"The isthmus was heavily inundated with Germans. It was one of their most strategic strongholds," Alex continued. "Nazis were everywhere, guarding both bridges. But, crossing the canal on one of those overpasses was the only way I could get to Athens. How could I cross a bridge—heavily fortified by Hitler's army—without being confronted and taken into custody?"

Alex said that while he hid from the Germans in a thick clump of bushes—with a view of the bridge—he took lots of time to give his dilemma serious study. He decided the Nazi-guarded vehicle bridge was completely off-limits to him; there was no way to cross it undetected. "I finally spotted a long German military train crossing the railroad bridge. It was heading north toward the mainland. That was the direction I needed to go in, and I decided on a plan." Alex was about to turn into Superman's predecessor—the Phantom.

My intrepid brother patiently waited for the next north-going train. As the locomotive started navigating the militarily fortified railroad bridge spanning the Isthmus of Corinth, Alex told us that he leapt onto the rushing train, "Holding on for dear life to the *underside* of a railroad car so I would not be seen—I crossed to the other side of the bridge." Hearing this, Mother cringed, glanced up toward heaven and crossed herself. Alex smiled. "Except for that wild and noisy, two-minute, German train ride, I walked all the way to Athens from Parnion." My big brother's odyssey left me flabbergasted.

We also learned from Alex that the Nazis had viciously continued killing, dynamiting, and burning while they were in the act of leaving Greece behind them. But the long-awaited German withdrawal had not brought peace and quiet. My uncles and brother filled us in on the horribly violent situation that had detonated in Athens in December of 1944, prior to our February '45 arrival. While street violence and killings had exploded in the center of the city in December, the British army had arrived, in formidable force, to settle down civic violence. Greece was drowning in Byzantine-style chaos due to a state of affairs, which worsened during the Nazi occupation.

Back in 1943, the Germans had installed their quisling, Ioannis Rallis, as Greek Prime Minister. It was Rallis who had instituted the horrendous Security Battalions: units of pro-Nazi, Greek collaborators, which he officially dispersed throughout the country to spy on and betray the overwhelming majority of Greeks who were not pro-Nazi. I recalled Papadopoulos in Parnion—the collaborator who had brought the Nazi officer to question my mother at Grandpa's house—and the other who brought half-a-dozen Nazi soldiers to our door on another day. It took days for Mom to recover from those horrible encounters.

Ruthless collaborators had raided village homes to take whatever they wanted, even when not accompanying Nazi soldiers. Most Greeks despised collaborators and saw them as traitorous opportunists. Pursuing greed and power for themselves, members of the Security Battalions expected to rule Greece for the Nazis after the German victory—the reason they sided with Hitler. The unwarranted Nazi presence in Parnion, instigated by quisling Papadopoulos, resulted in false accusations of innocent villagers, killings, unmitigated fear, and the burning of sixty homes.

When the Germans withdrew from Greece, pro-German Prime Minster Rallis was imprisoned along with many Battalion combatants—but not all of them. Some of Rallis's collaborators were still on Athens' streets wielding violence, making brutal circumstances even more complicated and harmful.

Even before the war was over, the great fear in Great Britain and the U.S. was that when the Nazis lost the war, Greece would be taken over by communists from the north because neighboring northern countries Albania, Yugoslavia, and Bulgaria were all under the mighty thumb of the U.S.S.R. Supporting this fear was the fact that, during the war, many *antartes*, influenced by the north, had become zealous communists.

On the other hand, however, a great many fiercely, anti-Nazi, *antartes* backed democratic rule for Greece—that's why they had risked their lives to fight against Nazi fascism. Those *antartes* were not communists. The overwhelming majority of Greeks were solidly against establishing a communist government in their country; there was no question about that.

World War II was fought throughout Europe to wipe out vicious, fanatical fascism. While fascist Hitler was in power, Nazis fought communism because it threatened fascism. And clearly, neither fascism nor communism represent democracy.

Collaborators in Rallis's Security Battalions were pro-Hitler fascists—but as dedicated fascists, they were also anti-communist. Worse yet, the Security Battalions meted unspeakable violence to innocent Greek citizens in the name of putting down communism. It was similar to the McCarthy era in the U.S. when fearful, innocent citizens were squelched with the threat of unjustly being labeled "communists." Except that in Greece, the Battalions squelched fellow Greeks by jailing or killing them.

And here's where the Greek state of affairs in the 1940s worsened. The British, fearing that communism would overwhelm the Greeks, focused on supporting already organized groups inside Greece, which were loudly anti-communist—and the Security Battalions fit the bill.

Incredibly, the British overlooked the Battalions' brutal, pro-Hitler atrocities; they not only released Greek collaborators from prisons, but they also armed them. Recognizing the collaborators as anti-communist, the British chose to become allies of the hated Security Battalions. Many Greeks saw this as a betrayal by the British, who the Greeks had regarded as best friends and allies during the occupation.

As a result, multiple political divisions hacked apart the country. Three of the many ideologies included: conservative royalists who wanted a monarchy, liberals who desired democracy over both a royalty-ruled Greece or a communistically ruled country, and the communists.

The liberals had hated Metaxas's 1930's dictatorship, and despised the Greek king because he had helped to install Metaxas's dictatorship; liberals were ready for a democratically ruled Greece.

But royalists felt comfortable slipping back into the days when Greece was a monarchy, and they were in favor of having the Greek king return. Great Britain, a constitutional monarchy, also favored restoring the Greek monarchy. And, the power-hungry Security Battalion members had *already infiltrated* the royalist side.

At the same time, the radically different, brutally aggressive, third point of view included the growing numbers of armed, ferocious, pro-communist *antartes.* This revolting set of extremely toxic circumstances would result in the appalling, violent, Greek civil war.

When it was all over and done with, non-communist Greek *antartes* unfairly got a bad name. Whereas in France and the Netherlands, resistance fighters were lauded with medals and memorials—in Greece they became unmentionable. Unjustly painting all *antartes* with the same red brush, as the saying goes, tragically extended an undeserved, unjust, Marxist reputation to those heroic Greek resistance fighters in WWII who were not communist, and who had helped rid the world of Hitler.

Even in the 1960s, hundreds of men and women, whose only crime was fighting the Germans, could still be found incarcerated in Greek prisons—a tragic ending to convoluted chaos. To show what chaos Greece suffered after WWII ended, during our one-year stay in Athens, alone, between early 1945 and early 1946, the Greek government went through five prime ministers.

Mother stayed away, as far as possible, from political turmoil. She only wished for us to get out of Greece and return to the U.S. as soon as possible. But not knowing how much longer we would have to remain there, Mother enrolled Nikki and me in a private school, almost immediately after we arrived from the village. Public schools were still closed.

"War and lack of schooling didn't bring amnesia, I hope," my mother teased. "You still remember how to read, write, add, subtract, and all the rest, don't you? I can't be bringing ignorant children back to your father."

Nikki and I walked a mile from our rented room to school. On our first day, we passed the National Archeological Museum, closed since the start of the war. I don't know if ancient treasures had been moved from there and hidden during the occupation. But what was both fascinating and creepy about the place in 1945 were the unruly prisoners incarcerated in the museum's cellar. A crowd of dirty, bearded, discontented men shouted at passers-by, non-stop, from behind heavy, iron bars, installed into glassless window frames at ground level—they terrified us.

The grubby prisoners became scarier when we heard them yelling, "Freedom or Death!" "We're innocent!" "Demand Free Elections!" while wildly rattling the windows' iron bars. "The people must rule!" "Demand democracy!" they insisted. The two of us handled the situation by silently staring straight ahead, and pretending not to notice blatantly noticeable, angry, raucous men.

When Nikki told Mother about the prisoners, she found us another route for getting to school.

Not knowing, as a kid, that Greek jails were filled to the brim with political prisoners and that the country was on the brink of civil war in early 1945, I wondered what those guys were doing locked up in the museum basement. As an adult I learned that the power-hungry Security Battalions, backed by the British, had arrested so many of the opposition that they had run out of prisons. So they utilized the closed-for-the-war, well-fortified museum as a jail. When I comprehended the reason the revered building's basement had been transformed into a prison, I finally understood the rhetoric we had heard prisoners shouting to pedestrians.

Mother was keeping her focus on getting back home to America, and needed to do some basic shopping to prepare us for travel. But she encountered a major glitch when she attempted to withdraw money that Dad had sent for her to use. My father had been informed to send her funds via an account at the American Embassy in Athens.

The first time Mother arrived at the embassy to take out some cash, she learned that her name was not on the account. My father had been advised to put Uncle Petros's name on the account instead. So every time she needed money, she had to go through Petros, "the middleman" she had been hoping to shake off, even when we were back in Parnion. Petros persisted in complaining about Mother's sensible requests, and griped that going out of his way to reach the embassy took too much of his precious time. Mom grew to detest the complicated but necessary process.

Dad also sent us several "care" packages while we lived in Athens. He had personally packed, wrapped, and addressed the large boxes, which brought forth a variety of nonperishable foods and some clothing. Receiving packages in the mail from America was the equivalent of experiencing Disneyland for the first time, after four years of having next to nothing. And opening gifts from our very own father was like getting presents from Santa Claus. Nikki and I couldn't have been more thrilled.

Several boxes contained clothes, but Dad was obviously not adept at judging sizes; we shared items that didn't fit us with others because shortages, of every category, abounded in Athens. People were happy to get free clothes, even if they didn't fit perfectly; seams could easily be taken in.

The most exciting packages from Dad contained food. I remember delectable cookies with the mysterious word "Nabisco" printed on colorful packaging and luscious chocolate bars enclosed in dark brown wrappers, labeled "HERSHEY." Spam made a big hit; Mom cut it up and fried it with eggs. I also recall Ritz and Saltine Crackers, Quaker Oats, Cream of Wheat, Uncle Ben's Rice, and a variety of canned goods. Some tins, labeled "Del Monte," produced sweet sliced peaches. Cans were opened with a gadget Mom referred to as the "opener," which Dad had thoughtfully enclosed in one of his surprise-filled cartons. Mother shared some of our goodies with my uncles, to smooth over relations with Petros, but they may not have been quite as dazzled with our strange American food as we were.

Dad sent a canned ham in one box. When Mother began turning the attached key to break the seal on the metal container, a foul smelling liquid gushed out, spurting up into the room, like Old Faithful. We jumped away from the exploding ham in disbelief. Ignoring our complaints about the rotten stench, Mother sent Nikki and me off to find old rags and buckets of water to wash away the putrid liquid, which dripped off the ceiling onto everything below.

"Well, the ham's gone bad," Mom, gingerly announced. "What a waste. It's so wrong to throw meat away when so many people are hungry. And I'm sure your father paid good money for it. I detest seeing food wasted, but eating this meat would certainly kill us." "Ham" was a new concept for me; I wasn't familiar with anything like it. When I looked at the reddish/pinkish rotten substance, it reminded me of bullet wounds I had seen on dead bodies in Parnion. Mother quickly disposed of the tin and its contents and we opened up the window to air out the apartment. I

298

didn't taste ham again until we were in Ann Arbor; even then I was suspicious of the strange, pink meat.

Athens, Greece's signature metropolis, was more ruined than the ancient, marble buildings on its two thousand-year-old Acropolis. Athenians suffered in many ways. The famine had taken its toll, but at least the city was no longer gripped with famine as it had been in 1942-1943: still, no one was "overstuffed with food." Disease was rampant, as it had been in Parnion. Some Athenians resembled walking corpses. As in the village, skinny people with grayish complexions walked around in worn, patched clothing, three sizes too large. Alex told us that in the midst of the *katohi* (occupation), dead bodies had piled up on Athens' boulevards because the bereaved were too poor and too weak to bury loved ones. Wooden carts had regularly collected bodies from neighborhood streets. Recovery from the evils of war was decades away.

In post-war Athens, skinny kids like me peddled various and sundry wares on street corners to help their families survive. A boy I made friends with in the neighborhood told me that when the occupation began, his family fled from Athens to his mother's village, near Tripolis. Wartime inflation had become so destructive to the Greek economy that his father sold a piece of property in Peloponnesos in exchange for one suitcase full of cigarettes. After negotiating the strange swap, his father had died. Now, at fourteen, the kid stood on Athens' street corners hawking those same cigarettes, one by one, to enable him and his mother to buy food. He said, "If we didn't have these cigarettes, we would not eat. It turned out, my father's trade was a good one."

When we arrived in Athens, Alex had already applied for passage home. Mother was deeply relieved in early summer of 1945, when, as a party of one, he was offered a berth on a ship leaving right away. Meanwhile, we three waited for space to accommodate all of us together.

After Alex's departure, Mother received Parnion news in a letter from her brother George. No word had arrived yet about

Aunt Joanna. Observing the confusion and destruction that had been wreaked on broken-down Athens, my mother was not surprised that they had not yet located her sister. George reported that villagers continued suffering, and it would take years to recover; we weren't surprised.

More tragic Parnion news concerned our good neighbors, Artemis and Phillip. Mom, Nikki, and I wept when we read that our good neighbor Phillip had experienced a bizarre accident. He had been kicked in the head by their ornery, post-war donkey while shoeing the obstinate animal. Phillip suffered serious injuries—and died. Shocked, we sorely grieved at the tragedy. Honest, hardworking Phillip had survived the war, but was suddenly gone.

"If Germans had not stolen his first donkey, the gentle critter he was used to working with everyday, Phillip would probably still be alive," I cried. "And now he'll never drive a truck, like he wanted to, because of that damned donkey and the damned Nazis."

Sixty-plus years later I realize proper medical treatment for serious head injuries did not exist in the village in 1945; there was no emergency transport to get Phillip to a hospital for help that might have saved his life. Back in Parnion, heartbroken Artemis lived the rest of her years without the love of her life. Mother wrote our condolences to her, reminding us, "Funerals, whether we like attending them or not, children, are a part of life on earth, in war and in peace."

After countless trips to the U.S. Embassy to stand in infinitely multiplying lines, we finally received our new American passports and tickets to sail to New York on Swedish America Line's *SS. Gripsholm*, the same ship on which Alex had sailed home before us.

We departed from Piraeus in early February of 1946, elated and excited about arriving in New York where, Dad had written, he would be waiting for us. We were grateful that we were leaving Greece during a very narrow time-gap—before the full-blown outbreak of civil war.

Our voyage was scheduled to take at least 14 days—a rather slow crossing. Ships, like the *Gripsholm*, which were sailing the Atlantic in the post-war period, needed to take additional time to detect and avoid suspected explosive mines left behind by Germans. We boarded with great excitement, but were disheartened to learn that, according to the immense ship's sleeping regulations, I would be separated from my mother and Nikki. They were assigned to women's quarters, and as a thirteen-year-old male, I was required to bunk with the men.

Nikki and I would meet on deck to watch all the activity together. Proceeding smoothly through the Mediterranean, the *Gripsholm* stopped in Naples and Marseilles to take in more passengers. My sister and I stood wide-eyed at the railing, enthralled by the commotion in these colorful, exotic cities—so much livelier than our village cocoon.

On board, we were also impressed with the diversity of our fellow passengers. One day, we saw a beautifully dressed woman at an adjacent table, out on the ship's deck, drinking a beverage of remarkable color: a luscious caramel sparked with burgundy. She sipped the mysterious liquid through a straw from a glass filled with intriguing ice cubes (a new phenomenon for us). The ice sparkled in the sunlight and jingled when she lifted her glass.

As she conversed with her companion in English, I wondered, "What superb beverage can this pretty woman be drinking?" After we were in Ann Arbor I spotted the luscious beverage again at Dad's restaurant. When I asked my father about it, he gladly filled a glass with the magic elixir and served it to me with ice cubes and a straw: my first taste of ice cold, refreshing Coca-Cola.

Waters were calm as we sailed through the Azores at night. I focused on black silhouettes of the silent islands protruding out of the dark sea like intimidating phantoms. But, after the ship began crossing the great ocean, the roaring, tumultuous waters of the Atlantic in February turned our voyage into a white-knuckle ride. Mom and I, both of us nauseous and dizzy, suffered from serious bouts of *mal de mer* and permanently kept to our segregated cabin bunks. The *Gripsholm* fiercely tossed about, like a coffin caught in white-water rapids. Adult men around me groaned; they were as terrified as I was.

When the immense ship's bow rose high out of the water—the stern became fully submerged in the dark ocean. Horrific thoughts drifted through my dizzy head as I rode my mattress like a rodeo champion: "What's happening to Mom and Nikki?" I worried. The vessel violently rocked up and then down again—for days. From my pillow, I chanced to glimpse around at men in other cabin bunks; like me, they were sick, green about the gills, and vomiting. The ship also produced loud, creaking sounds, which made us gasp. I shut my eyes to avoid looking at the porthole—it was submerged under the Atlantic's bleak waters.

Would the huge vessel split in two and spit us out into the unforgiving ocean? Would Mom, Nikki, and I see each other for a last time, before our bodies silently drifted to the bottom of the icy sea? Yet, the smiling ship's crew went about their business, unperturbed, incredibly relaxed, and smiling—providing me hope that we might survive.

My sweaty hands held tight to the sides of the bed frame and I sealed my eyelids to avoid looking at a ceiling in motion above my swaying *Gripsholm* mattress. Asleep or awake—it was difficult to know the difference—I "dreamed" snippets of my life in Greece. They flashed by like Technicolor coming attractions. Some memories were pleasant: Mother enjoying the sight of a flock of sheep; Bebba grazing in green fields; cozy nights, listening to stories by Grandpa's fireplace.

But as the ship lurched on, good memories faded to black, and bad ones flickered onto the screen in my head. Again, I felt sickening dread when my furious mother yelled at a Nazi officer following the theft of Martha's ewe. In my seasick nightmare, I watched the Germans set fire to our house. I replayed the Nazi curfew, when I waited to explode in gunfire while gripping bloody goat's liver. But by the time we reached New York, I was relieved to know, for sure, that incredible scenes of terror were from my past—ended. Crushing fear was finally over.

The ship finally passed into calmer waters nearer New York. And we all emerged from our respective cabins. Mom appeared haggard, but Nikki was hale and hearty. I was puzzled that Nikki's ocean journey had been vastly different than mine. She enjoyed every moment of the trip, ate heartily, explored the tempest-tossed ship with gusto, and even strummed a borrowed mandolin to entertain other vigorous passengers.

***

Japanese surrender finally brings WWII to an end—1945:

- ❖ *September 2: Wars ends in Asia and the rest of the world with formal Japanese surrender*

- ❖ *October 5: "Meet the Press" premiers on radio*

- ❖ *Americans are singing Johnny Mercer's hit "Ac-Cent-Tchu-Ate the Positive"*

- ❖ *Popular American movies: "Bells of St. Mary's" with Bing Crosby and Ingrid Bergman; "Without Love" with Spencer Tracy and Katharine Hepburn*

- ❖ *Chicago Cubs win N.L. pennant race but lose World Series to Detroit Tigers*

33 | NEW YORK TO ANN ARBOR

The excitement of reaching New York replaced my seasick misery. Keyed up, I attempted to watch the giant *Gripsholm's* docking through a steamy porthole, but didn't see much. Dark, heavy clouds hung down from the sky; snowflakes were falling.

"Come on Johnny, it's time to go." Nikki's voice, accompanied by her forceful tug on my sleeve, pulled me into line for disembarking. The three of us waited for our journey to end in a queue of other eager, shoving passengers.

"Shove back. Don't let them get in front of us," I urged Nikki.

At once, Mother gripped my elbow. "Don't push! We've waited eight years. We can tolerate a few more minutes, John."

Yielding to the human exodus, Nikki and I reluctantly let fellow voyagers thrust themselves ahead of us. Everyone on that ship yearned to walk on reliably firm land again—particularly the American variety. The immense Swedish ocean liner had finally delivered us from millennia-old, war-desecrated Greece, to the pristine, up-to-date New York City of February 20, 1946. Alex had arrived in the U.S. on the same ship, seven months before.

Inching toward the *Gripsholm's* exit deck, Mom, cool on the outside but surely more eager than the rest of us on the inside, restlessly scrutinized Nikki and me in our new winter coats, personally buttoning them, with collars up. Mother was savvy about northern Februarys; my sister and I were not. Dad had sent money to her in Athens to buy us wool coats when he realized we would be arriving in the dead of winter.

The moment finally arrived when it was my turn to cross over the ship's steel threshold into the great outdoors. Stepping into unexpected whiteness, I was startled to find myself engulfed in cold, heavily falling snow—tons of it—and more thrilled in that extraordinary instant than if it had been a white Christmas Eve.

The surprise winter storm stirred already excited passengers: some laughed, most gawked up into it. But when I glanced over at Mom, I saw her silent and pensive. Her eyes were fixed on the dock ahead of us: American *terra firma*.

Mere yards away, on the other side of the ship's icy railing, the U.S.A. came closer, but was still out of our reach. Firmly gripping her light bag and proceeding, step by blessed step, toward home, Mother held Nikki close with one arm and pulled me toward her with the other. Ice-frosted bureaucrats, peeking out under snowy caps, gazed at our papers for an umpteenth inspection before we departed the ship via the slippery gangplank.

And when we, at last, stepped upon solid, snow-covered America, I sensed exhilaration, as though we had achieved an incomparable triumph—like winning an Olympic medal.

Mom unexpectedly took us out of line, after we had officially reached the U.S., to let other passengers pass around us. Moved to tears, she struggled to clear her throat. "We're home, at last, children. Let's slow down, and thank God for bringing us back safely." Like Nikki, who had endured the crossing like a seasoned admiral, I crossed myself, more than grateful our tumbling, winter voyage on the Atlantic and all that had preceded it were over. The tempest-tossed journey infused in me an aversion to ships and sailing that has lasted to this day.

Nikki and I breathlessly turned our faces every which way to take in delightful, feathery white snow. And in an instant my eyes locked on fairy tale silhouettes of tall buildings soaring in the fuzzy distance. Barely visible, my stare questioned their reality. "Skyscrapers?" Mom smiled at me reassuringly, with that warm smile that had sadly evaporated during the war years. "They're real, Johnny. We're in America."

Walking away from the towering ship at dockside, we passed a Red Cross booth fragrant with the enticing aromas of hot coffee and crispy little cakes that Mom told us were "donuts." Mother, too anxious and excited to eat anything, encouraged Nikki and me to try them. Gracious, smiling, American ladies, in navy blue, wool capes and white nurses' caps embroidered with Red Cross logos, generously introduced us to an American indulgence.

I selected a powdered sugar covered goody, thinking to myself, "This must be the American version of *kourambiedes*" (the butter cookies I had bolted down during the wartime village wedding). The ancient gods' ambrosia could not have satisfied a newly repatriated boy citizen better than gratis, powdered-sugar donuts did. I couldn't believe the donuts were free—and served with a smile too. I have had a warm spot in my heart for the American Red Cross since that day.

With delectable donuts lining my empty stomach, Mom, Nikki, and I were guided through continuously falling snow toward a long line of waiting taxis. I was thrilled to step into an authentic, American car—a dream-come-true for the kid who grew up in rural Parnion. "Sophocles would love to own this taxi," I remarked to my grinning sister, who was as excited as I was. The frosty, yellow cab drove us a short distance to the port reception area where a huge crowd waited for new arrivals from the *Gripsholm* to descend from the queue of arriving taxis. "Those are Americans!" I realized.

A first glimpse of my fellow-Americans found them dressed in serious winter attire: pulled-down hats, pulled-up boots, thick overcoats, colorful scarves, gloves and mittens in multicolored permutations. I had never seen such clothing before. As our taxi slowly approached the curb, Mother calmly and silently pointed to a man in the crowd, standing next to a wall, about twenty feet away. He was anxiously peering inside each taxi that went by him.

The fidgety American on the curb was wrapped in an ankle-length, heavy coat of brown wool tweed; a yellow and brown plaid scarf tightly guarded his neck, and the snowy brim of his gray fedora hat half-concealed his face. He dashed over to our cab as it pulled to the curb, glanced into the icy back window, and then hurried away to inspect the snowy cab behind us.

Since Mom had pointed him out, seconds before, I continued following the movements of the unknown man in the funny looking, very long coat. And as I did, I watched his high-top galoshes hesitate on the slushy sidewalk. Next I saw him turn around to rivet his attention on our taxi for a second time when I heard Mom say, "*That* is your father."

A jolt like an electric shock ran through me. Shut off from everything American, I had forgotten how to speak English and even more embarrassing, I had forgotten my very own father's face. Yet Mom, who had not seen him for almost eight years, recognized him immediately, even as he stood in blinding snow. I curiously continued staring, trying to see his face, which was still shaded by the icy fedora.

When our driver stopped at the curb, Mom quickly grabbed the door handle, opened the taxi door, and pulled herself out of the back seat to face my father in the falling snow. Nikki and I followed.

Dumbfounded, I stared at him while he, in turn, absorbed the reality that we were there, actually standing in front of him. Wordless, he smiled as he embraced my mother tightly and for a long time; the only word she uttered as she hugged him back was his name, "Andrew." Then he turned to clasp Nikki and me—both at the same time—one arm around each of us, in a firm, long-lasting, double squeeze. When his heavy brown wool coat enveloped me in an elated, bear hug that morning, I felt relief that, at last, we were together again.

Smiling, and with tears streaming down his cheeks, Dad's first words included the traditional Greek welcome. "I have waited a long time to say, *Kalos oresate.*"

"Too long," Mom replied, looking relieved and happy to see him.

"I didn't know if you were alive during those years before the war ended…" Dad's voice wavered and he stopped talking; tears in the corners of his eyes began running down his cheeks.

In spite of the emotions pouring out of him, I was surprised to find my very own father looking robust and healthy. Clean-shaven, he appeared younger than I expected. Most adult men I interacted with for almost a decade wore mustaches; by war's end their faces were gaunt and emaciated. When Dad had finally removed his hat, I noticed his teary hazel eyes, light complexion, friendly features, and full head of graying hair, cut short, Spencer Tracy-style. The heavy tweed coat concealed the medium build of a sturdy man who, to me, looked as American as the Stars and Stripes.

Beaming, he thanked our cabdriver in what sounded like perfect English, then turned to us and spoke in flawless Greek. I may have forgotten his face, but the mystery man I yearned to be with for eight interminable years was, at that moment, valiant George Washington fused with ancient, noble Athenian Pericles. Reunion with my father brought on long-absent comfort: innate calm. He was my newly reclaimed, genuine hero—my very own father—our safe haven.

I may not have remembered his face, but Dad had recognized us, although his tremor of recognition had hesitated when he watched our taxi pulling to the sidewalk. His shock at our appearance was obvious. He anticipated that Nikki and I would have grown, of course, but he didn't expect us to look bony and sallow; Mom's silver hair surprised him too. Dad didn't know, yet, the nitty gritty of what we had been through, even if he had already heard plenty about the war from Alex. My brother had been living in Athens for much of the occupation and did not personally know the war as we had lived through it in the village.

Right away, Dad said, "After we check in at the hotel, I have a special 'welcome home' treat for you. And, we'll be seeing New York City together for a few days before taking the train home to Michigan." He saw to it that our belongings were removed from the first taxi's trunk, and he tipped the driver. Then Dad hailed a second cab and the four of us crowded into the back seat together for our ride into Manhattan.

Snow was falling heavily while the driver slowly inched us through snow-covered architectural canyons on deserted city streets. Yellow cabs and green-checkered taxis were the only vehicles trudging through the surrealistic storm. Red backlight auras from taxis we followed trail-blazed us through blinding whiteness; the cab's clacking windshield wipers sluggishly brushed aside persistently accumulating snow.

Mom's wartime anger at Dad's failed plan had quickly dissolved when the war ended. Now, fatigued by the long, grueling journey, she was elated to be with him again and paid little attention to the drama of the blizzard. Riding together in the taxi, she asked about my brother. With his arms around Nikki and me, my father cheerfully responded to Mother's concerns.

"Alex," Dad proudly told her, "is in Ann Arbor attending his classes at the University of Michigan." His eyes twinkled when he smiled, even though they occasionally filled with tears. While our parents discussed Alex's new life, Nikki and I twisted our amazed heads left, right, and upward to view the sights of an extraordinary, American city. But, Dad studied the three of us, instead of the skyscrapers.

Following our check-in at the Diplomat Hotel on 43rd Street, he hurried us off, by foot, toward his special treat in Times Square, linking his arm through Mother's to protect her from falling on the slippery sidewalks. Astonishing sights in every direction grabbed my attention. Celebrated New York skyscrapers had lost their heads in thick, gray skies, while immense neon signs, touting stuff I'd never heard of, boldly flashed on and off in garish colors. American lights were dazzling, far brighter than the crude oil lamp that had lit Grandpa's house.

Even with mounds of snow filling sidewalks, New York City appeared to be a naturally flat place. "Perhaps skyscrapers are its mountains," I thought to myself. My father pleasantly nodded to heavily dressed men shoveling snow off ample sidewalks; they nodded back. Surprised he was acquainted with these New Yorkers, I asked him how he knew them; after all, he didn't live in the city. Dad cheerfully explained that he enjoyed the friendly American practice of nodding pleasantly to strangers when walking down the street.

"Americans are friendly people?" I asked.

Smiling, he assured me, "Far more often than not." As we approached the Times Building, Dad pointed to last minute February 20 news: "TRUMAN SIGNS EMPLOYMENT ACT." Mesmerized, my eyes fixed on illuminated words crawling, non-stop, around *New York Times'* headquarters.

His surprise awaited us in Times Square, at Broadway and 43rd Street. Glistening store windows revealed white linen-covered tables set attractively with stemmed glass, matching china, and cleverly folded napkins: Toffenetti's Restaurant. Entering through a tricky, fast-moving revolving door, Nikki's eyes widened at the bustling scene of waitresses delivering huge trays of steaming dishes to well-dressed diners. I was as impressed as Nikki.

A polite gentleman in white shirt, dark suit, and tie seated us at a table covered with cloth, china, glass, and silver. Realizing that Nikki and I were probably unfamiliar with American breakfast choices (and he was right), Dad gave our food order to a cheery waitress dressed in a black and white uniform. In no time at all, she delivered two glasses of milk to our table for Nikki and me, along with two cups of hot coffee for Mom and Dad.

Attempting to shyly break the ice a little more with my father, I volunteered a piece of our previous life with him. "I have a goat in Parnion, Daddy. Her name is Bebba... she's with Uncle Vasili now. Bebba gave us milk."

Mother promptly explained Bebba's role in our survival. "Johnny kept his goat well-fed so she could produce milk. And he kept her hidden, so she would not end up in a Nazi dinner. Bebba kept us alive, Andrew."

Wide-eyed at our first reference to previous suffering, Dad somberly contemplated Mom's explanation. But in an effort to keep our reunion easy and carefree, he instantly smiled again and unexpectedly raised high his steaming coffee cup to proclaim, "I propose a toast—to Bebba. She helped my family come back to me...alive." Tears filled our parents' eyes again.

Dad told me, later, that he took us to Toffenetti's—first—because he felt it was his responsibility to feed us as soon as possible. "All three of you, though beautiful in my eyes, looked awful. You were emaciated!"

I gladly cooperated with his Toffenetti plan, gratefully devouring luscious, warm, crispy waffles and pancakes soaked with rich butter and warm syrup, multiple slices of luscious bacon, buttered toast smothered with a variety of fruit jams (I used them all at once), washed down with several glasses of cold, fresh cow's milk. Toffenetti's morning fare was a memorable banquet. Mother enjoyed her first American cup of coffee and full breakfast in almost a decade.

"I want to absorb and forever remember this incredibly blessed reunion," Mother said as she glanced around at the three of us. "Here we are... finally safe... together... and eating a great American breakfast in this wonderful restaurant. I wish Alex could be here too. I'm so happy he's enrolled at the university, and I know he'll do well there." Relaxing her shoulders, Mom's face was serene again as she crossed herself. "I thank God for this joyous day—our day to celebrate."

Tenderly gazing at Dad and surveying Nikki and me, Mother's eyes took on the radiance of Easter candles. The tranquil, warm, and joyous look that had been missing from my mother's classic features for almost a decade, along with her exquisite smile, were permanently resurrected in Mr. Toffenetti's restaurant. But a question from Nikki broke the enchantment. "Daddy, is your restaurant as big as this one?"

"No, Nikki, my Busy Bee is a fraction of this place. You'll see it when we go home to Ann Arbor this week. You can eat anything you want at the Busy Bee. I'll make hot beef sandwiches with mashed potatoes and gravy for you, your mother, and Johnny. As many as your stomachs can hold."

Now happy and content, Nikki remembered, "During the war, Mama used to tell us about those sandwiches, Daddy. I can't wait to eat one."

Four days later, a yellow cab deposited us at cavernous Grand Central Station for our trip to Ann Arbor. Dad plowed us through a surging crowd inside the immense waiting room: African-Americans, Asians, men and women in American military uniform. The immense railroad station was chock full of the most wide-ranging assortment of human beings I had ever seen. "It's best not to stare at people, Johnny, It's not considered polite in America," Dad confided.

Shiny glass and metal doors led us into a vast, darkish place attached to the bright waiting room where multitudes of unending, side-by-side rails glistened in cold darkness. Colossal black locomotives, silvery streamliners, and sleek passenger cars hissed, spewed out steam, and radiated a tremendous, pent-up energy: they were steel giants clearly indicating they were ready to go someplace.

We enjoyed Dad's company, ate good food together, and looked out train windows on our exciting overnight ride. Buildings in America were modern looking and well-kept, not broken, like buildings in Greece were after the war. I was intent on taking in every detail of my recovered homeland while the train streaked west, through snowy eastern America. When my breath iced the window, I used my fingernails to scrape away the kaleidoscope of crinkly frost.

The train finally arrived at Ann Arbor, Michigan, a city buried in snow. As I stepped down off the train to the cleared-off platform, my eyes fell on an icy stream within sight of the railroad station. "What's that, Daddy?" I asked, never having seen a body of water with chunks of ice in it. "The Huron River," he replied.

Dad hailed a taxi and gave the driver an address. We skidded along Ann Arbor's icy streets under leafless branches, freshly frosted with exquisite snow. Trees gracefully arched high above the slowly moving cab—trees were everywhere. And when the taxi pulled over to stop at a buried curb on Second Street, Dad proudly pointed to the two-story, brown, brick house on the corner and announced, "Welcome home!"

Focusing on our new "digs," I blurted out, "Wow! A downstairs and an upstairs!" Enthralled by tons of snow burying an entire city, including our "new" house, I didn't know on my arrival that shoveling and removing the icy, white stuff from front walk, steps, porch, and both public sidewalks adjacent to our corner lot would become my sole responsibility for as long as I lived in the house.

Two bare trees emerged from both sides of five stone steps leading up to the front door; windows graced both sides of the inviting entrance. A pair of second-story windows peered out between naked tree branches, and four skinny, white, wooden columns held up an attached roof that shaded the wide front porch—not quite Mount Vernon, but not usual in the Greek village houses I was used to. Various shapes of older houses, like ours, lined Second Street, as far as the eye could see.

Taking a few seconds to consider our new home, Mom crossed herself again. "My prayers are answered. It's a beautiful house, Andrew. I can't wait to see our Alex again." After almost nine years, Mother was content and ready to move on—we were home and safe. She had put Dad's near-fatal decision into the past, and my father smiled at her approval. "You'll see Alex soon, Katherine," he explained, "when his classes are finished for the day. The university is quite convenient—walking distance from home."

A few hours later, we happily reunited with my brother. Now really at home, we easily began to settle into our new residence. Indoor plumbing, a gas oven and stove, electricity, and central heating instantly improved our life-style—homemaking became easier for Mom. And, right away, on the second day, Dad walked very anxious Nikki and me, on neatly shoveled sidewalks, to enroll us in Bach Elementary School, at Jefferson and 4th Streets.

My first glimpse of distinctive Bach Elementary impressed me: it was magnificent. The two-story, kindergarten through sixth grade, school stood out in a neighborhood of typically Mid-Western, single-family homes. The handsome stone and red brick exterior, with decorative turret at roofline, was embellished with shiny, two-story high windows. Entering the first floor, I saw a wide, interior staircase traveling upward along the extremely tall windows that overlooked the street. Colored glass vases had been placed on shelves built into the windows; they glistened like stained glass as sunlight poured through them.

It was hard to believe that this splendid building was an elementary school. "If this is grammar school, what must the university look like?" Nikki whispered to me. An image of Parnion's primitive schoolhouse popped into my head as we shyly gazed around our new school.

But Nikki and I began our American school life at a disadvantage—we couldn't speak English. Dad assured our teachers that he had already hired a private tutor for us to re-learn English, at home, after school. Therefore, as a result of our forgotten English skills, we were placed in classes with younger children; I was embarrassed to be the oldest boy in 6th grade. Worse yet, the other kids couldn't figure out why these foreigners, perhaps from outer space, couldn't communicate in English, the language everyone else knew so proficiently.

Again, we were exotic strangers plunked into a company of kids who had known each other since kindergarten. Not being understood and not understanding what others were saying was imprisonment—in a frustrating twilight zone. Yet, Nikki and I were so intent on learning English words "by the book" with the help of Mr. Verros, our tutor, that I became an "A" student in spelling.

By June, even though we had not yet completely mastered English, our teachers felt Nikki and I could skip seventh grade—

and we were advanced to eighth at Slauson Jr. High School. I don't remember being teased by my classmates at either school about my imperfect English. If there were bullies at Bach, or Slauson, they didn't approach me. And with time, and a concerted effort to fit in, both Nikki and I learned English well, and comfortably made friends. Slauson was another American school with impressive facilities: football field, spacious gymnasium, science lab, cafeteria, and ultra-modern air conditioning. From my perspective, Ann Arbor schools were extraordinary.

When 1946's winter snows melted, Mom's sister Ellie and two of her adult children, Mary and Bill, drove to Ann Arbor from Chicago to welcome us back. Gracious Aunt Ellie was relieved to see that we had survived, intact, and she was intent on hearing about the war and about all the relatives we left behind in Parnion. The visit was filled with more female tears than I could stand.

Cousin Mary, whose framed college graduation photo graced the walls of Grandpa's house, was even lovelier and nicer than I remembered. Both she and Cousin Bill were great fun. He was a discharged U.S. Army Air Corps veteran who had been drafted before the war had begun, and was assigned to spend the war years Stateside. Bill riveted his attentions on our wartime experiences, labeling most of them with a new English word I learned from him: "incredible." Many delightful visits with my aunt and cousins were to take place in the years to come, when war memories finally began to fade.

During our first American springtime, Mom planted a vegetable garden. In May and June, she was delightfully surprised when our backyard came alive with well-established, billowy, gorgeous, bright pink peonies, left in the garden by the house's previous owner. In the warm, somewhat humid summer (humidity was new to us), we found sticky relief in the shade of Ann Arbor's trees. In fall, millions of leaves, from those many, many trees, tumbled down on homes, schools, businesses, and streets in rich autumn shades of crimson and gold.

We remembered the seasons in Parnion, as we went through our first year, but our occupation experiences were still too recent. Sweet nostalgia for our temporary village home was usually soured by an ugly wartime memory.

***

Memorable 1946:

- ❖ *Our family is reunited again at our home in Ann Arbor, Michigan, U.S.A.*

- ❖ *U.N. General Assembly meets for the first time (in London)*

- ❖ *George Orwell's "Animal Farm" is published*

- ❖ *Trial against Nazi war criminals begins in Nuremberg, Germany*

- ❖ *"Tide" detergent debuts*

- ❖ *UNICEF (United Nations Children's Fund) is established*

- ❖ *Frank Capra's "It's A Wonderful Life" premiers*

- ❖ *U.S. President Harry S. Truman officially proclaims the end of World War II*

34 | THE HOMEFRONT

As noted throughout these pages, we reconnected with Dad after the war by sharing our stories with each other in our Ann Arbor home. Instead of shivering by the hearth, as we had during Parnion winters, we enjoyed cozy central heating. After a hard day of work at the Busy Bee, Dad would settle in his favorite chair, the green lounger, and the rest of us would settle near him, on the cushy brown sofa.

I had imagined that my father was living a problem-free existence in the United States while we were trapped in WWII. Wasn't everything always abundant, untroubled, and cheery in America? But Dad's experiences were far different than what I had assumed.

After we had sailed away on the *Aquitania* in 1937, he continued working in Chicago as a temporary cook in everything from plain-Jane diners to high-end hotels, because he wasn't able to secure a permanent chef's position. "I learned a lot," he said, "but I wasn't making enough money... it was damn frustrating. I earned just enough to send money to you in my letters while you lived in Kalamata."

I recalled Mother's relief every time she had received one of those letters. It turned out that Dad was barely surviving himself, much less thriving enough to provide for us when we returned. I felt a pang of guilt at this, hearing of it in my post-war life. While we had struggled, I had not understood that my father had money problems of his own.

"John," he said to me, "not only was I walking on sore feet from one restaurant to another looking for a job, but when I was finally hired, I had to stand on my aching feet for hours and hours in hot, steamy kitchens, shoveling coal into sizzling ovens to bake and roast and cook all kinds of food. I learned a lot about restaurant cooking. And I guess 1941 was the year I finally started accumulating some savings." By mid-1941, Dad was working in Joliet, Illinois.

"But then, the Germans invaded Greece," he said, "and I suddenly lost my connection to you. I contacted the U.S. State Department. I contacted the Greek Embassy in Washington. I contacted the Red Cross. I badgered them with letters, telegrams, and long-distance telephone calls. No agency, government or otherwise, could help me because they told me you were trapped behind enemy lines.

"Can you even imagine how I felt when I was told my family was trapped—behind enemy lines?" Dad angrily asked with tears in his eyes. Even though we were safe now, sitting with him in our living room, he felt anguish, all over again, remembering the daunting questions that had plagued him all through the war.

"I didn't know if you remained in Kalamata—or were in a German concentration camp." He looked around, staring at each of us with his shoulders shrugged. "Were you bombing victims? Were you alive? Or dead? Nightmares haunted me. I was besieged with worry and terrible guilt. I hated myself. After all, *I* had sent you into that chaos." Dad's words reminded me of how Mother had cursed my father when she was down and out. But as angry as she had been at him in those moments, it was nothing compared to how angry he was with himself.

"I almost had a stroke when I read your mother's letters about going to court. My very own brother cruelly mistreating your mother…incredible! Denying her rights to the orchard?" Dad held his head in his hands, and told us he was shocked and disgusted with his brother Antoni's behavior. "I had trusted my brothers. We never recorded our joint purchase of the land on paper."

Dad said that when he and his two brothers had worked together on the railroad, before the 1920s, he contributed nearly half the money toward buying the orchard, but agreed on dividing ownership three ways. "I was staying in the U.S.—earning good wages. They were going back to Greece, where it was hard to make a living. They needed my help."

He told us that one weekend in early 1942, he went to visit some distant relatives in Detroit. On a side trip to Ann Arbor, he decided it was the perfect location for opening a little restaurant. Ann Arbor reminded him of Geneva, Illinois, where we had lived some happy days together as a family, before the Depression. And, he went on, "It's the home of a great university." Dad was already planning for his children to become educated—not "slave away" in the restaurant business as he had done.

The move to Michigan was his first step in preparing for our return. Yet, at that juncture of history, the war had started; millions of American men were being drafted into the Armed Services and the draft had led to a severe shortage of civilian male workers. That's when great numbers of women entered the work force to fill the labor gap. Factories in Ann Arbor worked around the clock for the war effort, and the downtown Busy Bee needed to be open around the clock too.

Dad began hiring women. He said he had not wanted to give "the ladies" hard, dirty restaurant work to do. He felt they should be home with their families at night, not working in his restaurant. "So I wound up working the night shift too. You know, John, I'm almost sixty years old. Hard work has drained me. The Busy Bee isn't open 24 hours anymore, because I'm worn out. I'm *tired.*"

Nationwide rationing of basic foodstuffs, initiated in spring of 1942, ensured that men and women in the Armed Forces had ample food to eat. Therefore, food shortages resulted in the civilian American population. "Victory Gardens" sprang up all over the U.S. My father faced his own food shortages. They were nothing like ours in Parnion, but enough to make his business difficult. Meat, sugar, fats, cheese, and coffee were rationed. But my father was a skilled chef, and his customers still praised his soup, meatloaf, and gravy.

"That gravy! Mother talked about it a lot in Parnion. What's the secret, Dad?" I asked. He leaned forward in his green easy chair to share the answer: "Bones! They were virtually free. And gave more than enough flavor," he said. Making beef stock from bones was a Depression-era trick that served him well.

"Johnny, don't think that those of us who lived in America weren't afraid." Dad explained that the American people took part in a *unique* kind of sacrifice in WWII. "Our sons marched off to risk… sacrifice… their lives in countries all over the globe. They were fighting in countries that we hadn't even heard of. Every day we mourned losing those kids who were being killed so far away from home—kids like you and Alex and Nikki.

"My customers brought in photos of their soldier-sons to show me at the restaurant. Worried men walked into my Busy Bee, proud to share a picture of their good-looking, baby-faced kid in uniform." But too often, Dad said, he saw those same proud fathers wearing black armbands when their kids were gone, forever. Dad's description reminded me that I had noticed great numbers of men in Athens wearing black, cloth bands around their arms to indicate that deaths had occurred in their families.

"Too many of our soldiers never came back," Dad said. "Many who survived… lost eyes and returned blind; others had arms and legs blown off; and some returned with sickness in their heads from the horrendous killing and dying they had witnessed. Did that scare us, Johnny? It scared the hell out of us.

"Sudden air-raid drills with screaming sirens… a blast of sound that could wake the dead… reminded us we weren't safe here at home," he explained. "Newspaper headlines about ominous Nazi and Japanese saboteurs infiltrating our mainland terrorized us. German submarines were regularly detected off America's Atlantic shore. The Japanese navy was sighted off the west coast.

"Every day, we were reminded that the bombing and invasion of America were possible. We didn't live through hell like you and the men and women of our armed forces did—but Americans weren't as comfortable as you thought we were. Remember, at the same time I was worried. I was sick, worrying about all of you. I regularly contributed to the Red Cross, hoping somehow their help would eventually reach you.

"Dear Katherine and children, the war was a bloody nightmare for us and for millions of others. The torment of violence is finally over, even though mourning continues, and will go on for decades.

"However it's time for us to put the war behind us... to move on with our lives now that we are back together. We've got to look to the future—your schooling—your careers—your mother and I growing old together. In the meantime, governments and people need to make sure that this was really 'the war to end all wars.' Going through something so atrocious, so unbearable, again, would be an abomination... an insult... to the millions who have died."

***

We learned from each other, and about each other, via our shared accounts with Dad regarding the previous eight years. In time, I came to realize that even within our one family, WWII was experienced in five different ways—Dad's, Mom's, Alex's, Nikki's, and mine.

And, thanks to Mom and Dad, during the years that followed our snowy introduction to Ann Arbor, the five of us were able, peacefully and comfortably, to settle into what might be called "ordinary" U.S. life. "Ordinary" may be mundane sounding. But "ordinary" life was a blessed and welcome relief for my family.

Ann Arbor, Michigan, became the splendid American city of our repatriation. It's where, like every American kid, I learned to play baseball and football, and where I learned to ride a bicycle. Dad bought me one to facilitate my first paying job: delivering *The Detroit News* and *The Detroit Free Press* in tranquil neighborhoods where there were no enemy soldiers to fear. Carefree in summer, I journeyed on my two wheels through middle-class, tree-filled neighborhoods, which were dotted with flower and vegetable gardens, proudly planted by the homeowners of frame and brick homes. On special occasions, I treated myself to a real American, Ann Arbor delicacy: the Washtenaw Dairy's luscious ice cream cone.

When I was older, like Alex and sister Nikki, I worked at Dad's restaurant while attending high school and the university. The three of us conveniently walked to school from home, right through earning master's degrees. My memories of Ann Arbor are full of contentment because my family and I lived in peace, in the first real home that actually belonged to us, with no strings attached.

And after seventy years, I joyously remember the awe-inspiring snowfall we experienced on our New York arrival and during our train trip to Ann Arbor. The tons and tons of magnificent pure, white snow covering the northeastern U.S. presented us a matchless homecoming welcome. American snow awarded my mother, my sister, and thirteen-year-old me a pristine slate on which we could begin new lives with Dad and Alex in our beloved U.S. homeland.

EPILOGUE

A year or two after our arrival in Ann Arbor, we received tragic news in a letter from Uncle George. The ship Mom's sister Joanna took from Lemnos during the war had been lost at sea in 1941 and never found; the vessel never reached Athens' port in Piraeus.

Did explosive Nazi mines in the sea cause the sinking? Had it been sunk by bombing from the air? Or did a German submarine destroy it? We speculated, but real facts were never known. We only knew that somewhere in the legendary Aegean, Nazi brutality sank, to the bottom of the sea, an entire ship, crowded with innocent people.

What unimaginable terror those travelers, my elderly aunt among them, must have endured in their wretched, final moments as they struggled to survive overpowering, choking waters, without hope for rescue. Lost to their loved ones for five years, they remained unmourned in hope of eventual reunion.

How many more ill-fated victims, from previously peaceful cities, towns, and villages scattered throughout the world, suffered similarly horrendous, war-related fates at the hands of the enemy, from the invasion of Ethiopia in 1935, the "rape of Nanking" in 1937, and the incursion of Poland in 1939, until the final ending of WWII in 1945? We will never know exact numbers.

Reading Uncle George's letter, my mother wept quietly and finally grieved the loss of her older sister. Mom insisted on wearing black for a year, a color that resurrected ugly war memories in me. We were relieved when blackness evolved to dark gray, then to navy blue, and eventually to brighter colors.

Mother never reunited with her siblings in Parnion. In their later years, Dad suggested to her that they take a pleasure trip together to the "old country" to see the Parthenon, visit Parnion, his native village, and their surviving siblings, nieces, and nephews. Incredulously listening to his idea, Mother paused, took a deep breath, and drilled a fiery stare into his kind, hazel eyes. "Don't you get it?" she asked. "Dear Andrew, my answer is— *NEVER!*"

Sadly, Mother and Dad passed away during the 1960s. Our parents' deaths have left holes in our family, and we still miss them. I regret that our son and his cousins did not get to know them. Meanwhile, the ensuing years have zipped by; Alex, Nikki, and I are now our family's senior citizens.

At various times during family visits, our parents, relatives, and the people we knew in Parnion come to mind as we talk about our adventures and tribulations during the war, when we were children. I'm still in contact with my Parnion cousin and boyhood friend, Demetri. During occupation, he and I had spotted a "stranger" when we were on our way to deliver dinner to his father Paul, at the village mill. Eventually, we learned the unidentified man was a British soldier protected by Uncle Paul and other villagers.

Demetri immigrated to the U.S. in the 1960s, received his degree in economics, married, had a family, and is now retired. Even though we live in cities separated by several thousand miles, we regularly chat on the phone, often recalling Parnion and our wartime childhoods.

Studies by learned scholars show that family dynamics, finances, and our childhood experiences, whether or not war is involved, directly impact our adulthoods. I wonder how many scholars have studied the influences war inflicts on children who personally experience enemy violence? With hindsight on my side, I've made my own simple observations about those of us who endured occupation. My observations focus on the Greek WWII experience, since that is what is familiar to me.

It is no surprise to me that each one of us outlived WWII in a unique way because war in one village was not the same as war in another. City experiences were diverse. Child survivors of the German occupation in Greece, with both father and mother present, survived occupation differently than a widow's children, or the kids of an American woman, temporarily parted from her husband who was living in the U.S.

All families were not penniless; every home did not burn; Nazi troops did not use every Greek home as a gratis hotel. Collaborators' offspring fared differently than *antartes'* children. And while a few of my own childhood memories, like playing with Bebba, are pleasantly recalled, another survivor told me, "I grew up too fast in the war... I never had a childhood. I don't know how to be playful. What does 'fun' mean?"

We kid-survivors display a wide spectrum of personality traits, which are influenced by economics, family structure, and personal inter-play with the enemy. War took the spirit out of many, installed mistrust in most, and instilled bouts of chronic depression in a few. Suspicion comes easily because it's almost impossible to feel absolute trust.

We matured, believing that what we suffered would not happen to anyone else, ever again. We surmised that the world had seen the last of war. Yet, catastrophically, it hasn't happened. That's why fear for the future is prevalent in so many of us: having been through one life-shattering hardship, we fear another may be lurking around the corner. At the same time, those miserable years created positive thinkers who have an "If I survived the war, then I can survive anything" attitude.

At times, we, survivors, can be indulgent, even lavish. One friend told me, "Extreme deprivation made me aware of the value of having 'things.' I enjoy luxury—yet I always look for a bargain." Another insists on buying everything "brand new"— wouldn't be caught dead in a hand-me-down, or shopping in an antique store or re-sale shop. A good friend tells me she cannot throw shoes away: "Because I walked barefoot too long." And, I'm acquainted with a survivor who is a genuine hoarder—saves everything. Conversely, a financially well-off kid-survivor says he can't see owning two sweaters: "I can only wear one at a time." Underneath it all, most of us are frugal. We abhor "waste;" we know how to "get by" with less. Staggering occupation left us with a multiplicity of scars and frailties.

On another focus, I ask myself did anything *good* come out of our 1937 journey and the ensuing German occupation? Now that I am older, retired, and with more leisure time to ponder the question, I finally have a one-word answer that applies to my own life—connection.

Living in a Greek village through the war allowed me to learn and benefit from extraordinary connections. They are not the kind of "connections" that "fix" parking tickets or bring in a windfall of money; I'm referring, instead, to warm links that benefit the soul. Many kids of immigrants, raised purely in America, were completely cut off from extended families back in the old country. In my case, I made exceptional bonds with our family in Greece. I never would have known my elderly grandmother, gracious aunts, kind uncles, and good-hearted cousins if we had not taken that fateful journey.

And early in my life, Parnion and its villagers provided me with the unique opportunity to connect with the earth. That familiarity instilled in me an appreciation for life as it perseveres, so magnificently, in the extraordinary nooks and crannies of this planet. Those connections taught me how fundamental earth's life-sustaining gifts are to our survival. Having lived in a village under somewhat primeval circumstances, I better understand the responsibility we humans bear in taking care of our precious earth. Tending my own vegetable garden is important to me; driving the latest model car is not.

In Parnion, we endured an ordeal that impacted the way I think as an adult and the way I completely wear out a pair of shoes before discarding them. Recycling comes naturally to me. I am reluctant to throw away items that I don't need anymore. I glean lost screws, nails, and discarded wooden boards. I make a concerted effort not to waste water because I remember filling that *niftera* full of water at St. Nick's fountain multiple times a day, when I was a kid, and then lugging it back to Grandpa's house. I never waste food, either. I purposely grow dandelion greens in my vegetable garden because they saved my life. I am not the person I would have been had I lived in the United States during those formative eight years.

Most certainly, I have never forgotten the connection I enjoyed with a gentle, companionable, life-saving nanny goat. Bebba is permanently etched in my memory with gobs of affection and appreciation. Whenever I'm with children at a petting zoo or county fair, I seek out and pet the goats. I never partook of Bebba's "family member," her kid that accompanied us from Parnion to Athens in 1945. I couldn't even be in the same apartment with our uncles in Athens when they savored every roasted morsel.

On an amusing note, I still maintain a nostalgic connection to our old beat-up trunk. It sailed the Atlantic with us on the *Aquitania* in 1937; was robbed of its contents at the Greek customs office on our arrival; and escaped with us from Kalamata to Parnion when the war started. More than once, German soldiers invaded its dark interior, searching for absent valuables. Yet at Grandpa's house, it provided us with a hiding place from vicious soldiers. "Buddy" has survived his adventures and enjoys his well-earned retirement in my garage.

I appreciate that my stint in Parnion connected me to my ancestors' treasured culture. Traditions abound in Greece. Name a custom! The Greeks have, most likely, honored it sometime in the last four thousand years. Greek esteem for hospitality, passed down through centuries, put food in my stomach during the 1940's famine.

And, as a kid, I learned a language so rich that it has given birth to millions of words in so many other languages. Greek words helped me excel in a high school biology class: they link me to ancient wisdom, and to Christianity's compassionate beginnings.

Paramount to all connections in my wartime upbringing, however, was the very best of all childhood bonds: the constant presence, guidance, protection, and love of my courageous, persevering mother. Her faith may have wilted, at times, but it never vanished. When wartime famine hit us hard, she sacrificed so that I could put food into my stomach. Certainly, overcoming her innate sense of propriety was agonizing for her. Yet, she painfully put aside pride and self-esteem, to humbly beg others to feed me, if they had a crust to spare. Mother not only gave life to Alex, Nikki, and me—she tenderly and selflessly ensured its continuance.

Now my question to myself is: what, if anything, did my mother eat? I still don't know. With innate grit and intelligence, she bore the loving sacrifices that parents willingly and gladly make for the wellbeing and survival of their children. Mother gave credit to God and to *tychi* (luck) for our survival, when the war ended. But as I see it today, Mom was both for us: God's exceptional gift to her three children—and our blessed *tychi*. Mother was my most precious, beloved, preeminent connection.

Unlike Mother, we in the younger generation have returned to Greece, to maintain our connections there. Alex, Nikki, and I have each taken our spouses and children to visit our cousins and their children, most of them living in Athens now. Certainly, I introduced my family to my mother Katherine's birthplace: Grandpa's house in Parnion. I admit that memories of occupation do come flooding back to me at the start of each visit. But those scenes quickly dissipate when I view the village as it was meant to be: without the pallor of war. Parnion is endowed with natural beauty, and I was proud when my wife and son took a liking to it.

Obvious changes were evident when we revisited. Homes have been updated and remodeled. Running water flows in every modernized kitchen; each house has a television set; many have computers; most villagers walk around with cell phones. Newer homes replaced properties burned down in the 1944 inferno. Yet, there are still a few burned-out ghost houses peeking out from decades of persistent vegetation. The charred, broken-down memorials bring reminders of "The War" to older citizens. But most youngsters, still ignorant of village history, have no inkling of why the old wrecks burned down in the first place.

I recently learned about a newer village improvement. The building, across from Grandpa's house, war-torn when we left in 1945 and still dilapidated when I last saw it, has been generously donated to the village by its American heirs. Skillfully refurbished, it was transformed into a computer center and library with the largest, flat screen TV in Parnion. Villagers gather to watch soccer games on the big screen, to use the computers, and to simply hang out together.

Updated, but still charming, old Parnion continues to lie beautifully perched on the western slopes of Mt. Parnon. "My village" is sparsely populated now, except in summer when those who had been born in Parnion and their progeny return to enjoy its refreshing summer climate, the view over the ravine toward the Byzantine monastery, the quiet of its streets, its invigorating greenness, and the continuously running lion fountain in the main square. On bright summer mornings visiting youngsters ride their bikes in circling patterns in the main square, near the lion-head fountain and St. George's Church.

Now, Grandpa's house, restored to antique beauty by my cousins, enjoys modern electric and plumbing conveniences. And just a few hundred feet up the road—crystal clear, revitalizing water still runs all day and all night from St. Nick's fountain, just as it flowed in World War II, as it did, still earlier in Grandpa's time, and for generations and generations before that.

My boundless love and gratitude will forever accompany the cherished memories of my dear parents and those in Greece, the land of their birth, who helped us survive the war.

My heartfelt, eternal appreciation is extended to all those who sacrificed on "the home front" and to the men and women of the Allied forces, from privates to generals, who courageously liberated Europe, Asia, Africa, and the rest of the world from the sick, diabolical strategies and deeds of the Axis powers. If it had not been for these courageous citizens, I would not be alive to tell my story.

For those 50 million around the globe who lost their lives during World War II— may their memories be eternal.

BIBLIOGRAPHY

BOOKS

Brave Men; by Ernie Pyle; University of Nebraska Press, 2001; originally published H. Holt; 1944

Campaigns of World War II, Day by Day; by Chris Bishop and Chris Mc Nab; Amber Books; 2003

Ethnic Chicago; by Melvin G. Holli and Peter d'A. Jones; William B. Eermans Publishing Company; 1984

Greek Americans, Struggle and Success, Third Edition; by Peter C. Moskos and Charles C. Moskos; Transaction Publishers; 2014

Heroes Fight Like Greeks, The Greek Resistance Against the Axis Powers in WWII; by Ronald J. Drez; Ghost Road Press; 2009

Hitler's Strategy 1940-1941 the Balkan Clue; by Martin van Creveld; Cambridge University Press; 1973

Inside Hitler's Greece, The Experience of Occupation, 1941-44; by Mark Mazower; Yale University Press; 1993

When Paris Went Dark: The City of Light Under the German Occupation, 1940-1944; by Ronald C. Rosbottom; Back Bay Books/Little, Brown and Company; 2014.

Yannis; by John (Yannis) Giannaris; Pilgrimage Publishing Inc.; 1988

INTERNET

"Ancient Roots;" November 18, 2014; from "Finding Your Roots;" Henry Louis Gates; PBS.org historyorb.com

Preservation of American Hellenic History; Greek/American Operational Group Office of Strategic Services (OSS); by Andrew S. Mousalimas

theguardian.com; November 30, 2014; "Athens 1944: Britain's Dirty Secret;" by Ed Vulliamy and Helena Smith

To Greece, Chapter 21; by W.G. Mc Clymont; 1959; from *The Official History of New Zealand in the Second World War 1939-1945*; Victoria University of Wellington Library

World War II Today, Follow the War as It Happened; Apr. 28, 1941 Last Ditch Stand at Kalamata

NEWSPAPER ARTICLES

"Remembering the 1944 December Uprising, 70 Years;" by Dr. Andre Gerolymatos; The National Herald, November 15-21, 2014

"Dueling Narratives about December 3, 1944 in Greece;" by Amb. Patrick N. Theros; The National Herald, November 29-December 5, 2014

ABOUT THE AUTHOR

Constance M. Constant, a graduate of Chicago's De Paul University and a retired elementary school teacher, has always been fascinated by history. Her books reflect both her vocation and her avocation. *Austin Lunch*, Constant's first book, colorfully relates how two children witnessed their hardworking immigrant parents' integrity and resolve in enduring the Great Depression. In *American Kid*, Constant reveals a child's-eye-view of his courageous mother's agony and strength of mind in struggling to ensure her American children's survival during WWII.

ALSO AVAILABLE FROM THIS AUTHOR

Austin Lunch: Greek-American Recollections

1930s and '40s through a Greek immigrant child's eyes. Mama defies convention in 1931 and goes to work in her husband's restaurant, the Austin Lunch. Located on Chicago's historic but seamy Near West Side, Papa's restaurant hosts a parade of inner city characters and becomes the proving ground for children Helen and Nicky.

Cosmos Publishing (ISBN: 978-1932455083)

Made in the USA
Charleston, SC
10 November 2016